W9-BYX-959

The Last Days of Hitler

Hugh Trevor-Roper (Lord Dacre of Glanton) has been Master of Peterhouse, Cambridge, since 1980. He was previously Regius Professor of Modern History, University of Oxford, from 1957 to 1980. He was born at Glanton, Northumberland, and was educated at Charterhouse and Christ Church, Oxford, where he read classics and modern history. From 1937 to 1939 he was a Research Fellow of Merton College, and subsequently a Student of Christ Church and University Lecturer in History. His numerous other books include *Archbishop Laud*, *Religion, the Reformation and Social Change* and *Hermit of Peking*.

Hugh Trevor-Roper

The Last Days
of Hitler

Sixth Edition

The University of Chicago Press

NEW HANOVER COUNTY
PUBLIC LIBRARY
201 CHESTNUT STREET
WILMINGTON, NC 28401

The University of Chicago Press, Chicago 60637

© Hugh Trevor-Roper 1971, 1978, 1987
All rights reserved. Sixth edition published 1987
University of Chicago Press edition 1992
Printed in the United States of America

09 08 07 06 05 04 03 02 01 00   4 5 6 7 8 9

Library of Congress Cataloging in Publication Data

Trevor-Roper, H. R. (Hugh Redwald) , 1914–
    The last days of Hitler / Hugh Trevor-Roper.
        p.   cm.
    Originally published: 6th ed. London : Papermac and
Macmillan Press, 1987.
    Includes bibliographical references (p.   ) and index.
    I. Title.
DD247.H5T7   1992
943.086´092—dc20
[B]   92-19709
                                                          CIP

ISBN 0-226-81224-3 (paperback)

∞ The paper used in this publication meets the minimum
requirements of the American National Standard for Information
Sciences—Permanence of Paper for Printed Library Materials,
ANSI Z39.48–1992.

NEW HANOVER COUNTY
PUBLIC LIBRARY
201 CHESTNUT STREET
WILMINGTON, NC 28401

CONTENTS

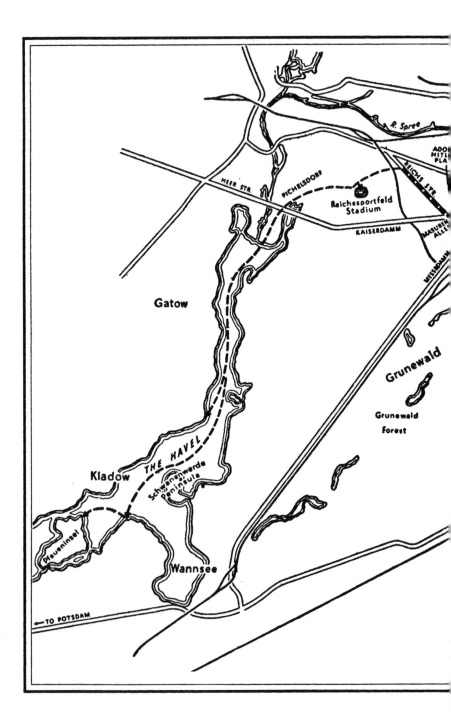

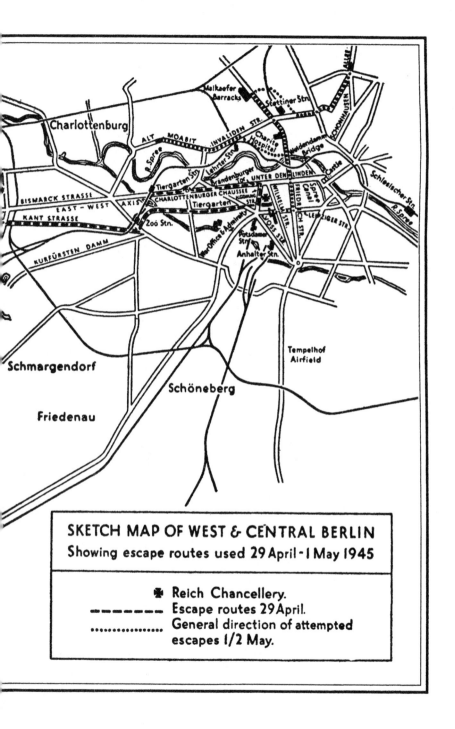

SKETCH MAP OF WEST & CENTRAL BERLIN
Showing escape routes used 29 April - 1 May 1945

✿ Reich Chancellery.
------- Escape routes 29 April.
.... General direction of attempted escapes 1/2 May.

PREFACE TO SIXTH EDITION (1987)

I<small>N</small> this new edition of *The Last Days of Hitler* I have omitted a few now obsolete footnotes but I have left the text unchanged. However, since some questions were insoluble in 1947, and were dealt with by me in later editions, I have included, from those editions, such additional matter as seems necessary to complete the story.

The long introduction to the third edition (1956) was occasioned by the release, in that year, of the German witnesses whom, being prisoners of the Russians, I had been unable to question during my enquiry in 1945. I took that opportunity to give a full account of my enquiry, and of the tortuous policy of the Russian Government in respect of the death of Hitler. This introduction has been included in all subsequent editions and I now regard it as an integral part of the book.

In the years after 1956 the Russian policy of mystification (or disinformation) continued, and the problem of the fate of Martin Bormann remained unsolved. However, by 1982 it was possible to end speculation on that subject and in the fifth edition of my book I dealt with both matters. For the sake of completeness I have therefore reprinted here both the preface to that edition, which deals, I hope finally, with the case of Bormann, and the appendix (Appendix II) which deals with the Russian evidence on the death of Hitler.

INTRODUCTION TO THIRD EDITION (1956)

IT IS now ten years since this book was written. In those ten years some mysteries of the last war have been resolved, others deepened. Eyewitnesses who were unattainable in 1945 have at last re-emerged from their long imprisonment in Russia. New books and articles have been written, and old judgments challenged or changed. But no new revelation has altered the story of Hitler's last ten days of life as it was first reconstructed in 1945 and published in 1947. Therefore—apart from trivial corrections such as occur in any reprint—I see no reason to alter the text for this new edition of my book. No doubt there are additions which I might make here or there; but since there are no substantial errors to correct or significant omissions to repair, I have decided to follow the wise example of Pontius Pilate and say, What I have written I have written. I have considered that any book which is worth reprinting at all can afford to carry the evidence of its date; and if there are any new comments which I think worth making, I have been content to confine them to footnotes or to this new introduction. The curious may, if they wish, detect the new footnotes by the date 1956 which I have added to them. In this new introduction I shall attempt two things. First, I shall give a full account of the original inquiry which led to the first publication of this book—an account substantially the same as that which appeared in the second edition, published in 1950. Secondly, I shall summarize such evidence as has since come to hand—evidence which does not alter the story as told in the book but which does, I think, shed interesting light on other matters and, in particular, upon the Russian attitude towards the last days of Hitler.

In September 1945 the circumstances of Hitler's death or disappearance had been for five months dark and mysterious. Many versions of his death or escape had become current. Some stated that he had been killed fighting in Berlin, others that he had been murdered by officers in the Tiergarten. He was supposed by some to have escaped, by air or submarine, and was alleged to be living now in a mist-enshrouded island in the Baltic, now in a Rhineland rock-fortress, sometimes in a Spanish monastery, or on a South American ranch, or among the friendly bandits of mountainous Albania; and the Russians, who were in the best position to illuminate the facts, had they wished to do so, preferred to perpetuate the obscurity. At one time they declared Hitler dead; at another they doubted their declaration; later they announced that they had discovered the corpses of both Hitler and Eva Braun and had identified them by the teeth; later still they accused the British of concealing Eva Braun and probably Hitler in the British Zone of Germany. It was at this stage that the British Intelligence authorities in Germany, believing that such mystification was an unnecessary embarrassment, decided to collect all available evidence and to determine, if possible, the truth. I was appointed to carry out this task. I was given all necessary facilities in the British Zone; and the American authorities at Frankfurt promptly and generously offered to put all their material at my disposal, to allow me to interrogate their prisoners, and to ensure the co-operation of their local counter-intelligence organization, the CIC.

What was the state of the evidence at this time? The ultimate authority on which the report of Hitler's death seemed to rest was a broadcast statement made by Admiral Doenitz to the German people on the evening of May 1st, 1945. In this statement Doenitz had announced Hitler's death that afternoon, fighting at the head of his troops in Berlin. This statement had been accepted as true at the time, at least for certain practical purposes: an obituary notice of Hitler had appeared in *The Times* next day, Mr de Valera had expressed his condolence to the German minister in Dublin, and Hitler's name (unlike that of Bormann, about whose fate there had been no such statement) had been excluded from the list of war criminals to be tried at Nuremberg. On the other hand there was no more valid reason for believing Doenitz's statement than for accepting certain other assertions. Doenitz's statement was indeed supported by a certain Dr Karl Heinz Spaeth of Stuttgart, who deposed on oath during his holiday at Illertissen in Bavaria that he had personally attended Hitler, when he was wounded in the lung by Russian shellfire at the Zoo Bunker on the afternoon of May 1st, and had pronounced him dead; but another authority, a Swiss woman journalist, Carmen Mory, deposed at Hamburg with equal protestations of veracity that Hitler, to her certain knowledge, was living on an estate in Bavaria with Eva Braun, her sister Gretl, and Gretl's husband Hermann Fegelein. Carmen Mory offered to investigate this matter herself, through numerous channels at her disposal (for having been imprisoned as a spy in a German concentration camp she was well supplied with means of information); but she warned the British authorities that any attempt to dispense with her services would be fatal: at the approach of anyone in uniform, all four would infallibly commit suicide. Since both these stories could not possibly be true, it was clear that mere affidavits could not be accepted as evidence in this matter.

Anyone who undertakes an inquiry of such a kind is soon made aware of one important fact: the worthlessness of mere human testimony. It is a chastening thought to a historian to consider how much of history is written on the basis of statements no more reliable than those of Admiral Doenitz, Dr Spaeth, and Carmen Mory. If such statements had been made and recorded with reference to the disputed death of the Czar Alexander I in 1825, plenty of historians would have been ready to take them seriously. Fortunately in this case they were made by contemporaries, and it was possible to check them.

The English historian James Spedding said that every historian, when faced with a statement of fact, must ask himself the question: Who first said so, and what opportunities had he of knowing it? Subjected to this test, much of historical evidence is found to dissolve. In search of Dr Karl Heinz Spaeth I went to the address which he had given in Stuttgart. I found that it was not a private house but the Technical High School. His name was unknown there, nor did it occur in any Stuttgart directory. It was clear that he had given a false name and address; and since his affidavit was mendacious on this subject, there was no reason to credit it in other matters where ignorance would have been more excusable. As for Carmen Mory, her whole saga dissolved at the mere touch of criticism: she had never seen Hitler or spoken to anyone who could have known the facts. The facts she gave were demonstrably wrong, and the arguments whereby she connected them with her conclusions demonstrably illogical. Her whole statement, like that of Dr Spaeth, was pure fantasy.

Why did these people make these false affidavits? Human motives can never be confidently interpreted, but they can sometimes be guessed. Carmen Mory, while in a German concentration camp, had become an agent of the Gestapo, selecting victims for its murders and experiments from among her fellow prisoners. This fact was well known to them, and when the camp had been captured by the Allies and its occupants liberated, it could only be a matter of time before Carmen Mory was accused of her crimes. Probably she thought that by inventing a story which she herself would be required to investigate she might both delay retribution and acquire British supporters. If so, she thought wrongly: her assistance was not required, and shortly afterwards she was condemned to death by a military tribunal, and forestalled execution by suicide.

The motives of Dr Spaeth seem to have been less rational. The source of his story is clear. It is an amplification, with circumstantial detail and a personal part assigned to the narrator, of the broadcast statement by Doenitz. Doenitz had said that Hitler had been killed fighting at the head of his troops on the afternoon of May 1st: Dr Spaeth had accepted and embellished this minimum of apparent fact, had added local colour and detail, and had introduced himself as a central figure. His motive was probably not rational but psychological: a delusion of vanity such as leads raconteurs to introduce themselves into the anecdotes they repeat, or convinced George IV that he had personally led a cavalry charge at the battle of Waterloo.

For mythopoeia is a far more common characteristic of the human race (and perhaps especially of the German race) than veracity; and the evidence for this statement has increased formidably since these incidents made it obvious to me. Even in December 1947 a German airman calling himself Baumgart deposed in Warsaw that he had flown Hitler and Eva Braun to Denmark on April 28th, 1945. The story is plainly fiction. One of my earliest steps in the inquiry had been to trace Hitler's two pilots, SS Obergruppenfuehrer Hans Baur and SS Standartenfuehrer Beetz, and I had established that both of them had left the Bunker with Bormann on the night of May 1st. Beetz had been last seen on the Weidendammer Bridge, and his wife and friends had never heard of him since. Baur had been captured by the Russians, and his wife had shown me a message which had been conveyed from him in Poland to her in Bavaria in October 1945. Besides, we have Hitler's own signature on his own will and marriage certificate 'given in Berlin on April 29th', the day after Baumgart claimed to have flown him to Denmark. But reason is powerless against the obstinate love of fiction, and although Baumgart afterwards retired to a lunatic asylum in Poland, those who wish to believe him will no doubt continue to do so.

Of course not all legends are pure fabrication: there are degrees of human invention, and some myths have a basis of fact or at least of wishful thinking. Such was the legend spread by Schellenberg after his surrender in Sweden, and eagerly accepted by the credulous. Schellenberg maintained that Himmler had poisoned Hitler. But how did he know? Schellenberg had not seen Hitler since 1942[1]. His sole evidence was his own wish: he wished to believe that Himmler had accepted his advice, and by a judicious and selective misinterpretation of Himmler's remarks he had succeeded in persuading himself that he had done so. A few questions to Schellenberg, an examination of Himmler's entourage, a reference to the contemporary reports of Count Bernadotte, and Schellenberg's legend dissolved as completely as those of Spaeth and Mory.

Thus the evidence of Hitler's fate shrank on examination to the statement of Doenitz. But what opportunity had Doenitz of knowing the facts? It was known that Doenitz had left Berlin on April 21st, and had never seen Hitler since. His broadcast speech had been made from Ploen, 150 miles from the incident which it claimed to describe. How then did he know? The answer to this question was easily discovered. When the so-called 'Flensburg government' was arrested, all its papers were also seized, and among these papers was a series of telegrams which had passed between Doenitz and Hitler's

[1] So, at least, he said under interrogation in 1945. In his *Memoirs*, he remembered seeing Hitler on a later occasion.

headquarters. The last in this series was a telegram from Goebbels to Doenitz[1] on May 1st. This telegram informed Doenitz that Hitler had died 'yesterday'—*ie* on April 30th—'at 15.30 hours'. Doenitz had no other evidence, for none of those who had been with Hitler at the end had been able to join him: the last eyewitnesses who had reached him from the Bunker were Ritter von Greim and Hanna Reitsch, who had left nearly two days before the end. His statement that Hitler had died fighting at the head of his troops was pure invention, and his statement that Hitler had died on May 1st was unsupported by the only evidence at his disposal, which clearly stated that he had died on April 30th. Thus Doenitz too joined Spaeth and Mory and the imaginative journalists as a worthless and rejected authority. The only evidence of Hitler's death was a telegram signed by Goebbels, who could not be cross-examined because he was dead, and his body, unlike Hitler's, had been found by the Russians.

There was, however, at least one other possible source of evidence. On June 9th, 1945, Marshal Zhukov, the Russian commanding general, had announced to the press that before his death or disappearance Hitler had married Eva Braun. This startling fact (for Eva Braun had hitherto scarcely been heard of even in Germany) was revealed, Zhukov said, by the diaries of adjutants which the Russians had found in the Bunker. These diaries, if they existed, would clearly be an important source of evidence, and I therefore decided to ask the Russians for access to them; but I decided first to collect such evidence as I could find in the areas under British and American control, and to use this to elicit from the Russians both the diaries and any other evidence that the Russians might be shown to possess. For if none of those who had offered information could survive the tests to which they had been subjected, there must be others who had really been in a position to observe the events in Hitler's Bunker before it was captured by the Russians.

For certain facts could be established with certainty. There were in Allied custody several men who had been with Hitler until about April 22nd—including Doenitz, Keitel, Jodl,

---

[1] The text of this telegram is given on pp. 239–40.

Speer, and several lesser figures—so that up to that time there was no mystery. But on April 22nd Hitler had held the famous staff conference at which his nerve had at last given way, and after which he had ordered his staff to leave while protesting that he would stay in Berlin. It was the period from April 22nd until the Russian occupation of the Chancellery on May 2nd that was the dark period of which no witnesses had come forward. And yet there must have been witnesses. The question was, Who were they? The task was to find them.

Neither such a question nor such a task is really difficult. Those who remained with Hitler were simply those of his customary entourage who had been with him before April 22nd and had not left on that day: generals and politicians, civil servants and adjutants, secretaries, guards and soldiers. A list of those who customarily attended Hitler in the Chancellery was not difficult to draw up: it only remained to find those who had left on April 22nd, most of whom had been captured either in Flensburg or Berchtesgaden, and by cross-examining them to discover whom they had left behind them in Berlin. It was necessary to look for representatives of all classes—for guards and typists were as likely to prove good witnesses as politicians and generals. I therefore began by locating as many of the fugitives as I could find, whatever their status, in accessible Allied captivity. I was soon rewarded. Politicians and generals were represented by the Flensburg prisoners Keitel, Jodl, Doenitz, and Speer. Two of Hitler's secretaries, who had left on April 22nd, Frl. Wolf and Frl. Schroeder, were found at Berchtesgaden. Hitler's detective guard was called *Reichssicherheitsdienst Dienststelle 1*; about half of its members had been evacuated to Berchtesgaden on April 22nd, and captured there. I was able to interrogate them in their camps at Ludwigsburg and Garmisch-Partenkirchen. Hitler's SS Guard, the *Fuehrerbegleitkommando*, had remained behind in Berlin, but one officer from it, SS Hauptsturmfuehrer Bornholdt, had left on a special mission on April 24th and had not returned: in due course he had become an Allied prisoner and I was able to question him about his comrades at Neumunster in Schleswig-Holstein. Thus from every stratum of society in Hitler's Bunker representative members were found who had left on or about April 22nd; and these, under cross-examination, were able to designate the comrades whom they had left behind in Berlin. From their answers it was possible to construct a complete list of all those men and women, of whatever status, who had stayed behind in Berlin after the great exodus of April 22nd. These, if they could be found, would be the witnesses of the dark period.

How could they be found? Here again the problem is less difficult than may appear. They were all described as 'missing'; but in fact people do not disappear or evaporate, even in a period of catastrophe. They either perish or remain alive: there is no third possibility. The word 'missing' applies not to them but to the evidence. If they are dead, their value as witnesses is over; if they are alive, they are either prisoners or free. If they are prisoners, they can be found in prison camps—at least if they are prisoners of the Western Powers; if they are free they must be sought elsewhere, and most probably in their own home districts, where friends and local knowledge will enable them to survive, but also where enemies (and German enmities are strong) may easily betray them. In collecting the names of possible witnesses I was therefore careful to obtain all possible information about their homes, and if their names did not occur in the registers of Allied prison camps, they were sought and sometimes found in their homes. By these methods seven witnesses of the dark period, from different and independent groups, had been located and interrogated, and other relevant material had been discovered and centralized, by November 1st, 1945, when the report of my conclusions was due. The seven witnesses were Hermann Karnau, a policeman from the detective guard who was imprisoned at Nienburg and had been examined by Canadian and British authorities before he was cross-examined by me; Erich Mansfeld and Hilco Poppen, two other policemen, who were detained at Bremen and Fallingbostel; Frl. Else Krueger, Bormann's secretary, who was detained at Ploen in Schleswig-Holstein and interrogated by me; Erich Kempka, Hitler's transport officer, who had been captured at Berchtesgaden and was interrogated both by American officers and by myself at Moosburg; Hanna Reitsch, the test pilot, who was detained in

Austria and was interrogated by American officers; and the Baroness von Varo, a casual visitor in Hitler's Bunker, who had been discovered by a British journalist in Berlin, and who was traced and interrogated by me in her mother's home at Bueckeburg. Other relevant material included the diary of General Koller, since published,[1] the diary of Count Schwerin von Krosigk, captured with its author at Flensburg, and the papers of Admiral Doenitz and his 'government'. Based on evidence from these sources, my report was submitted by the Intelligence Division in Berlin to the British government and to the Quadripartite Intelligence Committee in Berlin. At the end of the report I suggested certain other sources of evidence which might still become available: in particular I mentioned that Hitler's pilot Hans Baur and the head of the *Reichssicherheitsdienst* Brigadefuehrer Rattenhuber, who had ordered the burial of Hitler's body, were reported captured by the Russians in an official Russian communiqué, and that certain other important witnesses might have been taken at the same time; and I asked for access to the captured adjutant's diaries which had been cited by Marshal Zhukov as his authority for the marriage of Hitler and Eva Braun. The Russians noted these requests but never answered them.

At the same time an abbreviated version of the report was issued to the Press.[2]

The evidence for Hitler's last days increased considerably between the issue of the report of November 1st, 1945, and the writing of my book in the summer of 1946, but since it did not alter the conclusions except in two trifling details,[3] I

---

[1] Karl Koller, *Der letzte Monat* (Mannheim, 1949).

[2] The text of this Press report is given in William L. Shirer, *End of a Berlin Diary* (New York, 1947). It is summarized in the British and American newspapers of November 2nd, 1945.

[3] In the report of November 1st, 1945, I ascribed the wedding, in the absence of definite evidence, to the *evening* of April 29th. Subsequent evidence showed that it really took place in the small hours of the *morning* of April 29th. In the report I also accepted Gebhardt's statement that he visited the Bunker 'about April 23rd–24th'. Subsequent evidence convinced me that this could not be true, and I afterwards established, by cross-examining Gebhardt, that his visit had been on April 22nd as stated in my book.

18

shall pause at this stage to answer certain questions or criticisms which were made at the time of its presentation.

For the report of November 1st, 1945, it must be admitted, was not equally popular in all quarters, and that not entirely because of any defects of logic or lucidity which may have disfigured it. Throughout the summer and autumn of 1945 many resourceful journalists had been pursuing phantoms of Hitler with energy and enthusiasm, and the pleasant lakes of the Swiss frontier and the romantic Tyrolean Alps and the comfortable resorts of Upper Austria were frequently visited by devoted investigators whose scrupulous consciences forbade them to ignore even the most inconsiderable clue. In the course of these researches many engaging theories were propounded; but as winter drew near, and personal excursions became less attractive, the consensus of opinion began to allow that Hitler had really remained in Berlin, and the mystery of his fate was one that could best be solved not by strenuous travel in an inclement season, but by ingenious meditation in well-heated saloon bars. Consequently my report, which stated that Hitler had died in Berlin on April 30th, as Goebbels had said, and that all other explanations of his disappearance were 'contrary to the only positive evidence and supported by no evidence at all', was found unacceptable by many. The critics did not indeed deny the evidence that was produced, but they maintained that there was still a possibility of escaping so final a conclusion; they maintained that the body that had been burnt was that not of Hitler but of a 'double' introduced at the last minute, and they echoed the sentiment if not the words of Professor Hanky on a similar occasion: 'No matter though nine-tenths of the marks and measurements corresponded, so long as there is a tenth that does not do so, we should not be flesh and blood if we did not ignore the nine points and insist only on the tenth.' Alternatively they maintained that the witnesses on whose evidence the report was based had all been carefully briefed; that their evidence was a deliberately pre-concerted cover story and should be rejected altogether; and that in the total absence of evidence thus happily restored there was room for the unlimited development of any theory that might seem attractive to its inventor.

19

Such a suggestion can, in my opinion, be easily disproved. It is only necessary to consider its logical consequences. If half a dozen or a dozen people are all told to tell the same story under interrogation, then it may be assumed (supposing that their memories are infallible and their loyalty firm) that they will do so, even if the circumstances of the rehearsal (amid shellfire and battle) were somewhat distracting and the circumstances of the interrogation (isolated from each other, and six months later) somewhat difficult. But even in these ideal conditions the witnesses, who will begin by agreeing in every detail, so long as they are questioned within the brief that they have prepared, will inevitably disagree when the interrogator presses them on unconcerted matters, and their answers must be drawn not from a common prepared text but from their separate imaginations. On the other hand if the witnesses are speaking the truth, as far as they can, about an experience which they have really shared, the development of their answers will be in precisely the opposite direction. At first their replies will differ, because their opportunities of observation and recollection have been different; but as interrogation detaches those differences of circumstance, the essential agreement will become clear. Any interrogator soon becomes familiar with these facts, and by appreciating them, can often detect whether a story has been concerted or not; and on the strength of those facts I consider that the various witnesses whom I have interrogated, directly or indirectly, on the subject of Hitler's death were undoubtedly telling not a preconcerted story, but their own attempts to recollect the truth.

One small instance may be given to illustrate this point. The guard Karnau persistently affirmed that he saw the corpses of Hitler and Eva Braun burst suddenly, as if by spontaneous combustion, into flame. The chauffeur Kempka maintained that Guensche had set them alight. These two versions seem incompatible, but cross-examination reveals that they are simply two aspects of the same fact. Guensche lit the bodies by throwing a burning rag upon them; but he threw it from beneath the porch of the Bunker, and was therefore invisible to Karnau who was standing by the tower. The truth of the incident is attested by the rational discrepancy of the evidence.

Had Karnau and Kempka been taught their parts, they would never have disagreed at the start.

The report of November 1st had solicited certain information from the Russians. This information was never produced, but from other sources evidence continued to come in to enrich although not to alter the main conclusions. For by November 1st the inquiry had only lasted six weeks, and it was impossible for all available witnesses to be identified, traced, found, and interrogated in so short a time. Among the most important additional witnesses who were arrested and interrogated after November 1st was Artur Axmann, who had succeeded Baldur von Schirach as head of the Hitler Youth and who was arrested in the Bavarian Alps in December 1945 after a long and complicated Anglo-American intelligence operation. But the most significant and dramatic addition to knowledge was supplied by the discovery, in the winter of 1945-6, of a set of documents which strikingly confirmed the conclusions of the report of November 1st: Hitler's private and political testaments and the certificate of his marriage with Eva Braun.

At the end of November 1945, when I returned to Oxford on leave, I received a signal from British Headquarters at Bad Oeynhausen that a document had been discovered which purported to be Hitler's will, but that its authenticity was uncertain. Now I already had some information about Hitler's will, for in the same telegram in which Goebbels had reported the death of Hitler to Doenitz he had mentioned the Fuehrer's Testament of April 29th which had made certain political appointments, and which was being sent to Doenitz. Doenitz had furthermore stated that he had sent a plane to meet the bearer, but that the pilot, having been in touch with the bearer at the Havel, had lost him and returned empty. Since the document which had now been discovered was dated April 29th, and contained several political appointments, including those mentioned in Goebbels' telegram, there were good grounds for supposing it genuine. But Goebbels' telegram, which seemed to establish the authenticity of this document, also seemed to show that there were no less than three such

21

documents, addressed separately to Doenitz, Field-Marshal Schoerner (then commanding an Army Group in Bohemia), and the Party Archives in Munich. It was therefore clearly important to investigate the circumstances of this discovery.

In the summer of 1945 a Luxembourg journalist, Georges Thiers, had approached the British Military Government in Hanover. He had wished for employment, and had explained that he was usefully informed on many topics and could provide information on such interesting subjects as life in Hitler's Bunker in Berlin; but as he could give no valid explanations to account for his alleged intimacy with these high matters, his application had been ignored. Later, however, he had fallen under the suspicion of using false papers: he had been arrested and had admitted that in fact he was not a Luxemburger but a German, and that his name was not Georges Thiers, but Heinz Lorenz. He had been interned, and in November 1945, in the course of a routine search, a set of papers had been found sewn in the lining of his clothes. These appeared to be Hitler's personal and political testaments and a document signed by Dr Goebbels and entitled 'Appendix to the Fuehrer's Political Testament'.[1] Under interrogation Lorenz admitted that he had been in Hitler's Bunker at the end and had been ordered to deliver these documents to Munich. He confirmed Goebbels' statement that there had been, in all, three sets of documents; and he explained that he had been accompanied in his escape from Berlin by two other men: Major Willi Johannmeier, who was to carry Hitler's political testament to Field-Marshal Schoerner, and SS Standartenfuehrer Wilhelm Zander, who was to convey to Admiral Doenitz Hitler's two testaments and the certificate of his marriage to Eva Braun. To complete the evidence and establish the authenticity of the documents beyond a doubt it was therefore necessary to find Johannmeier and Zander.

Johannmeier was easily found, living with his parents in Iserlohn. A straightforward soldier, of unconditional loyalties and unpolitical courage, at first he denied all knowledge of the Bunker, then, finding it impossible to maintain this position, he insisted that he had merely been sent as a military escort

[1] The text of this document is given on p. 217.

to Zander and Lorenz, to guide them through the Russian lines. What their mission was he did not know: it had been none of his business to ask. Nothing could shake him from this position, and in spite of the discrepancy between his evidence and that of Lorenz, he almost convinced his interrogators. At any rate it was clear that no progress could be made till further evidence had been obtained from Zander.

Zander's home was in Munich, but all the evidence proved that he had not visited it since the defeat of Germany. His wife was found living with her parents in Hanover, and confirmed that she had never seen her husband since the end of the war. She explained that she still hoped for news, and willingly provided photographs of Zander and addresses of his mother and brothers in the hope that she might obtain information about him; but no clue led anywhither, until it was realized that all this was part of an elaborate stratagem designed to mislead the pursuers. Visiting Munich in December 1945 I soon obtained casual information which convinced me that Zander was alive, but in hiding, and that Frau Zander, in her zeal to conceal his existence, had even persuaded his own mother and brothers that he was dead. After a minute examination of local evidence it was established that Zander was living under the false name of Friedrich-Wilhelm Paustin, and had worked for a time as a market-gardener in the Bavarian village of Tegernsee.

From that moment the arrest of Zander was only a matter of time. The local records of Tegernsee soon revealed his movements, and after an abortive raid on his address in the village, he was tracked down to the little village of Aidenbach near Passau on the Austrian frontier. Thither I went, accompanied by members of the American CIC, and there, at 3 am on December 28th, he was found and arrested. He was staying with Bormann's secretary. Under interrogation he revealed himself as a disillusioned Nazi idealist who saw that his former world was shattered and spoke freely. His story agreed with that of Lorenz: he had brought his documents to Hanover and thence, seeing that delivery to Doenitz was impossible, had walked to Munich and concealed them in a trunk. The trunk was now deposited with a friend in Tegernsee; but another visit to Tegernsee proved unnecessary. Alarmed by the previous raid, the custodian of the trunk had voluntarily surrendered it to the local CIC while I was in Aidenbach looking for Zander. The documents were found in it: they consisted, as Lorenz had stated, of Hitler's two testaments and the marriage certificate.

After the arrest of Zander, interest returned to North Germany, to the irreducible Johannmeier, whose story of ignorance was now assailed by the independent but unanimous testimony of his two companions. Nevertheless he held firmly to his version. He had no documents, he said, and therefore could produce none. It was clear that he was actuated merely by loyalty. He had been ordered on no account to allow the documents to fall into Allied hands, and these orders he intended to fulfil, in spite of the evidence. Impervious to fear, indifferent to reward, it seemed that nothing would move him except reason. I appealed to reason. He could give us nothing that we had not got; we could not accept his story against the agreement of all other evidence; we had no interest in holding him and yet must do so unless he could explain away this obvious difficulty. For two hours Johannmeier firmly resisted even this appeal; even proof seemed uncertain against his single-minded insistence. Ultimately it was a pause in the proceedings which achieved his conversion. In interrogation pressure must be uninterrupted, but persuasion needs pauses, for only during a pause can a man reason with himself and catch up with the argument. In this pause, Johannmeier reasoned with himself and convinced himself. He decided (as he explained afterwards during the long drive to Iserlohn) that if his companions, old and highly-promoted Party men, could so easily betray a trust which, to them, was connected with their alleged political ideals, then it was quixotic in him, who had no such Party connections (for he was simply a regular soldier), to suffer longer in their cause or defend the pass which they had already sold. So after the pause, when the seemingly endless business began again, he observed at last "*Ich habe die Papiere.*" There was no need of further words. He accompanied me by car to Iserlohn, and there led me into the back garden of his home. It was dark. With an axe he broke

24

open the frozen ground and dug up a buried bottle. Then, breaking the bottle with the axe, he drew out and handed to me the last missing document: the third copy of Hitler's political testàment, and the vivid covering letter in which General Burgdorf told Field-Marshal Schoerner that it was 'the shattering news of Himmler's treachery' which had driven Hitler to his last decision.

After the discovery of all these papers the evidence of Hitler's last days was substantially complete, but the inquiries which had once been begun continued to yield fruit. In January, a fortnight after the capitulation of Johannmeier, Lieutenant-Colonel von Below was found, studying law in the university of Bonn. He had been the last to leave the Bunker before Hitler's death, and had been the bearer of his last valedictory recriminations to the General Staff. Then, in the spring and summer of 1946, Hitler's two secretaries, Frau Christian and Frau Junge, were at last found and interrogated: Frau Christian had been dodging arrest since the autumn of 1945, when I had missed her by a few days at her mother-in-law's house in the Palatinate. These and other captures, and the interrogation of a number of subsidiary characters, added detail and colour to the story, and resolved small remaining doubts, but they altered nothing significant: the main lines of the story were clear and unchanged since the first report of November 1st, 1945.

Such is the history of the inquiry which I carried out in 1945, and on the basis of which I afterwards, with the permission and support of the British Intelligence authorities, wrote this book. When the book was published, it at once excited a good deal of opposition from those who preferred to accept other conclusions; but since the world has not chosen to remember my critics, I shall not now, by naming them, disturb that decent oblivion. I shall pass on to consider the new evidence which has been produced since the publication of my book and which might have confirmed, completed, or challenged my findings. In particular, I shall deal with the evidence of those witnesses who, when I began my inquiry, had already disappeared into Russian prisons but who now,

25

ten years later, have at last been released and have been able to tell their story.

The principal witnesses whom I sought and failed to find in 1945 were five. They were Otto Guensche, Hitler's SS adjutant, and Heinz Linge, his personal servant, both of whom undoubtedly saw Hitler dead and took part in the burning of his body; Johann Rattenhuber, who commanded Hitler's detective bodyguard and who, I believed, knew the place of his burial; Hans Baur, Hitler's personal pilot, who was with him to the end; and Harry Mengershausen, an officer of the bodyguard who was reported to know about the burial of the bodies. There were of course other important witnesses whom I had missed, but it was these five whom I particularly sought because I had positive evidence that they were still alive. Guensche and Linge had both been seen and identified among Russian prisoners in Berlin, and the Russians had themselves included the names of Baur and Rattenhuber among their prisoners in an official communiqué which they had published on May 6th, 1945. However, as I have said, these requests were unavailing: the Russians declined to answer any questions and in the end I wrote my book without the help of these missing witnesses. Nevertheless I did not entirely lose touch with these Russian captives. In the following years I occasionally had news of them from more fortunate fellow prisoners who had returned to Germany. Thus I learned that some of them were still alive in the Lubianka Prison in Moscow, or in the Arctic prison of Vorkuta or the great prison camp at Sverdlovsk. I sometimes even received, at secondhand, snatches of their stories of the last days in the Bunker. Then suddenly, in the autumn of 1955, after Dr Adenauer's visit to Moscow, the prison gates opened, and by January 1956 all five men had returned. It is true, one of them has remained inaccessible. Guensche, still classified by the Russians as a war criminal, returned to East Germany—only to vanish again into another Communist prison in Bautzen.[1] But the other four, having returned to Western Germany, have been

[1] In May 1956, Guensche was set free and moved to West Germany; but his statements to the Press simply confirm what I have written.

able to tell their stories to the world. Linge in Berlin, lost no time in publishing his account in the Press.[1] Baur, Rattenhuber, and Mengershausen freely answered all the questions which I put to them in private interviews at their homes in Western Germany.

What is the result of these revelations? The essential fact is that they everywhere confirm the story as already told by me from other sources. At no point do they conflict with it or even modify it.[2] But do they perhaps extend or complete it? In particular, do they shed any light on those mysteries which I had been obliged to leave unsolved? To answer this question, we must first ask, what are these unsolved mysteries? They are two. First, what was done with the bodies of Hitler and Eva Braun after they had been burnt in the Chancellery garden? Secondly, what happened to Martin Bormann?

Concerning the ultimate disposal of Hitler's and Eva Braun's bodies I had, in 1945, no first-hand evidence. The best evidence I had was that of the guard Erich Mansfeld, who at midnight on April 30th, 1945, noticed that a bomb crater near the emergency exit of the Bunker had been newly worked into a rectangular shape, and deduced that the bodies had been buried there. There was further evidence that members of the detective guard had buried the bodies, and Artur Axmann, the Hitler Youth leader, stated emphatically, though without claiming to have seen it, that the burial was 'in one of the many bomb craters which exist around the Reich Chancellery'. On the other hand there were also other accounts which circulated in the Bunker, rendering certainty impossible, and so, in 1945, I ended by leaving the question open. But now it can be closed. Both Linge and Rattenhuber, when they returned to Germany in October 1955, stated circumstantially that although they had not witnessed the burial, they had been told that the bodies had been buried in the bomb crater.

[1] It was published in English, in the *News of the World* (October 23rd, 1955–January 1st, 1956) and in German, in *Revue* (Munich) (November 26th, 1955–February 11th, 1956).

[2] Certain newspapers, *eg The Observer*, October 9th, 1955, and *Manchester Guardian*, October 10th, 1955 reported Baur as stating that he watched Hitler shoot himself. This is a misunderstanding, and the statement is disowned by Baur.

Rattenhuber added that he had himself been asked to find a flag in which to wrap Hitler's body for such burial but had been unable to provide it. Three months later Mengershausen arrived in his home town of Bremen and confirmed these statements, admitting that he had actually dug the grave. The bodies, he said, were not consumed by the fire or even unrecognizable, and he buried them on three wooden boards three feet deep in the ground. He was helped by a colleague called Glanzer who, he says, was afterwards killed in the fighting in Berlin. Thus Hitler's burial place in the Chancellery is no longer a mystery. On the other hand, this does not finally settle the matter since, as will appear, we now know that the body was afterwards exhumed and transferred to another and still unknown destination.

So much for the first question: what of the second, the question of the fate of Martin Bormann? In 1945 the evidence on this question was conflicting and uncertain. Several witnesses maintained that Bormann had been killed in a tank which exploded when hit by a *Panzerfaust* on the Weidendammer Bridge during the attempted breakthrough on the night of May 1st–2nd. On the other hand, all these witnesses have admitted that the scene was one of great confusion and none of them claims to have seen Bormann's body. One of them, Erich Kempka, has even admitted that he was himself blinded by the same explosion, and it is therefore difficult to understand how he can have seen Bormann's death or anything else.[1] Further, even in 1945 I had three witnesses who independently claimed to have accompanied Bormann in his attempted escape. One of these witnesses, Artur Axmann, claimed afterwards to have seen him dead. Whether we believe Axmann or not is entirely a matter of choice, for his word is unsupported by any other testimony. In his favour it can be said that his evidence on all other points has been vindicated. On the other hand, if he wished to protect Bormann against further search, his natural course would be to give false evidence of his death. This being so, I came in 1945, to the

[1] Nevertheless, Kempka has obstinately persisted in describing Bormann's 'death' in this incident in his book *Ich habe Adolf Hitler verbrannt* (Munich, 1950).

only permissible conclusion, *viz*: that Bormann had certainly survived the tank explosion but had possibly, though by no means certainly been killed later that night. Such was the balance of evidence in 1945. How far it is altered by the new evidence of 1956?

The answer is, not at all. On the one hand both Linge and Baur state that Bormann was killed in the tank explosion—or at least they say that they think he was killed, for, once again, they admit that the scene was confused and that they never saw his body. On the other hand, Mengershausen declares firmly that Bormann was not killed in that explosion. He says that although Bormann was riding in a tank, it was not his tank which was blown up. And further, another witness has turned up since 1945 who states that he was with Bormann *after* the explosion. This is a former SS Major, Joachim Tiburtius, who, in 1953, made a statement to a Swiss newspaper.[1] In the confusion after the explosion Tiburtius says that he lost sight of Bormann, but afterwards he saw him again at the Hotel Atlas. "He had by then changed into civilian clothes. We pushed on together towards the Schiffbauerdamm and the Albrechtstrasse. Then I finally lost sight of him. But he had as good a chance to escape as I had."

Thus the evidence still obliges us to believe that Bormann survived the explosion, and it still does not give the support which Axmann's story requires before we can believe it. If we believe that Bormann is dead, it must be simply because no one has ever produced any acceptable evidence of his existence after May 1st, 1945.

Such is the contribution which the newly returned prisoners have added to the story as reconstructed in 1945. Seen in its proper perspective, it does not amount to very much. The conjecture that Hitler's body was buried in the bomb crater becomes a fact; the fate of Martin Bormann remains a mystery. But if these new witnesses do not add much to my story of the last days of Hitler, there is another subject upon which they shed new and interesting light: the attitude of the Russians to the problem of Hitler's last days. Already in 1950, in the second edition of my book, I was able to give some outline

[1] *Der Bund* (Berne), February 17th, 1953.

of Russian policy in this respect. Now, with the aid of these new sources, I believe I can complete the story.

In theory the Russians had no great problem, for it was they who, from the start, controlled all the evidence. On May 2nd, 1945, they overran the Bunker in which Hitler had perished. About the same time they captured, in a beer cellar in the Schönhäuser Allee, a number of Hitler's immediate attendants who knew the facts, and two at least of whom were identified within four days. The Chancellery garden which contained Hitler's bones, was—and still is—under their control. Moreover, even before they occupied the Reich Chancellery, they had had a formal statement of Hitler's death and perhaps an informal commentary on the circumstances of it. This statement had been given to them by General Hans Krebs.

Readers of this book will know that on the night of April 30th–May 1st, 1945, General Krebs was sent to the Russian headquarters with an offer of temporary local surrender by Bormann and Goebbels acting as Hitler's *de facto* successors. Now this General Krebs was not only Hitler's last Chief of General Staff and one of the witnesses of his last will and testament: he was also a former Assistant Military Attaché in Moscow. He spoke Russian fluently, knew the leading men in the Red Army personally, and had always been accounted a warm advocate of Russo-German co-operation, as a living symbol of which he had once been publicly embraced by Stalin. Thus the emissary who presented himself either to Marshal Zhukov or to the local Russian commander, General Chuïkov,[1] in the early hours of the morning after Hitler's death was no stranger. Further, he had to explain his commission, and why the letter of authority which he brought was signed not by Hitler but by Bormann and Goebbels.

[1] The official account of this meeting, published by Lt-Col P. Troyanovsky in the Red Army paper *Red Star* and elsewhere, states that Krebs saw Chuïkov. A much more circumstantial account, published in the Düsseldorf paper *Der Fortschritt* on May 19th, 1955, states that he saw Zhukov. According to this latter account, based on the reports of returned prisoners who presumably had it from Krebs on his return to the Chancellery, the meeting was friendly: Krebs was given a tumbler of vodka and questioned about the events in the Bunker.

According to a contemporary Russian report, Krebs said, "I am authorized to inform the Soviet High Command that yesterday, April 30th, the Fuehrer Adolf Hitler departed from this world at his own wish." This official Russian report is naturally bald and factual; we do not know whether, either during this visit or the second visit which he paid a few hours later, Krebs was called upon to amplify or substantiate it. All we can say is that, if so required, he could easily, as an eyewitness and a Russian-speaker, have done so. At any rate, the bare fact of Hitler's suicide was first reported to the Russians by Krebs within a few hours of the event.[1] All that remained was to verify it.

There can be no doubt that in the course of the next week the Russians set about verifying the report. For on May 13th Harry Mengershausen, the guard who had buried Hitler's body, was shown an important document. Mengershausen had been captured on the night of May 1st–2nd, but for ten days thereafter he had obstinately denied any connection with Hitler. In the face of this document, however, he now judged further denial useless, and surrendered at discretion. The document, which was dated May 9th, was a full and circumstantial account of the death of Hitler and his burial by Mengershausen, and it had been compiled for the Russians by another German who had evidently taken part in the proceedings, possibly Guensche.[2] This document was (at least)

[1] In the introduction to the second edition I referred to the action of the Czech Government in demanding the trial of Krebs as a war criminal. But in fact that demand was not for Hitler's Chief of General Staff, but for another Hans Krebs, the founder of the German National Socialist movement in Czechoslovakia, afterwards honorary Gauleiter and Regierungspräsident in the Protectorate of Bohemia-Moravia. This Hans Krebs was duly handed over to the Czech Government and executed. General Hans Krebs seems to have committed suicide in the Bunker. At least General Weidling reported so to the Russians when he was captured by them, and this was announced by the Russians on June 9th, 1945, although Stalin, in Moscow, continued to say that Krebs was alive in hiding.

[2] Mengershausen is still unwilling to name the compiler of this document, from which I deduce that he is still alive. Of those still living Guensche is likely to have been the best informed. But there are other witnesses who could have given the Russians sufficient material, at least at secondhand.

the second piece of evidence which the Russians now possessed, and its validity was shown by the fact that it had served to break down the hitherto obstinate Mengershausen.

Immediately after admitting to the Russians that he had buried Hitler, Mengershausen was taken to the Chancellery garden and ordered to locate Hitler's grave. He took his escort at once to the bomb crater, only to notice that the grave had already been dug up and the bodies of Hitler and Eva Braun removed. Clearly the Russians had acted on the earlier evidence, which Mengershausen had thus confirmed.

In fact it is now clear that the Russians had exhumed the bodies on May 9th—the very day on which they received the document describing the death and burial. For on that day two Russian officers, a man and a woman, called at the surgery of Dr Hugo Blaschke, in the Uhlanstrasse. Dr Blaschke was Hitler's dentist; but he was not at home to the Russians. He had fled to Munich, and his practice was now being carried on by a Jewish dentist from Silesia who had replaced him, Dr Feodor Bruck. The Russians asked Dr Bruck for Hitler's dental records. Bruck replied that he had no knowledge of Blaschke's work and referred them to his assistant, Frl. Käte Heusemann, whom he had inherited from Blaschke and who, by an odd coincidence, had been a refugee in the Chancellery during the siege of Berlin and had witnessed many details of Hitler's last days. Frl. Heusemann told the Russians that Hitler had never come to Blaschke's surgery—Blaschke had always gone to the Chancellery, and it was in the laboratory of the Chancellery, if anywhere, that his dental records must be sought. She herself had often accompanied Blaschke on these visits and was thoroughly familiar with Hitler's teeth. They had, she said, certain peculiar characteristics: in particular, identifiable bridges on the upper and lower jaws and a 'window-crown' seldom used in modern dentistry, on one of the incisors.[1] Thereupon Frl. Heusemann was taken to the

[1] The accuracy of these statements about Hitler's dentures is confirmed by X-ray photographs of Hitler's head taken in September 1944 (when Hitler was in the doctor's hands in consequence of the bomb plot of July 20th, 1944) and found among the medical records of Hitler's personal physician Dr Morell. I am grateful to Mr D. S. Hayton Williams who has kindly interpreted these photographs for me.

Chancellery, but no records being found there, she was taken on to the Russian headquarters at Buch. There a Russian officer showed her a cigar box. In it were an Iron Cross decoration, a Nazi Party badge, and a number of dental fittings. Asked whether she recognized these fittings, she replied that they were unmistakably those of the Fuehrer, Adolf Hitler, and—though these were less certain—of Eva Braun. On May 11th, Frl. Heusemann was released and returned to Dr Bruck's surgery to tell her tale. A few days later a boy brought her a message: she was to pack her bags for an absence of some weeks. That was the last Dr Bruck saw of her. Eight years later a woman prisoner returning from Russia told how she had left behind her in the prison of Butyrka one Käte Heusemann, who had regaled her fellow-prisoners *zum Überdruss—ad nauseam*—with the story of Hitler's last days and posthumous dentures.[1]

Frl. Heusemann's story is independently confirmed by another witness who was similarly summoned to identify Hitler's dental system. This was a dental mechanic called Fritz Echtmann who had actually made the fittings for Hitler in 1944, as well as certain other fittings for Eva Braun. He too was summoned by the Russians and shown the same cigar box, the same contents. He too identified them as the fittings of Hitler and Eva Braun. And he too, for his pains, was carried off to Russia—to the Lubianka Prison in Moscow. Later he shared a prison cell with Harry Mengershausen and was able to exchange reminiscences with him. In 1954 he was released and gave evidence of his experiences to the District Court of Berchtesgaden which was considering whether to declare Hitler legally dead or not.[2]

Thus by May 9th, the day on which Echtmann and Heusemann were arrested, it is clear that the Russians had already

[1] *The Times* of July 9th, 1945 (statement of Dr Bruck); *Süddeutsche Zeitung*, December 30th, 1953 (statement of Frl. Liselott Spalcke).

[2] *Süddeutsche Zeitung*, December 30th, 1953; evidence of Mengershausen; *The Times*, October 14th, 1954. Another dentist who had the misfortune to have been involved with Hitler's teeth, and so to have spent ten years in Russia, is Dr Helmut Kunz. See *Süddeutsche Zeitung*, October 21st, 1953.

exhumed the bodies of Hitler and Eva Braun. It also seems likely that they had exhumed them on that same day, for it was then that the memorandum had been submitted which had made it possible to locate the grave. The exhumation appears to have been carried out by a special detachment of the Russian Intelligence Service, the NKVD; for a member of this detachment, Captain Fjedor Pavlovich Vassilki, afterwards told the East Berlin police officer upon whom he was billeted how they had secured the bodies of both Hitler and Eva Braun.[1] "Hitler's skull," said Vassilki, "was almost intact, as were the cranium and the upper and lower jaws." Vassilki confirmed that its identity had afterwards been 'indisputably' proved by the teeth. This identification of the teeth had been followed by Mengershausen's identification by the grave on June 13th. Finally, at the end of May, the Russians took a further positive step. They confronted Mengershausen with the corpse of Hitler.

Mengershausen has described the incident. He was taken by car to a wood at Finow near Berlin. There he was shown three charred and blackened corpses each lying in a wooden crate. He was asked if he recognized them. To him, in spite of the ravages of fire and decay, they were unmistakable. They were the corpses of Goebbels, Frau Goebbels, and Hitler. Goebbels and Frau Goebbels were only superficially burnt. The body of Hitler was in a far worse state. The feet had been entirely consumed, the skin and flesh were blackened and burnt; but the facial structure remained clearly identifiable. There was a bullethole in one temple, but the upper and lower jaw were both intact. Having identified the corpses, Mengershausen was taken back to prison. He does not know what was afterwards done with them. Three months later he too, like Heusemann and Echtmann, was removed to Russia—for eleven years.

Thus by the beginning of June the Russians had learnt the circumstances of Hitler's death, and identified his grave and body, by a number of converging testimonies. Quite apart from the evidence of Krebs on the night of April 30th–May 1st, and any evidence which they may have obtained from

[1] *Das Bild*, January 26th, 1956.

other prisoners from the Bunker, they had the document of May 9th whose validity had been shown by its success in breaking down the resistance of Mengershausen, and they had the evidence of Mengershausen both of the grave and of the corpse found therein; they had the independent evidence of Heusemann and of other prisoners about the last days in the Bunker, and the separate technical evidence of Heusemann and Echtmann about Hitler's teeth. Further, the Russians had—or at least Marshal Zhukov stated that they had—certain 'captured adjutants' diaries' to which he afterwards ascribed his knowledge of the marriage of Hitler and Eva Braun. These 'diaries' may have been identical with the document of June 9th, which was evidently a reconstruction, not a genuine diary; but of course they may have been independent documents swelling still further the volume of evidence. Now all this evidence pointed clearly in the same direction, and although in theory it might conceivably have been concerted, in fact there were sufficient witnesses to make a serious and sustained conspiracy impossible. Altogether, by the first week in June, the Russians had a good deal more evidence (or at least the raw material for a good deal more evidence) for the last days of Hitler than I had for my reconstruction five months later.

Why then, we may ask, did they never publish their conclusions? Was it that they did not wish to discover the facts? Their whole attitude at the time—their search for records, arrest of witnesses, repeated identifications[1]—belies that assumption. Was it then that they were, in intelligence matters, incompetent? Their search in Hitler's Bunker itself was amazingly incomplete: they left Hitler's diary—a stout bound volume 14 inches by 7—lying in his chair for four months to be discovered by a British visitor. But no one can regard the Russians as unintelligent or unsystematic in their interrogation of prisoners and I do not think that we should flatter ourselves by supposing them less efficient than we are. If we wish to

[1] The Russians identified the body of Goebbels at least three times. Once on May 2nd, when it was identified for them by Hans Fritzsche, once about May 20th, when it was identified by Wilhelm Exkhold, Goebbels' personal security officer; and once at the end of May, as described above, by Mengershausen.

35

answer this question we must abstain from such assumptions and look closely at the actual facts in the case.

For there can be no doubt that in the first week of June the Russians in Berlin did admit Hitler's death. On June 5th, when the Allied Commanders-in-Chief met in Berlin to set up the machinery of quadripartite government, 'responsible Russian officers' told officers of General Eisenhower's staff that Hitler's body had been recovered and identified with 'fair certainty'. The body, they said, was one of four found in the Bunker. It was badly charred—a fact which they then ascribed (wrongly, as we now know) to the flamethrowers with which the Russian troops had cleared the place. The bodies, they said, had been examined by Russian doctors, and this examination had yielded 'almost certain identification'.[1] If the Russians did not make an official announcement of Hitler's death, that (said the Russian officers) was merely because they were reluctant to commit themselves so long as 'any shred of doubt' remained. But they made it clear that, as far as the evidence went, it seemed conclusive.[2]

Four days later, on June 9th, Marshal Zhukov made a public statement to the Press. He described the last days in the Chancellery. He related—it was the first time it had been published—the marriage of Hitler and Eva Braun, whom he described, incorrectly, as a film-actress. He based his knowledge of these facts, he said, on 'the diaries of Hitler's aides, which had fallen into Russian hands'. But on the crucial question of the death of Hitler, he faltered. He said nothing of Russian investigations, nothing of German revelations, nothing of the burning or the burial, the exhumation, the dentists,

[1] It is interesting to note that Artur Axmann, under interrogation in 1946, said that he was obliged to assume that, although it was not apparent from the corpse (which he had seen), Hitler, in shooting himself through the mouth, must have shattered his dental fittings, since otherwise it was inconceivable that the Russians should not have identified his body by them. In fact we know that these fittings were preserved and had been identified. In all the circumstances it is very difficult to suppose that there was room for genuine doubt by this time.

[2] The Russian statement as given in *The Times* of June 7th, 1945, contains some minor inaccuracies; but these are to be expected since it was given at secondhand by members of General Eisenhower's staff on their return to Paris.

or the teeth. 'The circumstances are very mysterious,' he said. 'We have not identified the body of Hitler. I can say nothing definite about his fate. He could have flown away from Berlin at the very last moment. The state of the runway would have allowed him to do so.'[1] Then the Russian military commandant of Berlin, Colonel-General Berzarin, spoke. He said that Hitler might well be alive. 'We have found several bodies that might be Hitler's, but we cannot state that he is dead. My opinion is that Hitler has gone into hiding and is somewhere in Europe, possibly with General Franco.' The ewith the subject was closed. From that moment Russian headquarters in Berlin never again mentioned the subject or circumstance of Hitler's death. Total silence enveloped the ostentatiously unsolved mystery, and this apparent repudiation of past admissions led, more than any other cause, to the growing belief that Hitler was alive after all.[2]

This gradual reversal of belief was clearly shown in the attitude of General Eisenhower. Up to June 9th, Eisenhower had publicly assumed Hitler to be dead. But on June 10th, the day after Zhukov's public statement, Eisenhower and Zhukov met at Frankfurt. Five days later, in Paris, Eisenhower bore witness to the change of doctrine which had followed this meeting. Previously, he said, he had accepted the fact of Hitler's death, but more recently he had met high Russian leaders who had great doubts.[3] These doubts were so strong that a week later, when the British published the story of Hermann Karnau, a member of Hitler's detective guard who had witnessed the burning of the bodies, it was generally disbelieved. In September the Russians carried their disbelief further: they accused the British of harbouring both Hitler and Eva Braun in their zone of Germany, presumably for eventual use against their Russian allies, and it was this accusation which led directly to my appointment to establish the facts. On October 6th General Eisenhower paid a visit to

[1] Zhukov's statement was published in *Pravda*, June 10th, 1945, and, in English, in *Soviet War News*, June 11th, 1945.

[2] As the *Sunday Express* wrote the day after Zhukov's statement, June 10th, 1945, 'these statements by the Russians will start a new hue-and-cry throughout Europe.' They did.

[3] *The Times*, June 16th, 1945.

Holland, and was quoted as telling Dutch journalists at Utrecht that although he had at first believed Hitler to be dead, now 'there was reason to believe that he was alive'. It happened that I was at General Eisenhower's headquarters at Frankfurt at the time, and was able to point out that, however defective the positive evidence of death might be, there was no reason to believe that Hitler was alive. On his return to Frankfurt General Eisenhower thereupon modified his statement. He himself, he said, found it hard to believe that Hitler was alive, 'but his Russian friends assured him that they had been unable to unearth any tangible evidence of his death'.[1]

Not only did the Russians insist that they had unearthed nothing themselves: they declined to show any interest in evidence unearthed by their allies. When they failed to find Dr Blaschke in Berlin, they never asked us to find him in Munich. They ignored Hermann Karnau and his story. On November 1st, 1945, when I made my report in Berlin, the Russians received it with complete lack of interest. It was not even mentioned in the Russian Press. My request that certain Russian prisoners might be interrogated was ignored. Eighteen months later, when my book was published, their attitude remained the same. Though it was translated into most European and some Asiatic languages, *The Last Days of Hitler* never penetrated behind the Iron Curtain. The apparent exceptions to this rule are in fact confirmations of it. The Czech edition was published before the Communist *coup d'état* of February 1948, the Yugoslav edition after the Titoist emancipation of June 1948; the Polish edition was stifled in the publisher's office, the Bulgarian edition destroyed by the police on its appearance. For years after June 9th, 1945, the official Russian doctrine remained unchanged, apparently unchangeable, by the evidence. It was never allowed that Hitler might be dead. It was assumed, and sometimes openly stated, that he was alive.

How can we account for this extraordinary reversal? Certainty indeed is impossible to attain; but there are suggestive straws of evidence. To detect them we must look not at Berlin, or any such subordinate office, but at the centre of Russian orthodoxy, Moscow.

[1] *The Times*, October 8th, and October 13th, 1945.

For during all this time, even when the Russians in Berlin had come nearest to announcing Hitler's death, Stalin in Moscow was firmly declaring that he was alive. Early in the morning of May 2nd, before the Russians had even captured the Reich Chancellery, the official Russian news agency, Tass, had declared the German broadcast statement of Hitler's death to be 'a fresh Fascist trick'. 'By spreading statements about Hitler's death,' it added, 'the German Fascists evidently hope to prepare the possibility for Hitler to disappear from the stage and go underground.'[1] On May 26th, while the Russians in Berlin were still collecting and digesting the evidence, Stalin, in the Kremlin, told Harry L. Hopkins, the representative of the American President, that he believed 'that Bormann, Goebbels, Hitler, and probably Krebs had escaped and were in hiding'.[2] This statement can hardly have been based on evidence from Berlin, where the body of Goebbels had long been found and identified, as the Russians in Berlin admitted, 'without any doubt'. It therefore seems to represent a personal prejudice of Stalin, who either believed it because he wanted to believe it, or stated it because he wanted it to be believed. Again, on June 6th, when Zhukov's staff officers were assuring Eisenhower's staff officers that Hitler's body had been discovered, exhumed, and scientifically identified, Stalin, in Moscow, was repeating to Hopkins not merely that he had no evidence of Hitler's death but that 'he was sure that Hitler was alive'.[3] Three days later Zhukov publicly changed his view. Stalin kept to his. On July 16th he came himself to Berlin for the Potsdam Conference. There, next day, he surprised the American Secretary of State, Mr James F. Byrnes, by saying that he believed Hitler to be alive, probably in Spain or Argentina.[4] Admiral Leahy, the representative of President Truman, also noted the remark. 'Concerning Hitler,' he records, 'Stalin repeated what he had told Hopkins at Moscow. He believed that the Fuehrer had escaped and was

[1] *Pravda*, May 2nd, 1945.
[2] Robert E. Sherwood, *The White House Papers* (London, 1949), p. 880.
[3] *Ibid.* p. 902.
[4] James F. Byrnes, *Speaking Frankly* (New York, 1947), p. 68.

in hiding somewhere. He said careful search by Soviet investigators had not found any trace of Hitler's remains or any other positive evidence of his death.'[1] Ten days later he repeated that his opinion was unchanged.[2]

Faced with this evidence, it is difficult to avoid the conclusion that Zhukov in Berlin had been corrected from Moscow: that he had been ordered, some time between June 5th and 9th, to abandon his belief, based on the evidence, that Hitler was dead and to substitute for it the view of Stalin, derived from some other motive, that he was alive, 'in hiding... possible with General Franco'.[3] Some plausibility is given to this conclusion by the fact that at precisely this time Andrei Vyshinsky, the first Soviet vice-commissar for Foreign Affairs, arrived in Berlin from Moscow, evidently in order to put Zhukov firmly in his place. On June 5th, in Berlin, Eisenhower had observed that 'Zhukov had seemed unwilling to reply to any of his questions without first consulting Vyshinsky'. Two days later, Hopkins, who had just been told by Stalin in Moscow that 'Zhukov would have very little power concerning political affairs in Berlin', noticed that Vyshinsky was 'in Zhukov's ear all during our conversation'. On June 9th, when Zhukov made his announcement that Hitler might be alive after all, Vyshinsky was standing beside him; and next day, when Zhukov visited Frankfurt and told Eisenhower of the change of doctrine, Vyshinsky came with him. At Frankfurt Zhukov, in Vyshinsky's presence, made a speech dwelling on the soldier's duty to obey the politician—a doctrine which he seems subsequently to have revised. There seems no doubt that at this time, as Hopkins told Eisenhower, 'the Russian Government intended to control General Zhukov completely'. A few months later, Zhukov—whom his German enemies had recognized as the ablest of Russian generals—was removed from Germany into virtual exile, first as Commander-in-Chief

[1] William D. Leahy, *I Was There* (London, 1950), p. 463.

[2] Byrnes, *loc. cit.*

[3] It is interesting to note this similarity between Stalin's view and what Colonel-General Berzarin described as 'my opinion', *viz*: that Hitler had taken refuge with Franco. It seems unlikely that Berzarin, a non-political soldier, would have ventured to express any view of his own on such a 'political' subject.

of Russian Home Forces, then, more ignominiously, as military governor of Odessa: an exile from which he only emerged—and he emerged with some *éclat*—on the death of Stalin.[1]

Why did Stalin thus correct Zhukov, and replace the 'almost certain' and at least legitimate conclusion that Hitler was dead by categorical statements that he was alive? Why did he require a veil of silence or denial to be drawn over the patient searches of Russian officers in Berlin, their interrogations, exhumations, identifications? Why did he refuse to accept from his Western allies evidence which would perhaps have clinched the matter, if there was any genuine doubt?[2] Was it that he regarded the belief in Hitler's death or survival as a 'political' question: that he judged it politically necessary, whatever the evidence, to maintain publicly that Hitler, so far from suffering a *Heldentod* in his ruined capital, had slunk away into hiding? Did he perhaps fear that an admission of Hitler's death might lead, if Nazism were to revive, to an identification of holy places, of pilgrimages, shrines, and relics, which in turn would sustain the spirit of later anti-Russian, anti-Bolshevik crusaders? Did he fear the political power of the successful Russian generals and so resolve to take this 'political' issue out of their control? His treatment of Zhukov, like his assumption of the title Generalissimo, suggests that he did distrust them, and the events after his death, when the Red Army leaders in general and Zhukov in particular took their revenge on his successor and his 'Georgian' party in Russia, suggests that there was a real opposition between them. Conceivably—when we remember the narrow and recondite fronts upon which inter-Bolshevik struggles are fought—the question of Hitler's death, and the official doctrine about it, may have been the symbol of some deeper tension in Russian politics. Or again, was Stalin perhaps preparing a useful stick with

[1] That Stalin was determined to disgrace Zhukov appears from several pieces of evidence. For instance, the history of the war was rewritten in Russia in such a way as to diminish or eliminate Zhukov's role in it. *See* Isaac Deutscher, *Stalin* (1949), pp. 483 note; 562.

[2] For instance, the Western allies obtained copious medical records from Hitler's doctors, including X-ray photographs of his head which would have been conclusive for the identification of the skull.

which to beat his *bête noire*, General Franco?[1] Or is all this too elaborate an analysis? May it not be that Stalin was simply wrong, and that his ill-considered dogmatism, like a papal indiscretion, became, by the mere machinery of ideological power, a necessary truth? We cannot exclude this possibility. By 1945 Stalin was already, in his own eyes, the greatest statesman, the greatest strategist, the greatest philosopher in the world, the Father and Teacher of Mankind; and thanks to a vast hierarchy of obedient yes-men beneath him his lightest observations could become infallible truths before which inconvenient evidence must bow and retire. It is quite possible that Stalin declared Hitler alive without any ulterior purpose, merely out of the abundant self-assurance of the great, and that the mere bureaucracy of ideological tyranny then converted this casual utterance into a dogma. At all events, the dogma prevailed. The Russians in Berlin knew the evidence against it. For them it was a dogma difficult to support and yet impolitic to deny. In such circumstances their best policy was silence. I now see how tiresome it much have been for them when, in response to that silence, their Western allies officiously offered to help them by producing what of all things they least wanted—more evidence.

However, the dogma did not last for ever. In 1950, when the second English edition of my book was published, its sway was still unbroken, at least in public. But meanwhile, in Russia, the ground was being silently prepared for a change. In 1949 a new 'documentary' colour film was being prepared. In June 1950 it was released in the Russian sector of Berlin. This film was called *The Fall of Berlin*.[2] It was produced by M. Chiaureli, and its chief characteristic was an unremitting,

[1] It should be remembered that Stalin was at this time demanding the overthrow of Franco to complete the victory over Fascism. As *Pravda* declared, in an article entitled 'Hitler's Agent, General Franco!' (July 6th, 1945), 'The interests of European peace and security require the earliest elimination of the Fascist hotbed in the Iberian Peninsula.'

[2] According to an article by M. Anzhaparidze and V. Tsirgiladze published in *IskusstvoKino* 1950 No 4, the script of *The Fall of Berlin* was completed in May 1948, after eight revisions, and the filming began in January 1949.

fulsome, indeed nauseating worship of Stalin, who was then still alive and enjoying the last stages of his apotheosis on earth. But in one respect the film deviated from the previous Stalinist orthodoxy. Hitler was now represented not as fleeing to Spain or Argentina, but as perishing, by his own hand, in the Chancellery Bunker, substantially as narrated in my book.

What had happened to cause this sudden, unheralded, unexplained *volte-face* in Russia, this sudden, new reversal of the Party line? Examinations of the prisoners newly returned from Russia gives some clue towards the solution of this problem. For after the *volte-face* of June 9th, the whole stage, the caste, and the stage-properties were all removed from Germany to Russia. By the end of August they had all arrived—including, it seems, the central figure in the drama, the charred and mouldering remains of the Fuehrer.[1] The witnesses, who had formerly been prisoners of the Red Army, were now classed as political prisoners, and as such were concentrated in the Lubianka prison in Moscow, but they were not allowed to communicate with each other. There were Baur and Rattenhuber, Mengershausen, Echtmann, Linge, Guensche, and others. They were known as 'the Reich Chancellery Group'. And now, when the stage had thus been reset, they were all separately and systematically re-examined. They were made to write down the full history of their experiences in the last days of Nazi Berlin. Wearily they repeated the facts which they had already stated in Germany. For long they were not believed. The Russians accused Baur, since he had been Hitler's Pilot of having flown the Fuehrer, or having arranged his flight, out of Berlin to safety. Was he not now in Spain or the Argentine? They accused Rattenhuber, since he had been responsible for Hitler's security, of having prepared his secret

[1] It is not clear precisely when the bodies were taken to Russia. The Russians apparently gave Baur the impression that they were available in Berlin in the summer of 1946 and were only removed to Russia then; but this impression may have been false, or the bodies may have been temporarily brought to Berlin together with the Reich Chancellery Group (see below). Vassilki seems to have implied that they were moved in the summer of 1945, and this seems a reasonable supposition. It is likely that the dead evidence and the living evidence was all transported together.

43

escape by U-boat to the Argentine. Always it was Spain or the Argentine, just as Stalin had insisted in May 1945. "Come," the interrogator once said to Rattenhuber, after he had told the old facts for the umpteenth time, "enough of these fairy tales. Tell us the truth." Ultimately, after almost a year of interrogation, Baur at least had the impression that the incredulity of his captors was beginning to melt. Then, in the summer of 1946, a new scene was enacted in this grim, insistent, slow, nagging Russian comedy.

The 'Reich Chancellery Group' were suddenly assembled and taken out of their prison. Without explanation they were put into a train and then into an aeroplane. They landed, and found that they were in Berlin. They were taken to the Chancellery; and there they were made to re-enact, on its original site, the whole scene of Hitler's death, burial, and burning.[1] This macabre incident seems finally to have satisfied the Russians. At one moment, while in Berlin, they even promised to show Baur and others the mortal relics of the Fuehrer; but this promise was never carried out. Then, having satisfied themselves of the conclusions, the Russians set to work to dissipate the evidence. They took the witnesses back to Russia and dispersed them to different prisons, some to the Arctic, some to the Urals; they laid waste the Chancellery, blew up the Bunker with high explosive; and as for Hitler's body, which he himself had taken such pains to hide from them, lest they should insult it, they now, having identified it, sought to hide it from the Germans, lest they should revere it. Three years later a German prisoner, brought from the Urals to the Lubianka prison and asked if he could recognize a photograph of the charred bodies of Hitler and Eva Braun, felt unable to give a positive answer. To give a positive answer, he said, he would need to see the bodies themselves. "Then you don't believe that the bodies are in Moscow?" asked his interrogator. The prisoner admitted that he did not. "Hitler's body," he was then told, "is in better keeping with us than under the Brandenburg Gate in Berlin. The dead can be more dangerous than the living. If Frederick the Great had not been buried

[1] A published account of this incident can be found in *Der Fortschritt* (Düsseldorf), May 5th, 1955.

in state in Potsdam the Germans would not have started so many wars in the last two centuries. The Germans like martyrs!"[1] But this martyr they were not to have. Though further knowledge has altered their circumstantial background, my original remark remains accidentally true: 'Like Alaric, buried secretly under the river-bed of Busento, the modern destroyer of mankind is now immune from discovery.'

Thus after long incredulity and in spite of official prejudices the Russians at last accepted the truth about the last days of Hitler substantially as it is recorded in this book. Their methods and their sources were different; their investigation was entirely—indeed gratuitously—independent; and they arrived more reluctantly at their conclusions. But their conclusions are the same as mine. Such agreement, in such circumstances, seems to me the strongest support that I could hope for, if indeed I felt the need for any support for conclusions already reached by rational methods. Before long such evidence will surely convince even the German lawcourts which still, in May 1956, hesitate to pronounce Hitler dead.[2]

I have said that the Russian version is 'substantially' the same as mine, for in one small detail I must admit that we differ. Both in their early admissions and in their later film the Russians suggested that Hitler had killed himself by taking poison. On June 5th, 1945, Zhukov's staff officers stated that Russian doctors had established, by an examination of Hitler's body, that he had died of poison. In their film Hitler is shown swallowing a poison-capsule. On the other hand I have stated that he shot himself through the mouth. Since the Russians

[1] The account of this former prisoner (who remains anonymous) is published in *Revue* (Munich), February 11th, 1956.

[2] A legal declaration of Hitler's death was sought, in 1952, in order to establish the Austrian government's legal title to a confiscated painting by Vermeer, *The Artist in his Studio*, which Hitler had acquired from Count Jaromir Czernin-Morzin in 1940. After a dispute as to competence between the courts (*Amtsgerichte*) of Berchtesgaden and Berlin-Schöneberg had been settled in favour of the former in July 1955, the victorious court of Berchtesgaden, in October 1955, postponed a final death certificate until all German prisoners should have returned from Russia.

45

had possession of Hitler's body and I had not, they were obviously in a more favourable position than I was to determine the cause of his death. On the other hand none of their pronouncements has been authoritative, reasoned, or even circumstantial. Their early statements, before June 9th, 1945, were unofficial and secondhand: in some respects they were certainly inaccurate—at least in the form in which they were reported; and their film was unashamed propaganda full of tendentious inaccuracies: it cannot be taken as scientific documentation. In these circumstances perhaps it is best to go behind their loose statements and re-examine the available evidence.

The first witness who was available in 1945 was Erich Kempka, Hitler's chauffeur. He had escaped from Berlin and had been captured by the Americans. Under interrogation he stated that immediately after Hitler's death, Guensche, who had inspected the body, had told him that Hitler had shot himself through the mouth. This of course, is only secondhand evidence; but Kempka added that after helping to carry Eva Braun's body out to the burning, he himself had gone into the 'death room' and seen, lying on the floor, two revolvers, one a Walther 7·65, the other a Walther 6·35. Seven months later this evidence was confirmed and completed by the Hitler Youth Leader, Artur Axmann, who had been at large in the Bavarian Alps and who is thus independent of Kempka. Axmann stated that he had been one of those who entered the 'death room' immediately after Hitler's suicide. "As we entered, we saw the Fuehrer sitting on a small divan, Eva Braun at his side, with her head resting on his shoulder. The Fuehrer was only slightly slumped forward and everyone recognized that he was dead. His jaw hung somewhat loosely down and a pistol lay on the floor. Blood was dripping from both temples, and his mouth was bloody and smeared, but there was not much blood spattered around . . . I believe that Hitler took poison first and then shot himself through the mouth, and that the concussion of such a blast resulted in the blood on the Fuehrer's temples."

Such was the evidence available to me in 1946. Now it is supplemented by the evidence of Linge and Mengershausen who, having spent the intervening decade in Russian prisons, have had no opportunity of collusion with either Kempka or Axmann. Linge is a first-hand witness: he too went into the 'death room' immediately after Hitler's suicide, and it was he who carried the body out into the garden. According to his account, when he went into the room, "there, almost upright in a sitting position on a couch, was the body of Adolf Hitler. A small hole, the size of a German silver mark, showed on his right temple and a trickle of blood ran slowly down over his cheek." After this statement, which exactly confirms the entirely independent account of Axmann, Linge goes on to confirm the details given by Kempka: 'one pistol, a Walther 7·65 lay on the floor where it had dropped from his right hand. A yard or so away lay another gun of 6·35 calibre.'[1] To this must be added the evidence of Mengershausen, who states that when he was shown the remains of Hitler's body about a month later, the head had a bullethole in the temple. Mengershausen adds that he believes, from the state of the head when he inspected it, that Hitler had shot himself through the head, not through the mouth as I had written. The hole in the temple seemed to him to be the hole of an ingoing, not an outgoing bullet. Had Hitler shot himself through the mouth, Mengershausen says, the air pressure would surely have broken the jaws; which, however, were intact. I am not competent to judge this matter, and the experts whom I consult give me such different answers that I am content to leave the matter in suspense. But the evidence seems clear that although Hitler may conceivably, as Axmann surmised, have taken poison as well,[2] he certainly killed himself with a revolver shot.[3]

Indeed, this is what I should have expected from his character. Hitler liked to remember, and to show, that he was a soldier. He liked to set to his generals, whom he distrusted,

[1] *News of the World*, October 23rd, 1955.
[2] Such a theory would account for any traces of poison which the Russians may have found in his body. But I am sceptical. Even to the Russians the bullethole in Hitler's head must have been more obvious than any traces of poison in his body. Since they were silent about the bullethole, why should we take seriously their statement about poison?
[3] The newly released Guensche now also states that Hitler shot himself.

an example of the correct behaviour of a true German soldier. Already two years before he had stated very clearly what that duty might be. It was in February 1943, when the news reached him that Field-Marshal Paulus had surrendered at Stalingrad. On hearing such news Hitler was beside himself with rage and treated his General Staff to a tirade on the subject. Why, he asked, had he made Paulus, at this last minute, a Field Marshal? Why, except to show that the Fuehrer was honouring him at his death? For of course he had expected Paulus and his commanders to commit suicide. They should have 'closed ranks, formed a hedgehog, and shot themselves with their last bullet'. Why should they not have shot themselves? "It is," he declared ominously, "the road that every man has to take some time." Even in peacetime, "in Germany about 18,000 or 20,000 people a year chose to commit suicide, even without being in such a position." How could there be any excuse for a defeated war leader? "When the nerves break down, there is nothing left but to admit that one can't handle the situation and to shoot one's self."[1] In April 1945 Hitler recognized that he had met his Stalingrad. I do not think he would have failed to follow his own prescription to the letter. He would have chosen the formal death of the soldier, with a revolver.

Why then did the Russians expurgate the revolver from their version of Hitler's death? There is a perfectly rational explanation which, though conjectural, may well be true. The Russians may well have concealed the manner of Hitler's suicide for precisely the same reason for which Hitler chose it: because it was a soldier's death. I myself suspect that this was their reason. After all, it is in line with their general practice. Previous tyrannies of the spirit have sought to crush defeated but dangerous philosophies by emphatic, public executions: the gibbet, the block, the bloody quarters exhibited *in terrorem populi*. But such spectacular liquidations, however effective at the time, have a habit of breeding later myths: there are relics of the dead, pilgrimages to the place of execution. The Russian Bolsheviks have therefore preferred in general a less emphatic method: their ideological enemies have slid into oblivion in nameless graves at uncertain dates and no

[1] *Hitler Directs His War* (New York, 1950), pp. 17–22.

relics of them are available for later veneration. I have already suggested that it was for this reason, and in accordance with this philosophy, that they concealed the circumstances of Hitler's death, hid his bones, and destroyed the scene of his suicide and his Nordic funeral. It may well be that when such total concealment was no longer possible and they decided to admit the facts, there was one fact which they thought it expedient to alter. The soldier's death might seem to the Germans heroic. Suicide by poison might well seem to the Russians a more expedient version.

If this is so, it raises an interesting general question. For my book was also written, in the first place, for exactly the same reason which made the Russians frown upon it: to prevent (as far as such means can prevent) the rebirth of the Hitler myth. It would thus seem that we and the Russians, in this matter, seek exactly the same end by diametrically opposite means: they by suppressing the evidence, we by publishing it. Which of these two methods is the more effective is arguable. I will only say that I personally believe in my own. For when has the suppression of the truth prevented the rise of a myth, if a myth is wanted? When has the absence of genuine relics prevented the discovery of false relics, if they are needed? When has uncertainty about a true shrine prevented pilgrimages to a false one? And besides, there seems to me in the Russian argument, if I have correctly described it, a somewhat sinister implication. If they fear the truth, does it not seem that they believe in its power: that they think that Hitler's reign really was inspiring, that his end really was glorious, and that secrecy is necessary to prevent the spread of such a view? It is a view which I do not share. It seems to me, having perhaps too naïve a faith in human nature and human reason, that Hitler's reign was so evil, his character so detestable, that no one can be seduced into admiring him by reading the true history either of his life or of his melodramatic and carefully stage-managed end.

For that these last days of Hitler were a carefully produced theatrical piece is, I think, clear. It was not merely because he wished to escape a public trial, or hide his body from the Russians, that Hitler chose his form of death. His whole previous history had been consciously theatrical, perhaps even operatic; and it would have been contrary to all his thinking if he had ended such a career with an insipid or bungled finale. Long before, in the days of his triumph, he had often declared that the only satisfactory alternative to apotheosis was a spectacular annihilation: like Samson at Gaza he would drag down with him the temples of his enemies. He had even indicated—long before he even conceived of failure—the ideal method of death. "In short," he remarked in February 1942, "if one hadn't a family to bequeath one's house to, the best thing would be to be burnt in it with all its contents—a magnificent funeral pyre!"[1] Little did he think, in those months of triumph, that he would so soon be following, even to the letter, his own prescription. Fortunately, when the time came, he had with him the essential man, the impresario of the Nazi movement, Joseph Goebbels, who for twenty years had devised the décor, the accompaniment and the advertisement of this dreadful Wagnerian melodrama. On March 27th, 1945, Goebbels' assistant, Rudolf Semler, recorded in his diary the preparations for this last act. 'Goebbels', he wrote, 'has persuaded Hitler not to leave Berlin. He has reminded him of his oath taken on January 30th, 1933. That evening Hitler had said to Goebbels in the Reich Chancellery, "We shall never leave this building again of our own free will. No power in the world can ever force us to abandon our position." Now all preparations are being made for the real 'Twilight of the Gods scene.'[2] This book is the record of that carefully prepared scene. It is also evidence of its skilful management. But does such a well-staged melodrama excite respect or inspire emulation? The reader must judge. Posterity will show.

[1] *Hitler's Table Talk* (1953), p. 316.
[2] R. Semler, *Goebbels, the Man Next to Hitler* (1947), p. 188.

50

PREFACE TO FIFTH EDITION (1978)

FOR the fourth edition of *The Last Days of Hitler*, in 1971, I did not find it necessary to make any changes from the previous edition of 1956, and I left the Introduction to that edition unchanged. Apart from the evidence of its date, it seems to me still adequate for all its purposes today, and I see no point in tampering with it.

The only new evidence which had appeared between 1956 and 1971 was the Russian evidence concerning the method of Hitler's death. The fact of the secret Russian enquiry, and its conclusions, were known to me when I wrote my introduction to the 1956 edition, in which I took account of them (see pp. 29–45). The subsequent publication of the secret did not add anything except the report of the official Russian autopsy. However, for the sake of completeness I added to the fourth edition a new appendix (Appendix II) which gives some account of the Russian publication and my comments upon it.

The remaining problem concerns the fate of Martin Bormann. In 1946 I recorded the evidence of Artur Axmann who stated that he had seen the bodies of Bormann and Stumpfegger lying in the Invalidenstrasse near the Lehrter station. This statement was unsupported and therefore could not be accepted without reservation, and in view of the confident, if conflicting, statements that were made about Bormann's survival, I decided to leave the question open. In the next 25 years nothing happened to change the balance of evidence, and in 1971, when the fourth edition of my book went to press, I still felt obliged to leave it open. However, in view of new evidence which has recently been found, I believe that it can now be closed.

The first clue came from Russia. In 1965 a Russian journalist, Lev Bezymenski, in the course of a work of Soviet propaganda designed to show (but by very feeble arguments) that Bormann had escaped to South America to serve the interests of U.S. imperialism (*Po Sledam Martina Borman*, Moscow 1965), incidentally referred to a diary of Martin Bormann allegedly found in Berlin. Mr. Bezymenski has since been allowed to publish this diary, with a lengthy commentary by himself, in Germany.[1] Internal evidence suggests that it is genuine. Although the history of this document has been variously reported, it seems that it was found in the pocket of a discarded leather coat near the Lehrter station – i.e. in the area where Axmann reported having seen the bodies of Bormann and Stumpfegger – and had been in Russian hands since 1945. After its existence had been disclosed, attempts were made to discover the bodies, but they were unsuccessful. However, in December 1972, in the course of building operations in the same place, two bodies were accidentally dug up which the German authorities have declared, after forensic tests, to be those of Bormann and Stumpfegger. Some of the circumstances of this enquiry, which was organised by a popular newspaper, aroused suspicion; but Dr. Reidar F. Sognnaes, a U.S. dental surgeon who has specialised in such identification, and has used the surviving dental records of Bormann's (and Hitler's) dentist, Professor Hugo Blaschke, is satisfied that the shorter of the two bodies has been correctly identified as that of Bormann.[2] Thus Axmann's evidence is at last independently confirmed, at least in essentials. Only in one inessential detail does it need to be modified. Seeing no wounds, Axmann assumed that Bormann and Stumpfegger had been shot in the back. The German authorities concluded that, despairing of escape, they had taken poison.

[1] Lew Besymenski, *Die letzten Notizen von Martin Bormann* (Stuttgart, 1974).

[2] Reidar F. Sognnaes, 'Dental Evidence in the Postmortem Identification of Adolf Hitler, Eva Braun and Martin Bormann', in *Legal Medicine Annual*, 1976.

CHAPTER ONE

HITLER AND HIS COURT

Now that the New Order is past, and the Thousand-Year Reich has crumbled in a decade, we are able at last, picking among the still smoking rubble, to discover the truth about that fantastic and tragical episode. It is a chastening as well as an interesting study; for we discover not only the true facts, but the extent of our own errors. If we are to understand the extraordinary tale of Hitler's last days, and appreciate the true character of Nazi politics, it is essential that we should first dispose of those errors. We must recognize that Hitler was not a pawn; that the Nazi state was not (in any significant use of the word) totalitarian; and that its leading politicians were not a government but a court—a court as negligible in its power of ruling, as incalculable in its capacity for intrigue, as any oriental sultanate.[1] Further we must know the true political significance of the Nazi doctrine, and the extent to which it retained its purity and determined events in these last days; and the nature of Hitler's struggle with the Army General Staff—the one dissident group which he could neither dissolve nor eliminate, and which, at one time, might have eliminated him. Unless such political facts and relations are understood, the events of

---

[1] The Reich Cabinet, though it existed in theory, had no significance in fact and never met. Lammers, the Nazi constitutional pundit, stated at Nuremberg that he had once tried to get the members to meet each other informally, to drink beer; but Hitler had forbidden such a dangerous experiment.

April 1945 will be quite incomprehensible, and the labour of collecting and arranging that complicated mass of evidence will have been, in one sense, in vain: for while solving one mystery of fact, it will have added a greater mystery of interpretation.

Some of these statements may seem paradoxical. How many people, in the past years, were unconsciously seduced by Nazi propaganda into believing that Nazi Germany was organized as a 'totalitarian' state—totally integrated, totally mobilized, centrally controlled! Had this been true, Germany might yet have won the war, for its advantages in time, resources, and preparation were enormous; but in fact the totalitarianism of Germany was something quite different from this. Only policy, not administration, was effectively controlled at the centre. Total war, to the Nazis, did not mean, as it meant to us (and perhaps only to us), a concentration of all effort upon the war, and a corresponding suspension of all irrelevant industry, for in Germany the production of many inessential luxuries was continued; it meant indiscriminate war by all methods and in all elements. In Nazi Germany neither war production, nor man-power, nor administration, nor intelligence, was rationally centralized; and Ribbentrop's protest at Nuremberg that foreign intelligence was not supplied by the Foreign Ministry but by thirty competing agencies is substantially true. The structure of German politics and administration, instead of being, as the Nazis claimed, 'pyramidal' and 'monolithic', was in fact a confusion of private empires, private armies, and private intelligence services. In truth, irresponsible absolutism is incompatible with totalitarian administration; for in the uncertainty of politics, the danger of arbitrary change, and the fear of personal revenge, every man whose position makes him either strong or vulnerable must protect himself against surprise by reserving from the common pool whatever power he has managed to acquire. Thus there is, in the end, no common pool at all. Irresponsibility of the ruler causes irresponsibility of the subject; the conception of the commonwealth no longer exists outside propaganda; and politics become the politics of feudal anarchy, which the personal power of an undisputed despot may conceal but cannot alter.

And how wrong many of us were about that despot too,

who has often been represented as a tool, but whose personal power was in fact so undisputed that he rode to the end above the chaos he had created, and concealed its true nature—even presiding from his grave over his weak and worthless subordinates in the dock at Nuremberg! If this absolutism was unchecked, uncontrolled, by any external force, it is vain to suppose that any internal resistance could have corrected it. No man can escape the corruption of absolute power. The inhibitions, the cautions, the introspections which may influence the exercise of power when it is limited by insecurity or competition do not survive those limitations; and in Hitler's last years it will be futile to look for the diplomacy and concessions of his more tentative days, or the reservations and occasional humilities of *Mein Kampf*.[1]

Then there is Nazism itself, the religion of the German revolution, which underlay and inspired its temporary but spectacular success, and was as important an element in its politics as was Calvinism in earlier convulsions. Many worthy scholars have examined this vast system of bestial Nordic nonsense, analysing its component parts, discovering its remote origins, explaining its significance, and disposing of its errors; but of all the works on that dispiriting subject, the best, the most illuminating, the most valuable, seem to me to have come not from the conscientious scholars, nor from the virtuous victims of the movement, but (since failure is often a better political education than either industry or virtue) from one disappointed Nazi. Hermann Rauschning, an East Prussian magnate, was one of those military aristocrats who joined the movement in its early days, hoping to use it for their own ends, and who, having made their contribution to its success, and been cheated of their reward, saw the final ruin of their class in the purge of 1944. More intelligent then the rest, Rauschning escaped early from the movement which he could neither control nor stop, and in two books exposed, with terrible

---

[1] Some of the contrasts between Hitler's theory, as published in *Mein Kampf*, and his practice during the war will be noticed as they become relevant—*eg* pp. 96–97, 101, 110.

clarity, the true significance of the Nazi movement. His motives had not been pure, either in joining or in leaving the Party. He was no democrat, no pacifist, no martyr (if these are pure professions); and the intellectual clarity he achieved was the clarity not of suffering but of disillusion. But truth is independent of the stimulus that has provoked its discovery, and the conditions that have guided its expression; and to say that Rauschning is no better than his class is an irrelevant criticism of his books. In those books he demonstrated, as none other has done, the essential nihilism of the Nazi philosophy. This nihilism, the expression of frustration by the existing world, had inspired the Nazi movement in its early days; it was obscured in the days of power by other, more positive interests which became parasitical upon it; but in the last days, with which this book is concerned, when all hope and profit had departed, when all rivals had been eliminated or had fled, and the Party, in indisputed power, had nothing positive to offer any more, it was to this nihilism that it returned as its ultimate philosophy and valediction. The voice that issued from the doomed city of Berlin in the winter of 1944 and the spring of 1945 was the authentic voice of Nazism, purged of all its accessory appeals, its noonday concessions, and welcoming once more the consequences of its original formula, World Power or Ruin.

For by the winter of 1944 the positive alternative of the formula had failed, as all knew except a few still blinded devotees. That positive alternative was described in general terms as 'world power', or 'historical greatness'; more particularly defined, it meant one thing only—the conquest of Russia, the extermination of the Slavs, and the colonization of the East. This was the real message of Nazism. It is the burden of *Mein Kampf*;[1] obscured by the more general terminology of destruction, it rings through the conversations recorded by Rauschning;[2] and in Hitler's last written message, composed when the Russians were already at the gates of the

[1] *Mein Kampf*, chap. xiv. All references to *Mein Kampf* are to the 45th edition, 1938 (2 vols).

[2] *Hitler Speaks*, chap. iii, etc. (Darré's wartime speeches fully confirm this account by Rauschning of his earlier utterances).

Berlin Chancellery, the last and only positive aim which he bequeathed to his people was still 'the conquest of territory in the east'.[1] This Eastern policy was essential to Nazism; all other positive aims—the conquest of France or Britain—were subsidiary and incidental to it. The offence of France was its traditional policy of Eastern alliances, which had enabled it, for three centuries, to intervene in Germany. The offence of Britain was its refusal to be content with a maritime supremacy, its insistent tradition of preventing the domination of Europe by a single Continental power. But the offence of Russia was the existence of Russia. As these offences were different, so the German response to each was different—at least until Hitler, in the intoxication of success, abandoned all discrimination and diplomacy. France was to be finished as a great power; it was to be reduced to second-rate status, and, thus reduced, might survive as a western Croatia or Slovakia, independent, but incapable of a European policy. Britain was to become a purely maritime power; it need not sink to second-rate status—Hitler was always prepared to 'guarantee the British Empire'—but it must never intervene in Continental politics again. Thus the Nazi policy in respect of the West would ensure to Germany freedom to deal unhindered with the fundamental problem of the East. For Russia there was no such indulgent solution. As Russia's crimes was its existence, so its judgment was extermination. The war in the West was a traditional war, a war of diplomatic aims and limited objectives, in which some residue of international convention was regarded; the war in the East was a crusade, 'a war of ideologies', in which all conventions were ignored. It is essential that we remember the basic anti-Russian significance of Nazism. All the general concepts of that terrible creed conceal a particular anti-Russian significance. Racialism means the supremacy of Germans to Slavs; 'living space' and 'geopolitics' mean the conquest of their territory; the rule of the 'master race' means the enslavement of their surviving population. Crusades require crusaders; and again it is in the anti-Russian character of Nazism that we find the significance of the SS, the most fanatical, most mystical missionaries of the

[1] See below, p. 225.

new gospel. It was they who preached racialism and 'living space', and practised extermination and enslavement; it was they who emphasized the crusade by organizing 'Germanic' foreigners into anti-Russian legions; they carried Nordic mysticism to lengths which even Hitler ridiculed; and in the end they were prepared to carry on the Eastern crusade at a price which even Hitler rejected—surrender in the West. It was not Hitler but Himmler, the high-priest of the SS, who expressed the Nordic gospel in its most outrageous form; and it was particularly in respect of Russia that he expressed it.[1] An appreciation of this anti-Russian character of Nazism is not only necessary to the understanding of Nazism itself; it will also explain, in part, the most significant opposition to Hitler inside Germany—the opposition of the Army General Staff.

Hitler's struggle with the Army General Staff is one of the most interesting features of Nazi history during the war, for the General Staff was the one centre of opposition which Hitler, though he succeeded in ruining it, was never able to conquer. In 1924, when Hitler wrote *Mein Kampf*, he looked back on the German General Staff as 'the mightiest thing the world has ever seen';[2] but once he had attained power, he discovered, with disgust, that the General Staff was not content to be a mighty instrument of his policy—it had a policy of its own. Just as it had dictated terms to the Kaiser, so it sought to dictate to the Fuehrer. Hitler liquidated the trade unions without a blow; he frightened the middle-classes into submission; he bribed the industrialists; he had no trouble from the Churches; and the Communists, since they had long surrendered their independence, supplied the easiest converts of all. But the Army refused to be converted or bribed or frightened; and since Hitler needed it, he could not ignore or liquidate it—rather, he had to increase it. At one time, in 1934, the Army even forced Hitler to crush his own radical wing and publicly to disown the Revolution of Destruction.[3]

[1] Compare his speeches quoted below, pp. 74, 77.

[2] *Mein Kampf*, p. 249.

[3] In a speech to the Reichstag after the liquidation of Roehm and his followers on June 30th, 1934, Hitler condemned those who regarded revolution as an end in itself; but this was only a tactical condemnation forced upon him by the temporary ascendancy of the Army.

Unable to storm this last citidel, Hitler set out to sap and mine it. By forced resignations and new appointments he partially succeeded—but only partially. In 1938, at the time of the Munich crisis, the General Staff, under Halder, decided to remove the demented government; but the sudden news that Chamberlain had accepted the invitation to Munich knocked the weapons from their hands as they were preparing to strike.[1] Hitler's success at Munich was temporarily fatal to the Army leaders. They never had any outside support; they represented only themselves; and they were powerless against a dictator who could achieve triumphs such as this. For a time, the opposition of the General Staff became again insignificant. Besides, the policy of the German Government for the next three years was not inconsistent with their own.

The leaders of the German Army believed in a policy of limited conquest. They wished Germany to be a great power, capable of supporting an efficient, well-paid and privileged army. Such a position could be achieved by a mere reversal of the events of 1918; in fact, a restoration of imperial conditions. In so far as Hitler was likely to gain for them that external support which they lacked, they were prepared to support him, and to connive at some of the incidental vulgarities of his movement; but as practical men, organizers and calculators, not mystics or prophets, they were opposed to any unlimited venture of which they could not foresee or control the consequences. In particular, they were opposed to any conquest which would alter the social structure of Germany, and submerge their own privileged but precarious class in a new millenary Nazi Reich. Thus they were consistently opposed to war with Russia. Russia was the traditional ally of the German Junkers, whose prejudices, though swamped in the middle-class officers' corps, still dominated the General Staff. The Bolshevik Revolution did not alter this alliance, for they were practical men, above mere ideological conceptions; and in fact it was through an agreement with Bolshevik Russia that they had contrived to keep a shadow army in

[1] The account of this abortive plot, first revealed by Halder, and since confirmed by other generals (eg Mueller-Hildebrandt), has been accepted as genuine by the authorities who examined it.

existence during the dark days after Versailles. Thus the interest of the German Army leaders was satisfied by the conquest of Poland and France, and in 1940 they would gladly have called a halt and stabilized the position on the basis of their gains. Unfortunately, what had satisfied them had merely inspired the confidence and excited the appetite of Hitler. The imperial frontiers of Germany were to him a contemptible ambition.[1] What was an end to them was only a means to him. In June 1941, flushed with success, and intoxicated by the propaganda which hailed him as 'the greatest strategic genius of all time', he set out to achieve the fundamental aims of the Nazi movement—the colonization of the East.

With the opening of the Russian campaign in 1941, the opposition of the German General Staff began again. Its ultimate achievement was the abortive Plot of July 20th, 1944; but it had passed through long underground channels before it broke out in that sudden, spectacular cascade. At first the generals had merely advised and protested. A Russian war was against their political interest; but their political interest no longer mattered. They had launched themselves on the brown Nazi current without making sure of its direction, and now they were adrift. It was against their military knowledge too; but that too was brushed aside, for now they were faced by the greatest strategical genius of all time, who of all things most resented the suggestion that there were 'experts' who knew more than he. That Russia could resist the German armies seemed to him a ridiculous belief. "You have only to kick the front door," he declared, "and the whole house will tumble down." When the chief of the Army General Staff produced figures of Russian tank production, Hitler flew into a rage and ordered the technical department which had compiled such 'defeatist' figures to be silenced.[2] So the generals meekly gave in, as the *bourgeoisie* had given in, as everyone

---

[1] *Mein Kampf*, p. 736.

[2] Halder, who witnessed it, has described this scene, when Hitler 'went off the deep end—he was no longer a rational being . . . he foamed at the mouth and threatened me with his fists. Any rational discussion was out of the question.' The offending department was the *OKW Wirtschaftsund Rüstungsamt*, under General Thomas. Speer has also described the incident.

(according to Hitler's philosophy) would ultimately give in, before a superior willpower; and the Russian adventure began. It is true the house did not tumble down at the first kick, but that was explained away. Just as Britain was only apparently unbeaten, so Russia was only apparently standing up. For practical purposes, Hitler announced in October 1941, the war was over; "the Russians no longer *exist!*" he would shout at doubting generals;[1] or in a more compromising mood he would explain that the Russian bear was dead—it merely refused to lie down; and to advertise his confidence he ordered the dissolution of forty divisions of the Army, the return of man-power to industry, and the cessation of armament production, all without reference to the Army Command. Nevertheless, the generals continued to doubt. In December 1941 Hitler took over the high command of the German Army. Nine months later, Halder, chief of the German Army General Staff, by common consent the ablest of German generals, the only successor in the great tradition of Moltke and Schlieffen, was dismissed. Meanwhile the OKW, or Combined General Staff,[2] had become a new political directorate of the Armed Forces, and suitable generals had been exalted within it— the grovelling Keitel, who believed in Hitler's strategical genius,[3] and the industrious Jodl who applied it. From the

[1] This phrase, according to Halder, was Hitler's 'theme-song', and the idea became a monomania with him.

[2] The OKW (*Oberkommando der Wehrmacht*), originally a co-ordinating committee of the three branches of the Armed Forces, was gradually developed by Hitler into an instrument of political control, which he used particularly to impose his will upon the OKH, or Army General Staff, the stronghold of military opposition. I have translated OKW throughout as 'Combined General Staff', as this gives a more accurate idea of its functions under Hitler than would a literal translation. Keitel was *Chef OKW*, Jodl *Chef OKW Fuehrungsstab* (operational staff).

[3] Keitel said at Nuremberg that 'every professional soldier would confirm that Hitler's grasp of strategy and tactics commanded admiration. Nights of the war were passed at his headquarters in study of all the General Staff books by Moltke, Schlieffen, and Clausewitz, and his remarkable knowledge not only of all the armies, but of the navies of the globe, amounted to genius. Far from the chief of the OKW (*ie* Keitel) advising Hitler, it was Hitler who advised him' April 5th, 1946). Hitler certainly showed an astonishing grasp of military detail,

Fuehrer's Headquarters in deep underground bunkers in Berlin and Rastenburg the war was directed by somnambulist decisions; the control of the Party over the Army was complete; and the opposition of the Army General Staff continued underground.

The existence of serious opposition to Hitler in the Army General Staff during the years 1941 to 1944 has sometimes been doubted. Hitler never made that error. It was the greatest mortification to his otherwise complacent spirit that the one instrument on which he must always rely was secretly but fundamentally opposed to him. He often said so. Often he declared that in 1941 the generals had lost their nerve, and only his iron will, his military genius, had saved the German armies in that first terrible Russian winter. Often he openly envied and praised the power, the foresight, and the thoroughness of Stalin, who had liquidated his General Staff by a wholesale purge before undertaking the risk of war. Often he raged at his own indignant officers, calling them liars and traitors to their faces, until, as some believed, resentment drove them to conspiracy. Personal antipathies increased his hatred of the whole class. However shrilly he might protest his strategical genius, however complacently he might listen to the flattering echo of his protestations, he could never convince himself of its universal acceptance. With his inner ear he always listened for the voice of mockery; and if anyone at court wished to ruin the career of an officer, he had only to whisper, in the right quarter, that his intended victim had referred to Hitler as 'the corporal'.[1] Nevertheless, though this opposition to the war existed since 1941, and though its leaders were planning the assassination of Hitler from January 1942 onwards, it could not, owing to the unrepresentative character of its leaders, express itself in action until the myth of Hitler's

[1] Statement by Keitel.

---

but such knowledge has not hitherto been understood to constitute strategical genius. A more critical judgment is that of Halder, that Hitler showed an extraordinary grasp of technical detail and a capacity for unlimited generalization, but that nearly all decisions of strategy must be taken in the middle region between these two categories—and there Hitler was deficient.

omnipotence had been shaken by defeat. By 1944 that condition seemed to have been fulfilled; but in 1941 the Party was triumphant as never before.

If 1941 marks the triumph of the Party over the Army, it also marks a further stage in the change within the government—the change from a cabinet to a court. Absolute power brings its own corruptions, and after the successes of 1940 a marked deterioration became apparent in the characters of all the Nazi leaders. There were also important changes in personnel. The ascendancy of Hitler, indeed, remained unchallenged within the Party till the end; even in the last days of all, when all power to compel or reward, all machinery to enforce his decisions, all hope of success or relief, all glory of achievement had departed, that demonic character, by mere force of personality, and perhaps the habit of control, reigned undisputed over his followers. But if he should die, who, among his eager flatterers, could hope to succeed to that vertiginous position? 'Relations between the various high leaders can only be understood', says the ablest and least corrupted member of the court,[1] 'if their aspirations are interpreted as a struggle for the succession to Adolf Hitler. The War of the Diadochi[2] started very early behind the scenes.' At first the succession had been vested, by a decree of September 1st, 1939, in Goering, who, though politically a coward, was still an able and important functionary—the founder of the Luftwaffe, the architect of the four-year plan, head of the Hermann Goering Werke, originator of the Gestapo and concentration camps—a man who had assumed responsibility for bloodshed before which even Hitler had quailed. After Goering, the next in succession, by the same decree, was Rudolf Hess, a harmless, simpleminded crank, unstable in his decisions and absurd in his beliefs. But in 1941 Hess had flown to Scotland on his crack-brained mission, and the question of the succession had to be reconsidered.

---

[1] Speer.

[2] The War of the Diadochi was the war between the successors of Alexander the Great.

Albert Speer, who was present at Hitler's chalet at Obersalzberg on the day of Hess's flight, has described how Hitler received the news of his deputy's eccentric gesture. Two of Hess's adjutants arrived at the chalet and announced that they had a personal letter from Hess to Hitler. One of them was called in and delivered the letter. Standing in the passage, Speer heard the loud voice of the Fuehrer raised in command; Martin Bormann, Hess's indefatigable assistant, who was already beginning to overshadow his nominal chief, was ordered to make immediate telephone connection with the satraps of the court, Goebbels and Ribbentrop, Goering and Himmler, who were all summoned to the presence. Hitler then called Udet, the air ace of the Luftwaffe, and asked whether Hess had any chance of reaching Scotland, flying alone in a twin-engined aircraft, without navigational aids. The reply of the Luftwaffe was a categorical negative; Hess, the experts were agreed, would come down in the sea, short of his destination. Encouraged by this, there were some who advocated that the whole affair should be hushed up: Hess would perish, and no one need ever know. But Hitler was unconvinced. He despised experts, and he knew Hess's ability as a pilot; he had sometimes remonstrated with him about his indulgence in these dangerous sports.[1] Lest the British should get in first with their version, and exploit the propaganda value of the incident, he at once issued a communiqué. Hess's two adjutants were arrested, and in 1945 were still in prison, although hitherto, observes the caustic Speer, 'the custom of punishing the bearers of bad news had been known only in Asiatic countries'.

When Hess flew to Scotland, he was already a back number in the Fuehrer's entourage, from which he was gradually being

---

[1] An incident described by Rauschning contains a pleasant element of dramatic irony. Hess had just been a successful competitor in a flying competition. 'You must give that sort of thing up in future,' Hitler told him. 'There are better things in store for you.' (*Hitler Speaks*, p. 18.)

ousted by the persistent Bormann. This molelike creature, who seemed to avoid the glare of daylight and publicity[1] and to despise the rewards and trimmings, was nevertheless insatiable in his appetite for the reality of power; by his invariable presence he gradually became indispensable to Hitler; and by his well-timed insinuations he succeeded ultimately in removing all rivals about his master's throne. At first, though private adviser and financial administrator to Hitler, he was nominally responsible to Hess; but his work inevitably drew him into the personal circle of the Fuehrer. Entrusted with the building of the Berghof, Hitler's chalet, and with the purchase of pictures for his collections, he soon found himself among the privileged favourites of the court, and lost no time in discarding his former associates; and Hitler, thinking he had found an industrious and reliable servant, did not detect, or at least never distrusted, in this unobtrusive secretary, the consuming ambition which thus innocently disguised itself. By 1941 Bormann, now personal secretary to the Fuehrer, had almost replaced Hess in the inner council. He was permanently there, while Hess emerged less and less frequently from embittered seclusion.

On the flight of Hess, Bormann was therefore a powerful candidate for his position as head of the Party Chancery. Goering, sensing a rival and personally detesting Bormann, warned Hitler against him, but in vain. A fortnight later, on opening his morning paper, he read that Bormann had been appointed to the vacant post. To the greater position, of second in succession to the Fuehrer, he could not yet aspire. By a decree of June 29th, 1941, the succession was vested in Goering alone, and no heir was mentioned. From now on, Goering was Bormann's greatest enemy, his next-intended victim, in the byzantine palace politics of Berlin, Berchtesgaden, and the mobile Fuehrer's headquarters.

Nevertheless, though Goering thus still occupied the greatest position in the state under Hitler, the real position bore little correspondence with its formal expression. From 1941 onwards, the corruption of power and the complacency of the *arriviste* began to consume, and ultimately to obscure, the

[1] Photographs of Bormann are regarded as a rarity.

once vigorous abilities of that formidable character until, at the end, he was popularly regarded as a mere voluptuary, a scented Nero fiddling while Rome burned. For by 1941 Goering had achieved everything that he had ever sought. He was Grand Vizier; he was Reich Marshal; enormously rich; and contented. The war (it was agreed) was won; there was no need of further effort. So Goering began to take his ease among his flatterers and neglect his offices. The Luftwaffe failed, the bombers came through, German industry creaked, but Goering came only rarely to Berlin. He was in Karinhall, his vast country palace in the Schorfheide, dressed (says an eyewitness) now like some oriental maharaja, now in a light-blue uniform with a bejewelled baton of pure gold and ivory, now in white silk, like a Doge of Venice, only studded with jewels, with the emblematic stag of St Hubertus on his head, and a swastika of gleaming pearls set between the antlers. There, in scenes of Roman luxury, he feasted and hunted and entertained, and showed his distinguished guests round the architectural and artistic wonders of his house—a study like a medium-sized church, a domed library like the Vatican library, a desk twenty-six feet long, of mahogany inlaid with bronze swastikas, furnished with two big golden baroque candelabra, and an inkstand all of onyx, and a long ruler of green ivory studded with jewels. Meanwhile his art gangsters came continually in from Paris and Rome, from Athens and Kiev, and some also from the museums of Germany, with their tribute of jewels and statuary, of old masters and *objets d'art*, of Gobelin tapestries and altar-pieces, of goldsmiths' work and Augsburg work, and old Roman bishops' staves, from the looted museums and gutted palaces of more ancient, famous states.

There, for the time, we may leave Goering; for whatever pose he may have been able to strike at Nuremberg, he was in fact, by the end of the war, a totally discredited figure, as will be evident in this narrative. He had taken Hitler at his word and behaved as if the war was won; and it was not. The Russian bear refused to lie down; the British refused to admit defeat; and soon there were the Americans to consider too. Doubts grew about the Fuehrer's somnambulist strategy;

under defeat in the East, and bombing in the West, and a universal mental perplexity, the brief unity of Party, Army, and People began to decompose; and other figures rose to prominence in place of the too soon contented Reich Marshal. To resolve the mental doubts, to refute the whispered heresies, the voice of the prophet Goebbels was once more raised after a long silence; for in time of victory, prophets are unnecessary distractions. To prevent heresy from hatching into plots and conspiracies, the power of Himmler began that rapid growth by which it ultimately seemed to overshadow even the authority of Hitler himself.

Joseph Goebbels was the intellectual of the Nazi Party—perhaps its only intellectual. Unlike most of the Party leaders, who sprang with monotonous regularity from Saxony, Bavaria, and Austria, he was a West German, from the Latin Rhineland; and it was the Latin lucidity of his mind, the un-German suppleness of his argument, which made him so much more successful as a preacher than the frothblowing nationalists of the South. Essentially Goebbels was a practical man, a restless, radical character who sought instant and complete results. If he was capable of seeing the truth, he was also capable of despising it: consequently he could use it; and since ideas were to him always currency, never objects of value, he could always prove what he wanted. So he persuaded the Germans that their defeats were always victories, that the enemy was only apparently superior, and that new weapons would make all old problems obsolete—until in the end he proved without convincing, and his constructive propaganda became ridiculous and of no effect. "I often had occasion to notice," observes Speer, "that Goebbels' style was 'Latin' not 'Germanic'. His propagandist principles were also essentially Latin. For example, it would have been much better if Goebbels had given the people the same watchword as Churchill gave his people, *Blood, Sweat and Tears*. This was a hard and honest watchword, and it would have suited the German people well. But Goebbels always raised false hopes among the people, which merely caused discrepancy between his propaganda and the trend of popular opinion." In fact Goebbels' position did not depend solely upon his propaganda. He was respected for his intelligence, his administrative ability, and his apparent personal integrity: he neither believed palpable nonsense, nor performed ludicrous antics, nor exhibited indecent opulence; he wielded no engines of terror or oppression; and he was a radical who preached not only total war but also total mobilization, which those (like Goering) who prized their privileged standard of living would never advocate. Nevertheless, propaganda remains his permanent achievement, his ultimate title to fame. Whatever else history may say of Dr Goebbels, it must credit him with one contribution to the science of politics—a terrible but a positive contribution which, like the atom-bomb, may be deplored but cannot be undone: he created a system of propaganda, ironically styled 'public enlightenment' which persuaded a people to believe that black was white. Certainly Hess and Goering and Bormann could claim no achievement comparable with this.

On Hitler's side, the sinister figure of Himmler grew daily in stature. In the public imagination Himmler is a real and terrible figure, a cold-blooded inhuman ogre ruthlessly exterminating millions of helpless prisoners by every refinement of sadistic torture; not a man, but an impersonal abstraction, a creature to whom the weaknesses of pity and forgiveness are unknown; an inexorable monster whose cold, malignant rage no prayers, no human sacrifices can ever for one moment appease. Certainly Himmler was implacable. His power seemed as unlimited as his ambitions of destruction. In the calmest, most dispassionate manner he ordered the destruction of whole races, the extermination of Jews and Slavs. He was quite pitiless; nothing horrified him. The thought of hundreds of thousand of men and women stuffed into 'humane' gas-wagons—incidents which frequently drove the criminal attendants mad—the knowledge that the torture chambers of Europe were peopled by his victims, and that at every hour of the day his name was being execrated by dying people in a whole continent—these things (if he thought of them) never interrupted the regularity of his meals, never disturbed the routine of his office, never disconcerted the puffy smoothness of that cold complacent expression. But Himmler was not a sadist. There was nothing terrible or volcanic in his character.

His very coldness was a negative element, not glacial, but bloodless. He did not delight in cruelty, he was indifferent to it; and the scruples of others were to him not contemptible, but unintelligible. 'But they are animals', or 'criminals', he would say, with ingenuous deprecation, when foreign ambassadors, or even his own subordinates, sometimes remonstrated at some particularly savage holocaust. In this monster there were many curious qualities, which have made him to some an incredible, enigmatical figure. He was extraordinarily ignorant and naïve. The man who, after such a career, culminating in total defeat, still regarded himself as a fit negotiator to meet the Allied commanders, and hoped to be continued in office by their permission, cannot have been a man of diabolical subtlety. He was also beloved by all of his subordinates—men of neuter conscience indeed, but in other respects apparently of only normal weakness. His adjutants and advisers remained, even after his death, unconditionally loyal to him. No one in the SS conspired against him. To the end he was its *Reichsfuehrer*; and its members spoke of him with affection as 'Reichsheini'. Brutality? his subordinates exclaim in naïve chorus, there were no signs of brutality in his private nature; hesitation seemed to them his most obvious characteristic. Himmler himself could never understand the reputation which he had acquired. In the end he despaired of understanding it; it was some strange foible of foreigners, he concluded; and he satisfied himself with making little jokes about it in his private circle.[1]

Nevertheless the character of Himmler is not as mysterious as these facts may suggest to those familiar with the variety of the human mind. In a civilized world, it is true, such men are seldom tolerated; but if we look back at the cataclysmic periods of society, at periods of revolution and violent social change, his prototype is there. It is the Grand Inquisitor, the mystic in politics, the man who is prepared to sacrifice humanity to an abstract ideal. The Grand Inquisitors of history were not cruel or self-indulgent men. They were often painfully conscientious and austere in their personal lives.

[1] Some such jokes are mentioned in Count Bernadotte's book, *The Fall of the Curtain* (1945).

They were often scrupulously kind to animals,[1] like St Robert Bellarmine, who refused to disturb the fleas in his clothes. Since they could not hope for theological bliss (he said), it would be uncharitable to deny them that carnal refreshment to which alone they could aspire. But for men who, having opportunities of worshipping aright, chose wrong, no remedy was too drastic. So the faggots were piled and lit, and the misbelievers and their books were burnt, and those gentle old bishops went home to sup on white fish and inexpensive vegetables, to feed their cats and canaries, and to meditate on the Penitential Psalms, while their chaplains sat down in their studies to compose their biographies and explain to posterity the saintly lives, the observances and austerities, the almsgivings and simplicity, of those exemplary pastors, knowing (as Cardinal Newman said) that it is better that all humanity should perish in extremest agony than that one single venial sin should be committed.

---

[1] 'We Germans,' said Himmler (in the course of a speech described at Nuremberg as 'one of the most monstrous documents ever penned'), *'who are the only people in the world who have a decent attitude towards animals*, will also assume a decent attitude towards these human animals [he was referring to Czech and Russian women], but it is a crime against our own blood to worry about them and give them ideals' (Nuremberg document 1919-PS). According to Kersten, Himmler hated bloodsports as 'cold-blooded murder of innocent and defenceless animals', and said to him: 'Goering, that damned bloodhound, kills all animals. Imagine, Herr Kersten, some poor deer is grazing peacefully, and up comes the hunter with his gun to shoot that poor animal. . . . Could that give you pleasure, Herr Kersten?' (Deposition by Kersten in Rijksinstituut voor Oorlogsdokumentatie, Amsterdam). In fact Goering would have repudiated the charge of cruelty: he held the orthodox view that animals enjoy being hunted; and at Karinhall he erected a pompous monument to himself on their behalf, testifying the gratitude of the animals of the Reich to their protector.

Such a comparison perhaps seems fanciful; but nature is fanciful in designing the human mind, and times of revolution do throw up into positions of eminence men who, in stable periods, remain unobserved in gaols and monasteries. Himmler himself, everyone is agreed, was an utterly insignificant man, common, pedantic, and mean. He was careful of money and incapable of thought; and yet he could not resist the temptation to speculate, to lose himself in the *O Altitudo*, and entangle himself in the theological minutiae, of the pure Nazi doctrine. Hitler himself, in one sense, was not a Nazi, for the doctrines of Nazism, that great system of teutonic nonsense, were to him only a weapon of politics; 'he criticized and ridiculed the ideology of the SS';[1] but to Himmler they were, every iota of them, the pure Aryan truth, which if a man keep not pure and undefiled, he shall without doubt perish everlastingly. With such a narrow pedantry, with such black-letter antiquarianism, did Himmler study the details of this sad rubbish, that many have supposed, but wrongly, that he had been a schoolmaster. He gave Speer the impression of being 'half schoolmaster, half crank'. During the war, while Goebbels was demanding total mobilization, Himmler was employing thousands of men and millions of marks in the projects of a religious maniac. In one department of his foreign intelligence service, a school of eager researchers studied such important matters as Rosicrucianism and Freemasonry, the symbolism of the suppression of the harp in Ulster, and the occult significance of Gothic pinnacles and top hats at Eton.[2] The SS scientific laboratories laboured infelicitously to isolate pure Aryan blood. An explorer was sent to Tibet to discover traces of a pure Germanic race believed to preserve the ancient Nordic mysteries in those unvisited mountains. Throughout Europe excavators sought for relics of authentic German *Kultur*. When the German army

---

[1] Speer.

[2] The department was *RSHA (Reichssicherheitshauptamt), Amt VII*.

prepared hastily to evacuate Naples, Himmler's only demand was that it should not omit to carry with it the tomb of Conradin, the last Hohenstaufen King. Meanwhile, rich business men, if they wished to join his exclusive Circle of Friends,[1] had to buy admission by subscribing perhaps a million marks to the *Ahnenerbe*, a 'scientific' institute that made expensive researches into Aryan origins.[2] Even in April 1945, when the whole Reich was tumbling in ruins, Himmler was contemplating the colonization of the Ukraine with a new religious sect mentioned by his masseur,[3] and in conversation with Count Bernadotte (having just maintained that he was the only sane man left in Germany), interrupted the discussion of war and peace to digress for an hour on runes. He was particularly interested in runes, the epigraphic alphabet of the Northmen of the Dark Ages. Studied with the eye of faith, they might, he believed, yield resemblance to Japanese ideograms, and thus prove the Japanese to be Aryans after all.[4]

In such a character no grain of subtlety is discernible. Himmler was an elementary believer. His fanaticism was not the difficult birth of fear and weakness, nor his hesitation the consequence of doubt. Doubt had not yet nibbled at the infantile serenity of his cosmic acceptances. It was because he could not follow the intellectual processes or the labyrinthine

[1] The *Freundeskreis des RfSS*, a group of mystical financiers, headed by one Wilhelm Keppler (see below, p. 116 note), who formed themselves into an 'exclusive' club under this name.

[2] It was the *Ahnenerbe* whose fine collection of human skulls was described at Nuremberg. Himmler welcomed the Russian war (among other reasons) because it would enable him to enrich this collection with the hitherto unobtainable skulls of that sub-human type 'the Jewish-Bolshevik commissar', and elaborate instructions were given to ensure that commissars should be killed without damage to their skulls. (Letter from Dr Wolfram Sievers, head of the *Ahnenerbe*, to Himmler's secretary, Dr Brandt, read at Nuremberg, August 8th, 1946.)

[3] The sect was that of the *Bibelforscher*, the German equivalent of the English and American *Jehovah's Witnesses*. Their normal fate was to be imprisoned in concentration camps, and Kersten, the masseur, interceded for them, as for so many of Himmler's victims. Himmler responded with this fantastic notion (information from Kersten and Schellenberg).

[4] Speer.

72

plots of his subordinates, that he would not become involved in them; because he was assured of their ultimate loyalty to him that he did not interfere with what must have seemed, and sometimes certainly were, their treasonable dabblings. For two years this *treuer Heinrich*, this 'faithful Heinrich', who really believed that he was unconditionally loyal to Hitler, allowed his favourite adviser to indulge in absurd, but serious attempts at peacemaking. He cannot have been altogether ignorant of the plans to substitute himself for his master; but he would neither condemn these activities nor accept their implications. His followers wrung their hands in despair at his interminable vacillation. In fact he simply turned a blind eye. The true believer can afford to let others speculate, provided their final loyalty is assured.

Of course if Himmler had been only a crank, we should have heard less of him. He was also, in an executive capacity, very efficient; and he had a capacity for choosing useful subordinates. It is true that his personal court contained some strange figures; that he took political advice from his doctor Gebhardt, the sinister adviser whom many regarded as his evil genius; that (like Hitler and Wallenstein) he was unduly influenced by his astrologer, Wulf; that his masseur, Kersten, had attained the position which more orthodox believers entrust to a father-confessor; and that his relations with Hitler depended on the illiterate jockey, Fegelein; but these were all personal advisers. On a purely executive level Himmler chose well—as far as it was possible to choose well in a world of illusion. In return, he was well served; followed even to his squalid grave by the devotion of his subordinates.

This dual character of Himmler, his impersonal efficiency as an executor, and his oceanic credulity as a thinker, is, I believe, the key to his fantastic career. Animated by an unconditional loyalty to Hitler, to whom, as he often protested, he owed everything, and inspiring, as such simple characters do, a similar loyalty among his own followers towards himself, both competent to execute and too unoriginal to conspire, he was, as long as this harmony continued, an ideal chief of police to a revolutionary leader. It is said that soon after his rise to power, Hitler once called, in Munich, on the aged philosopher

73

Oswald Spengler, in order to receive the blessing of that disreputable sage. The reply of the oracle was unusually laconic. "Beware," he said, "of your praetorian guards." On June 30th, 1934 Hitler took the necessary precautions. After that, the praetorian guard was in the hands of the stupid, devoted, ruthless, efficient, mystical Himmler; and Hitler felt safe. Safe that is, until the delicate balance of Himmler's personality had been fretted away; and then it was Himmler's unexpected defection that decided Hitler to end the tedious drama. Only if this dual character of Himmler is appreciated, can the extraordinary events of April 1945 be understood.

From the opening of the Russian campaign, the power of Himmler had continued to rise; for the Russian campaign, while it alienated the regular Army, or at least the General Staff, was the consummation of the long ambition of the SS. While Hitler and Goering, intoxicated with pride and assurance, 'cut up the giant cake' of European Russia, promising themselves the Volga and the Crimea, Bialystok and Baku, and awarding the unvalued scraps to their Balkan satellites, Himmler was fixing his more mystical eyes on a vaster, remoter horizon. He was demanding 'an open road to the east, the creation of the German Reich this way or that, the fetching home of thirty million human beings of our blood, so that even during our lifetimes we shall be a people of 120 million Germanic souls'.[1] The defeat at Stalingrad, which chastened more realistic thinkers, did not affect the transcendental views of Himmler (for facts do not trouble the bigot and the crank); and his practical activity as a policeman became only more necessary than ever. Throughout 1943 and 1944 his power continually grew. Already head of the SS, the Armed SS,[2] the Secret Police, and the Criminal Police, in 1943 he became Minister of the Interior, and the entire police system of Germany became united under his command. In 1944 he achieved a further signal triumph. The German Foreign Intelligence Service, or *Abwehr*, had hitherto been part of the

[1] Statement by Himmler quoted at Nuremberg, *The Times*, February 15th, 1946. The scene in which Hitler, Goering, Keitel, and Rosenberg 'cut up the giant cake' at the Fuehrer's Headquarters in July 1941 is described in a minute by Bormann, quoted in *The Times*, December 18th, 1945. [2] *Waffen SS*.

74

Combined General Staff. Under the negligent rule of Admiral Canaris, an enigmatical figure, more interested in anti-Nazi intrigue than in his official duties,[1] for the first two years of the war it had been borne along, a happy parasite, on the success of the German Army, and its well-paid agents had been able to enjoy the café and cabaret life of Madrid and Estoril, and to speculate profitably in the black markets of Belgrade and Sofia, with an easy conscience. But when the military initiative had passed to the Allies, the Party began to expect something more; it expected intelligence which might restore the failing balance of power; and since none came, it began to criticize. The criticism came loudest and most insistent from the SS, whose own foreign intelligence service was already growing in establishment and ambition under the control of Walter Schellenberg.

Among the universally parochial minds of the SS, Schellenberg, its youngest general, enjoyed an undeserved reputation. He was credited with understanding foreign affairs. It is true that his notions were a little less extravagant than those of some of his rivals, and the fact that he began to work his passage home as early as 1942 separates him from the crasser intellects of the Party. A North German, he was also exempt from the ideological gibberish of the Austrian and Bavarian Nazis. He believed not in force, nor in nonsense, but in subtlety; and he believed that he was subtle. This was perhaps his greatest mistake, for he was in fact a very trivial character; but he made other mistakes too. Like so many of Himmler's subordinates, he believed in Himmler, and aspired to be the good genius of his master, a counter-influence to monsters like Kaltenbrunner and Ohlendorf,[2] and tempters like Gebhardt,

[1] The account of Canaris as 'a personality of pure intellect', and the *Abwehr* as 'a spiritual organization', which was given at Nuremberg on November 30th, 1945, by Colonel Lahousen (one of its members) is highly idealized. The *Abwehr* can claim a few martyrs; but no saints or thinkers.

[2] Ernst Kaltenbrunner succeeded Heydrich as *Chef RSHA*, and was nominally Schellenberg's superior, although Schellenberg's direct access to Himmler reduced the significance of this subordination. Otto Ohlendorf was head of *RSHA Amt III* (also called SD or *Sicherheitsdienst*), and also Ministerialdirektor in the Reich Ministry of Economics.

who also shared the confidence and perverted the judgment of the Reichsfuehrer. He believed that Himmler alone was capable of purging the administration of its inveterate ignorance and corruption, and of rectifying the disastrous, arrogant foreign policy of Hitler and Ribbentrop. If only Himmler would be guided by him, if only the master of the greatest, most efficient organization in Germany would be directed by the subtlest and best-informed intelligence, then (so Schellenberg naïvely believed) there would be an authority which might yet rival the fatal maniac of Berchtesgaden, and, with a little good fortune and some careful preparation, might yet save Germany by negotiating a compromise peace.

Such, as they ultimately developed, were the plans of Schellenberg, the Gestapo officer who, in 1941, had taken over the control of Himmler's foreign intelligence service. To achieve them, two things were necessary. Firstly, he must create an intelligence service superior to all rivals in power and efficiency; secondly, he must build up some capital of goodwill in the Allied camp and among neutral powers, and seek, where possible, to mitigate the odium which clung, throughout the world, to Himmler's name. These two objects Schellenberg set himself conscientiously to attain. For two years he negotiated with Swedish and Swiss friends, arranged the escape of Jews and condemned prisoners of war, and sought to reduce the severity of Himmler's judgments and frustrate the savagery of Kaltenbrunner.[1] As time passed, he became more ambitious, more fanciful than ever. Like Hess, he believed that English public figures would listen to his overtures. He sent emissaries through neutral countries with tales so extravagant that they were dismissed with humiliating

---

[1] Schellenberg's motives, in thus saving life, were of course purely opportunist; for he was too 'realistic' to indulge any humanitarian fancies. As he explained to a friend, the extermination of the Jews would have been unexceptionable if it could have been carried out completely; but since two-thirds of the Jews were out of reach, such a policy 'was worse than a crime; it was folly' ('da aber nur ein Drittel in unserer Hand war, die übrigen aber ausserhalb unseres Machtbereiches lebten, sei die Art der Behandlung der Juden schlimmer als ein Verbrechen, es sei eine Dummheit gewesen.'—Schwerin von Krosigk's diary, s.d. April 15th, 1945).

ridicule; he even discovered a cracked psychologist who believed that, by ingenious psychotherapy, he could bring about 'the psychological revival of the Christian soul in the German people'. What better qualifications could be found for a peace emissary to the devout English? So Schellenberg planned to send the psychologist on a mission to Archbishop Temple.

At the same time he was building up his foreign intelligence service. Like so many Germans, he was an admirer, a despairing admirer, of the British Intelligence Service—an organization of which indeed he knew very little, but of which he had evidently read much in those amazing novelettes which filled the reference library of the Gestapo. From these he had learnt much about that all-pervasive, incessant engine which, founded by Edward III and perfected by Oliver Cromwell, has secured the otherwise unaccountable success of British diplomacy and politics, and which, operating through the YMCA, the Boy Scout Movement, and other dependent organizations, has overthrown dynasties, altered governments, and assassinated inconvenient ministers throughout the world. To create such a universal, 'totalitarian' intelligence service in Germany was the ambitious dream of Schellenberg. The first stage towards it would consist in the liquidation of the existing intelligence service, the *Abwehr*; and this, after two years of competition, during which he exploited every error, every failure of his rival, he secured. The *Abwehr* was well aware of the doom that was prepared for it; but it was helpless. Rotten with corruption, notoriously inefficient, politically suspect, it could do nothing; and the spasmodic efforts of certain conscientious staff officers to achieve some internal reform led only to disillusion and resignation. Meanwhile Schellenberg's service, if hardly more efficient, enjoyed all the advantages of attack. In February 1944, his bankruptcy demonstrated by a succession of glaring failures, Canaris was dismissed. In May Himmler took over. The surviving directors of the old firm were summoned to the Kursalon at Salzburg, and there they were met by Himmler with Schellenberg at his side. In a bombastic speech Himmler outlined his programme. The name *Abwehr*, he said, was un-German; it implied defence. He was going to

77

create a new, aggressive, totalitarian and pure Aryan intelligence service instead. And then, his imagination warming as he left the tedious details of organization for the mysterious generalities in which his idealist spirit was at home, he described the events which were about to follow. There was no room for defeatism now, he said; great things were coming. The Fuehrer was inspired as never before; his statesmanship, skill, and intuitive wisdom were yet to exhibit their masterpiece. He prayed that the infatuated plutocrats of the West might be foolish enough to invade the Continent. They would be hurled back and 'drowned in the seas of their own blood'. Then it would be the turn of the East. Within a year the Russians were to be chased headlong across the Volga, over the Urals, and into Asia, their barbarian home, whence a Chinese Wall, built by Slavonic slave labour, would prevent them from ever returning.[1] A fortnight later the Western Allies landed in Normandy. Two months after that occurred the most spectacular political event since 1934; the Generals' Plot of July 20th, 1944, which showed that the leaders of the German Army regarded the war as lost, and were at last prepared to break their alliance with the Party.

Many of the details of the Generals' Plot are already well known. Its importance cannot be overrated. After long preparation, a small section of the German people had at last taken the initiative. Ignoring, or overriding, the fumblings and hesitations of more timorous conspirators, it had made a positive, determined, and nearly successful effort to destroy the Nazi régime. That section was the East German aristocracy (appropriately it was in their home, in East Prussia, that the blow was struck), the rulers once of the German Army, now only of the General Staff, the colleagues of Rauschning, who had thought it possible to bend the angry spirit of Pan-Germanism to their will by accepting the Nazis as junior partners, and who now sought, by this desperate blow, to undo their disastrous error. It was too late; their error was

[1] This project of an Eastern Wall was seriously entertained by Hitler and often mentioned by him, *eg* in a letter to Mussolini of March 25th, 1943; and cf. Ulrich v. Hassell, *Vom andern Deutschland*, p. 276.

irreparable; as a class the Junkers are now gone for ever, as obsolete as the mammoth and the mastodon.[1]

Nevertheless the conspiracy had been well planned and was nearly successful. Several times the explosive charge had been sent to Hitler's headquarters, and had returned unused through some technical hitch, before Count von Stauffenberg finally introduced it, concealed in a briefcase, into the conference room at Rastenburg. When Hitler had taken his place, and the conference had begun, Stauffenberg laid his briefcase against the table-leg and made an excuse to slip out of the room. As he crossed the outer compound, he heard the noise of detonation. Then he climbed into his plane, flew to Berlin, and confidently announced the death of Hitler and the successful usurpation of a new government. It was a premature announcement. In the meantime Providence (as all good Nazis agreed) had intervened. How Hitler escaped is still not quite clear. Either he had moved away from his place in time, or the peculiar construction of the table had diverted the blast from him. When the dust and turmoil of the explosion had subsided, it was clear that the plot had failed. Hitler's eardrums were pierced, his right arm was bruised, his uniform was tattered, and he had fallen, dazed, into the arms of the everobsequious Keitel; but while four men lay dead or mortally wounded around him, he was alive. Had the conference taken

[1] It should be emphasized that the men of July 20th, Beck, Tresckow, Olbricht, Stauffenberg, and a few other General Staff officers, were a radical group among the opponents of the Nazi Government, and were not necessarily supported by the numerous other groups whose ineffective opposition is often discernible. Had Stauffenberg succeeded in killing Hitler, the other groups would doubtless have followed his lead; his failure, by frightening them back into mutual distrust and hostility, enabled the government, by prompt action, to destroy them all. The equal retribution which fell upon all groups alike, has given them the semblance of a unity of purpose and policy which they certainly never had. Thus the civilian groups of Goerdeler and von Trott zu Solz seem to have been separate from the Army group, which was itself subdivided. Rommel, for instance, while agreeing with the purpose of the plot, seems to have been genuinely shocked at Stauffenberg's methods.

place in the usual concrete bunker, instead of in a wooden hut, not one of the participants could have survived.

Almost every element in the German political situation was affected by the Plot of July 20th. From that time onwards Hitler knew that the Army, as an institution was in opposition; he knew that if he won the war, it would be in spite of the generals, not because of them. More and more, from that moment, he surrounded himself with officers from the Navy and the Luftwaffe. The German Navy might not have played a conspicuous part in the war, but it was untainted by treachery; the Luftwaffe might not have come up to expectations, but the blame for that belonged not to it but to Goering. As for the Army—the common soldiers were doubtless loyal, and Hitler came more and more to identify himself with them to the exclusion of their officers. If he trusted in any generals at all, it was in a few toadies only, in Keitel and Burgdorf; [1] as a class, he regarded them all as traitors, and their treachery was always in his mind and often in his mouth. Whenever an army retreated or a stronghold fell, he cried treachery; telegrams of hectic recrimination and angry strategic lectures issued ceaselessly from the Fuehrer's headquarters; and the sedulous Bormann screamed treble to his master's bass. At his last fullscale conference, Hitler accused the generals to their faces of deceiving him; and in his last written documents, the testaments that were to recommend him to posterity, he could not omit a last sidelong condemnation of the treachery of Army officers and the Army General Staff.

Drawing thus away from his generals into the safer company of his intimate admirers, Hitler inevitably hastened the conversion of his headquarters from a war cabinet to an oriental court of flatterers and toadies. How far the process had already gone is clear from eyewitness accounts of the scene shortly after the detonation. That same day, July 20th, Mussolini, now the puppet-ruler of Lombardy, was due to arrive at Rastenburg on a visit to his protector. His train reached the station early in the afternoon, and Hitler, white as a sheet,

[1] General Wilhelm Burgdorf was *Chef Heerespersonalamt OKH* and *Wehrmacht* adjutant at the Fuehrer's headquarters. He associated himself completely with the views of Hitler, Bormann, and Goebbels.

was there on the platform to receive him. As they left the station, Hitler explained the miracle of his escape, only a few hours ago; and arriving at his headquarters, he took his guest to see the scene of the incident. The room was a mass of debris, for the walls had caught fire after the explosion and the ceiling had fallen in. After wandering through the smoking shambles, they withdrew for a tea party. As so often, it is over the teacups that Hitler is seen in his most outrageous postures.

It was five o'clock when the tea party began, and the whole court assembled in the Fuehrer's headquarters. Conversation was naturally about the Fuehrer's escape, but it quickly deteriorated into recrimination. Voices were raised in high-pitched and bitter argument; and everyone in turn was blamed because the war had not yet been won. Ribbentrop and Doenitz raved against the generals because they had betrayed Germany to England, and the generals raved in reply against Ribbentrop and Doenitz. All this time Hitler and Mussolini sat quiet and reserved, as if mere spectators of the scene, while Graziani told them of his African adventures. Then, quite suddenly, someone mentioned that other famous 'plot' in Nazi history—the Roehm plot of June 30th, 1934, and the bloody purge which followed it. Immediately Hitler leapt up in a fit of frenzy, with foam on his lips, and shouted that he would be revenged on all traitors. Providence had just shown him once again, he screamed, that he had been chosen to make world history; and he ranted wildly about terrible punishments for women and children—all of them would be thrown into concentration camps—an eye for an eye, and a tooth for a tooth—none should be spared who set himself against divine Providence. The court fell silent as the Fuehrer raged for a full half hour; the visitors thought he must be mad—"I don't know," said one of them, "why I didn't go over to the Allies there and then." Mussolini looked embarrassed, and said nothing; Graziani sought feebly to break the spell by beginning a technical discussion with Keitel; and all the time footmen, dressed in white, circulated with their teapots among the gaping worshippers.

This scene was interrupted by a call from Berlin, where order had not yet been restored. Hitler seized the telephone and shouted his orders into the mouthpiece, giving full orders to shoot anyone and everyone. Why hadn't Himmler arrived yet? Then came the portentous statement of the megalomaniac: "I'm beginning to doubt whether the German people is worthy of my great ideals."

These words broke the spell of silence. At once the entire court competed to speak, each protesting his loyalty. In grovelling terms Doenitz sang the praises of the German Navy. Goering began a violent quarrel with Ribbentrop and made a pass at him with his field-marshal's baton; and the voice of Ribbentrop was heard above the tumult protesting, "I am still Foreign Minister and my name is *von* Ribbentrop." Only Hitler was silent now. The parts in the comic opera had been reversed, and the *prima donna* ceased while the chorus discordantly sang. He sat still; in his hand he had a tube of brightly coloured pastilles which he continually sucked;[1] only at intervals, like a still spluttering volcano, would he utter some savage phrase, the residue of his unexpended emotion, about blood, and Providence, and concentration camps.

This scene, as it is described to us,[2] is perhaps overdrawn; but not improbably. Absolute power corrupts absolutely, and we have too many accounts of life in that exotic court to doubt the authenticity, in its main lines, even of this. When a staid German general compared Goering to Elagabalus, he was not exaggerating. In the absolutism, the opulence, and the degeneracy of the middle Roman Empire we can perhaps find the best parallel to the high noonday of the Nazi Reich. There, in the severe pages of Gibbon, we read of characters apparently wielding gigantic authority who, on closer examination, are found to be the pliant creatures of concubines and catamites, of eunuchs and freedmen; and here too we see the *élite* of the Thousand-Year Reich a set of flatulent clowns swayed by purely random influences. Even Mussolini was embarrassed; but then Mussolini had after all, like Goebbels, a Latin mind; he could never be at home among these cavorting Nibelungs.

---

[1] The reader who will persevere as far as p. 112 will learn more about these pastilles.

[2] By Eugen Dollmann, Himmler's 'Highest SS and Police Leader' for Italy, who had accompanied Mussolini.

Goebbels, incidentally, was not present at this Mad Hatter's tea party; he was in Berlin, giving orders for the supression of the revolt.

The effect of the Generals' Plot on the career of Himmler was also decisive. It was both personal and political. Personally the Plot achieved a notable success; it brought Himmler to God. In April 1945 he described to a friend this signal conversion. "I know," he said, "that I am generally regarded as a heedless pagan, but in the depths of my heart I am a believer; I believe in God and Providence. In the course of the last year I have learned to believe in miracles again. The Fuehrer's escape on July 20th was a miracle; and a second I have experienced in my own life, this very spring. . . ." The second miracle was the convenient thaw on the river Oder, when Himmler commanded an Army Group there, and the Russians were about to break across the ice.[1]

Politically the Generals' Plot marked the beginning of Himmler's decline. To the outer world indeed Himmler never seemed so powerful as in the months immediately after the Plot, the months when many supposed that he had actually assumed control of the state, Hitler having been either killed by the explosion or imprisoned by the usurper. Certainly, after the Plot, Himmler increased his authority; for the policeman is never so necessary as when a widespread conspiracy has been disclosed. One of his first acts was to complete his victory over the old Army Intelligence Service, whose former chiefs figured largely among the conspirators and had actually supplied their explosive charge from their captured supplies. They had already been proved inefficient; now Himmler could show that they were disloyal. Against Admiral Canaris the evidence was inconclusive; he disappeared into prison, and nine months later was executed with medieval barbarity.[2] His successor, Colonel Hansen, was executed. General Freytag von Loringhoven, who, as head of the sabotage department, had supplied the explosive, committed suicide to avoid a more painful end. His predecessor, Colonel Lahousen, and some others, escaped

[1] Schwerin von Krosigk. Cf. below p. 146.
[2] He was strangled in Flossenbürg Concentration Camp on April 9th, 1945.

83

miraculously to tell the tale at Nuremberg and mortify Goering by their survival. But the old intelligence service was merely a department of the old General Staff; and the whole General Staff was involved, or suspected, in this extensive conspiracy. In the great blood-purge which followed—a purge more drastic even then the purge of 1934—over fifty General Staff officers perished, and hundreds of lesser figures were inconspicuously removed. General Halder, its now deposed chief, was thrown into a concentration camp on mere suspicion, and for four months never saw the light of day. His predecessor, General Beck, the acknowledged leader of almost every group in the conspiracy, was forced to an untidy suicide. His successor, Zeitzler, was dismissed. Stauffenberg and three other conspirators were shot at once on the orders of Fromm, who thus sought to conceal his own guilt—but in vain; for he too was hanged; Stuelpnagel, commanding the armies of occupation in France, who had rashly obeyed the orders of the usurpers and had imprisoned the Gestapo in Paris, shot himself in a wood near Verdun. Misfiring, he only blinded himself, and was executed instead. Kluge, the commander in the field, took his own life. Witzleben was executed; so was Fellgiebel—a philsophical general, he followed the best examples, and spent his last hours discussing with his adjutant the immortality of the soul. To Rommel, once Hitler's darling general, whose prestige had been deliberately and (as it now seemed) dangerously enhanced by propaganda, Hitler sent General Burgdorf, his most assiduous sycophant, with a revolver and a poison capsule. He was told that if he would commit suicide quietly, there would be no publicity and no reprisals on his family;[1] and he obeyed. One general, who was killed soon afterwards, was about to receive a state funeral when his complicity was discovered; the plans were changed at once, and he was hustled unattended to a criminal's grave. No wonder Hitler withdrew into a long privacy; no wonder he shrank from the company of his most competent military advisers, and listened only to the bombastic amateurs of the SS; he could no longer be sure

[1] This account of Rommel's death is given by Jodl and Keitel, and confirmed by other sources. Cf. Hans Speidel, *Invasion 1944* (Tuebingen, 1949).

of the loyalty of any officer. And no wonder Himmler seemed in those months to enjoy an extravagant measure of power. On the days of the Plot he succeeded Fromm as commander-in-chief of the Reserve Army. Shortly afterwards he took over from the Armed Forces the control of all prisoner-of-war camps. Within a few months this former sergeant-major was himself in command of an Army Group, vainly resisting the Russians on the Vistula Front.

Nevertheless, in spite of these apparent accessions of power, Himmler was in fact in decline. Though the attempt on Hitler's life made him for a moment more necessary than ever, the narrowness of its failure was proof that he too had failed. After all, it had been a very near thing. It was Providence (as Himmler himself agreed), not the police, that had saved Hitler's life. There were even some who maintained that so extensive a conspiracy could not possibly have been developed over so long a period without Himmler's knowledge; it was against nature, or at least against all precedent.[1]

Such doubts were not left unexploited by the patient, persistent Bormann. This 'evil genius of the Fuehrer', this 'Brown Eminence, sitting in the shadows', as one of the court[2] described him, 'Hitler's Mephistopheles', as he was more generally known, had by now achieved an undisputed supremacy such as had never been previously known in the immediate *entourage* of his master. Hitherto it had been, or at least it had seemed, Hitler's policy never to allow any of his ministers to attain to any singularity of position in his counsels. He had seemed always to play off one minister against another, and so himself to hold the balance among them. But now Martin Bormann, who, like Holstein in the cabinets of the Kaiser, had 'realized from the beginning the importance of representing his position as insignificant', had won the reward of his

---

[1] In fact it seems very unlikely that Himmler had any exact previous knowledge of the Plot; but it is certain that some of his *entourage*, including Schellenberg, knew about it in a general way, and although Schellenberg dared not mention the matter to Himmler, Himmler certainly had opportunities of knowing that his subordinates were coquetting with the opposition. Another of Himmler's subordinates who claims to have known about the Plot was Ohlendorf.

[2] Schwerin von Krosigk.

infinite patience. Never away from his master's side, even keeping the same eccentric hours as he—rising at midday and retiring at 4.30 or 5 in the morning—in sole control of the vast machinery of the Party, indispensable, indefatigable, and ubiquitous, he was now the sole custodian of Hitler's secrets, the sole channel for his orders, the sole method of approach to that ever more inaccessible presence. During the years of war every development had strengthened his authority. The Gauleiters were subordinate to him alone; he had increased their subordination and altered their character. The original Gauleiters had been old Party hacks who, having thumped their tubs and blown their trumpets obstreperously in the early days of the movement, had been rewarded with these lucrative and not too exacting offices. Bormann had changed that. One by one the old Gauleiters had gone, and new men had replaced them, younger, more energetic, more fanatical men, who owed everything not to the impersonal Party in the days when Bormann was unknown, but to Bormann himself. Throughout the war the Party machine, like the SS, had grown; like the SS, it had encroached on the functions of the Armed Forces, especially in matters of administration and supply, fortification and evacuation; like the SS, it had become more formidable, and more indispensable, with every defeat of German arms. Observers who watched the parallel development of these twin engines of power wondered what would happen when they began to conflict, when Himmler and Bormann, having absorbed or conquered all independent bodies, at last met face to face. In 1943, when Himmler was made Minister of the Interior, that interesting moment had come. Till then the relations between the two men had been excellent; thereafter sharp conflicts broke out. The slightest attempts by Himmler to exercise authority outside the SS were openly resented by Bormann. In the provinces, several Higher SS and Police Leaders[1] thought they could presume on Himmler's new authority and trespass on the preserves of the Gauleiters; they were quickly undeceived. 'Bormann immediately reported such cases to Hitler, and exploited them to fortify his own

[1] *Hoeherer SS und Polizei Fuehrer*; these were Himmler's regional deputies in Germany and occupied countries.

position. To our surprise [it is Speer who is speaking] it did not take him long to stalemate Himmler as Minister of the Interior.'[1] Such are the advantages of a central position.

In the same way, after the Plot of July 20th, Bormann was again quick to exploit the errors or omissions of his rival. While Himmler naïvely believed (since Goering was plainly out of favour) that he was the obvious heir-apparent to the throne, and took every promotion as confirmation of such a certainty, Bormann was in fact seeing to it that he was moving not upwards and towards the centre of power, but outwards and away from it. In the dark days of the last winter of war, Bormann achieved a further triumph; he secured the appointment of Himmler as Commander-in-Chief of Army Group Vistula, a new formation fighting a desperate battle against the Russians east of Berlin. Thus Himmler was moved away from Berlin, where he might still attract the favour of Hitler or interfere with the influence of Bormann; and Bormann, remaining safely in possession, indeed monopoly, of the Fuehrer's ear did not omit to ascribe the irresistible advance of the Red Army to the incompetence, perhaps even treachery, of his rival.

Nevertheless Bormann, though powerful, was not quite alone, not quite omnipotent, at Hitler's headquarters. Firstly, there remained Goebbels. Over all (or perhaps all but one) of Hitler's subordinates Goebbels enjoyed one indisputable advantage; he was able. Even Bormann recognized that to quarrel with Goebbels might prove fatal; and Goebbels, in his turn, recognized that Bormann had an undeniable vantage post through the regularity of his attendance upon Hitler. Between these two, therefore, though they differed to the end on many matters of policy, there subsisted, to the end, a working agreement. As an intimate personal friend, Goebbels always had

---

[1] A similar account has been given by Goering. It should be emphasized that the conflict between Himmler and Bormann was not solely a conflict of personalities and jurisdictions; it was also a conflict between the Party and the SS. The SS, as it was more fanatical, was also (in general) more disinterested than the Party, and entertained a bitter hatred for the corruption of the Party officials. This was the basis of the various plans in the SS to replace Hitler by Himmler. The fact was recognized even by the opposition. Cf. Hassell, *Von andern Deutschland*, p. 178.

direct access to the Fuehrer; nevertheless he thought it prudent to conciliate Bormann by using him as an intermediary in inessential matters, and only using his own special position on special occasions. And Bormann, on his side, recognizing this concession, did not seek to interfere with the occasional independence of Goebbels. In the last days of all, the actions of Goebbels and Bormann were symbolical of this practical compromise between the two surviving high-priests of Nazism. Their advice was different, their ambitions were different, their personal plans were different, but in the decisions of the Fuehrer, and in the mummery of his court, they agreed; and both officiated together at his last pagan sacraments of marriage and funeral before pursuing their separate courses to different fates.

The second character whose personality limited the empire of Martin Bormann was Hitler himself. Liberal refugees, theoretical Marxists, despairing reactionaries have pretended, or persuaded themselves, that Hitler was himself only a pawn in a game which not he but some other politicians, or some more cosmic forces, were playing. It is a fundamental delusion. Whatever independent forces he may have used, whatever incidental support he may have borrowed, Hitler remained to the end the sole master of the movement which he had himself inspired and founded, and which he was himself, by his personal leadership, to ruin. Neither Roehm nor Himmler, neither the Army nor the Junkers, neither high finance nor heavy industry, ever controlled that demonic and disastrous genius, whatever assistance they may at times have given or received, with whatever hopes or credulities they may have solaced their occasional misgivings, their frequent disappointments. And certainly, whatever ascendancy he may have gained over Goering, Hess, and Himmler, Bormann never controlled the uncontrollable will of Hitler, by whose favour alone he held office. His last political advice—to leave Berlin for Obersalzberg in April—was rejected; his dearest wish—to retain power after Hitler's death—was ignored. In 1939, when Sir Nevile Henderson suggested to Goering that he might use his influence to alter Hitler's mind, Goering had answered that once the Fuehrer had made up his mind, 'all the rest of us are no more than the ground under his feet'. It was a universal truth, as true of Bormann as of Goering, as true in 1945 as in 1939. Admittedly, says Speer, Bormann was to the end in complete control of all internal affairs; but at any time Hitler could have resumed direct control had he wished. 'He had always carried out the old principle, *Divide and rule.* There were political groups who were always ready to do away with others. A few critical words from Hitler, and all Bormann's enemies would have jumped at his throat.' If Bormann in fact exercised his power to the end, it was not in his own right, but by the sufferance of the formidable dictator whose incredible willpower whose hypnotic influence, compelled even his critics to worship and obey. 'Was Hitler, as an historic phenomenon, a product of the years after the first World War? Was he a sequel of the Versailles Treaty, the Revolution, and the events that followed? Was he a figure which these events would inevitably have produced?' So Albert Speer reflected in the philosophic leisure of the rock-perched fortress in which he was interned. But seeking to answer these questions, he was forced to re-envisage the character of the man whom he held responsible for Germany's downfall; and re-envisaging it, he replied that he was more than this. 'It is true that without these events Hitler would never have found the soil on which his activities could bear such rapid and prolific fruit; but the whole demonic figure of the man can never be explained simply as the product of these events. They could just as easily have found expression in a national leader of mediocre stature. For Hitler was one of those inexplicable historical phenomena which emerge at rare intervals among mankind. His person determined the fate of the nation. He alone placed it, and kept it, upon the path which has led it to this dreadful ending. The nation was spellbound by him as a people has rarely been in the whole of history.'

This conception of Hitler as a phoenix, rare in human centuries, a cosmic phenomenon exempt from ordinary laws, was not universally accepted inside Germany. It was not accepted by the generals, those hard-headed, unmystical, military engines. To them he was never more than a vulgarian of extraordinary power who fell short of their idea of genius. "When I was working with him," says Halder, the ablest of that class, "I was always looking for signs of genius in him. I tried hard to be honest and impartial, and not to be blinded by my antipathy to the man. I *never* found genius in him, only the diabolical." But one man accepted it completely, and his acceptance of it was the basis of its success. 'At long intervals in human history,' he wrote, 'it may occasionally happen that the practical politician and the political philosopher are one. The more intimate the union, the greater his political difficulties. Such a man does not labour to satisfy the demands that are obvious to every philistine; he reaches out towards ends that are comprehensible only to the few. Therefore his life is torn between hatred and love. The protest of the present generation, which does not understand him, wrestles with the recognition of posterity, for whom he also works.'

The author of that description is Hitler himself; and it is a self-portrait.[1] He had written it in prison, long before he had attained the power he contemplated. His own firm belief in his messianic mission was perhaps the most important element in the extraordinary power of his personality, which lasted long after the external reasons for its survival had disappeared; and the acceptance of this myth even by the intelligent Speer is the best evidence of its power.

[1] *Mein Kampf*, p. 231.

CHAPTER TWO

HITLER IN DEFEAT

SUCH WAS the setting of the stage, such the cast of the players, when the Allied breakthrough at Avranches in August 1944 opened the last act in the tragedy of Germany. The rest of the drama—the pace of the catastrophe, the inter-relation and concatenation of events—was determined by an external, uncontrollable force: the advance of the Allied armies. With every new crisis, with the fall of each great fortress, the passage of each great river, a fresh fever seemed to break out in Rastenburg, Berlin, or Bad Nauheim; but these were merely stages in the development of the drama not changes, or factors, in its course. Though strange errors still persisted in the politically illiterate court, though Himmler envisaged himself as a new colossus, and Ribbentrop to the last believed in an inevitable split between the Allies, in fact only two questions remained to which the answer was in any doubt: when would the end come, and how would the Nazi Party in general, and Hitler in particular, face it? For since the failure of the Generals' Plot, it was he alone who would decide the matter. By that last victory he had gained, not indeed the salvation or even the reprieve of Germany, but at least the power to ruin it in his own way.

To the first of these questions, no answer could rationally be made in Germany, for the answer no longer depended on Germany alone. The Party, of course, had an official answer: it would not come at all—at least, not in the form of a defeat for Germany. Never was the protest, 'We shall never capit-ulate!'—that cry which had already punctuated Hitler's utterances in 1933[1]—raised so frequently, so shrilly, and so unconvincingly, or repeated so obediently, as in the last winter of the war. Such an answer, had it really been admitted, would have rendered the second question irrelevant; but in fact not

[1] Rauschning, *Hitler Speaks*, pp. 15, 125.

everyone, not even the Party leaders themselves, could really believe in it; many of them were already making their plans for escape, or at least survival. Nevertheless, it was the official answer; no other answer was allowed; and a curious but inevitable consequence ensued. With slogans of victory on their lips, everyone was preparing for defeat; and since no official preparation could be envisaged, a total breakdown of discipline and organization became apparent. Plans for collective resistance, or even collective survival, were rendered impossible, because everyone, or almost everyone, was individually engaged in secret negotiations for surrender, or secret plans for desertion. Loud boasts were made of an impregnable bastion in the south, an Alpine Redoubt in the sacred hills of Nazi mythology, hills charged with legends of Barbarossa and sanctified by Hitler's residence; but when no one, except Hitler himself and a few overheated schoolboys, believed in such resistance, and everyone else was preoccupied with personal projects of surrender or disappearance, all such designs remained in the already overcrowded realm of German metaphysics. The same fatal flaw condemned the so-called German resistance movement from the start. In fact, there was never any such movement. A 'resistance movement', as defined by the circumstances of the war, is a movement of unconquered people in a conquered country. But it was the official doctrine of the Nazi Government that Germany not only would not, but could not be conquered. Indeed, since it had this implication, any mention of a German resistance movement was absolutely forbidden. Schellenberg has told us how, in these darkening days, a certain Major-General Gehlen, who had long been busy studying the Polish underground movement, drew up a careful plan for German resistance on similar lines; but how, when Schellenberg forwarded these plans to Himmler, their reception made him tremble for his life. "This is complete madness!" was Himmler's answer. "If I were to discuss such a plan with Wenck,[1] I should be denounced as the first defeatist in the Third Reich. The fact would be served up to the Fuehrer piping hot!"; and he went on to

[1] General Wenck was GOC German 12th Army, fighting on the Elbe. This army is of importance later in this history.

denounce 'high-class staff officers' who sat safely in evacuation areas nursing post-war plans instead of fighting. Even in February 1945, when the writing on the wall (one would have thought) needed no highly trained interpreters, General Staff officers received a circular reminding them of the severe penalties for defeatism, and naming three General Staff officers who had already been shot for that crime. Like the Roman augurs, who used to wink to each other over the obsolete religious ceremonies which they solemnly celebrated, many German Staff officers, whose secret plans had long ago been completed, must have smiled inwardly as they initialled, and passed on, this now meaningless document.

What then of the Werewolves? someone will ask. The answer is simple. The Werewolves do not contradict, they illustrate these facts. For a long time the facts were incomprehensible, because they seemed to conflict. It was known that an organization for guerrilla warfare, the so-called Undertaking Werewolf, had been secretly set under the authority of the now ubiquitous Himmler; and then the German radio announced the desperate character, the invincible determination, and the expected results of this formidable movement. It was assumed, naturally enough, that this was to be a resistance movement comparable to the underground armies which had fought against the German armies of occupation in Poland and France, in Italy, Denmark, and the Balkans. At the same time it was surprising to find that the leader of the Werewolves, SS Obergruppenfuehrer Hans Pruetzmann, was engaged, together with the Gauleiter of Hamburg and others, in negotiating, or seeking to negotiate, with the British, through the Danish underground movement, for a peaceful surrender. And when the surrender came, and the operations of the Werewolves should have begun, the reverse happened. In a broadcast speech, Admiral Doenitz, the new Fuehrer, ordered all the Werewolves in the West to cease their activity. He was obeyed. Of all the conquered countries of Europe, Germany alone produced no resistance movement.

The explanation of these facts, at first obscure, is now clear. In May 1945 Pruetzmann, the head of the Werewolves, surrendered himself at Flensburg. Unfortunately he succeeded in committing suicide before full interrogation; but the story which he knew has since been learned from other sources. The Werewolves were never intended to operate after defeat; since the mention, or suggestion, of defeat was forbidden, that was out of the question. They were intended as a paramilitary formation, an auxiliary arm, to fight behind the Allied lines as diversionary forces, and thereby to assist the German armies. Thus their activity was parallel to that of the regular armies, not in succession to it. They were never intended to operate independently of the German High Command. Indeed, the Werewolves themselves never expected to have to fight in civilian clothes; they assumed they would fight in uniform, and thus, when captured, be entitled to the treatment of prisoners of war; and the discovery that this was not so was responsible for many desertions.

Why then were the Werewolves ever regarded as a serious menace? Here again we must appeal to later information to solve an old riddle. On April 1st, 1945, a new development occurred which both obscured the real issue and vividly illustrates the condition of jungle war which made nonsense of so many Nazi plans and organizations. As the controlling centre of a wide organization, Pruetzmann's office, according to all who knew it, was inefficient and uninspiring. Pruetzmann himself was vain, idle, and boastful. The organization of his headquarters, says Schellenberg, corresponded with the mental capacity of its members—it was weak; and he adds that he personally remonstrated with Himmler about the whole business, as 'criminal and stupid'. But on April 1st a new instrument of centralization appeared. This was the Radio Werewolf, which first published the hitherto secret organization, and turned the name 'Werewolf' from a mysterious symbol into a public slogan. But this Radio Werewolf was in fact quite independent of Pruetzmann's organization; for the propaganda of the movement had been seized by Goebbels, who, still struggling, even at this eleventh hour, for the dwindling fragments of authority, thus hoped (it seems) to gain control of the whole organization. Goebbels had no relations with Pruetzmann whom he evidently thought insufficiently radical; but his use of Radio Werewolf, far from curing the defects of the movement, only made it more chaotic—for he used it to preach an ideological nihilism which had no connection with the real and limited aims of the Werewolf organization, and which often discredited and discouraged its members. The usurpation of Radio Werewolf by Goebbels is responsible for many of the popular misconceptions about the Werewolves, and for the ridiculous difference between their supposed aims and their actual achievements. It did the Nazi cause no good; if anything, by discrediting the movement, it probably hastened its collapse.[1]

Nevertheless Radio Werewolf is of importance; for in it is to be found the answer to our second question; how would the Nazi Party face the defeat which, openly, it refused even to contemplate? Because of this refusal there was, of course, no official, no direct answer, though it was always understood that Hitler would remain true to his original programme, *Weltmacht oder Niedergang*—world power or ruin. If world-power was unattainable, then (it was agreed by all who knew him) he would make the ruin as great as he could, and himself, like Samson at Gaza, perish in the cataclysm of his own making. For Hitler was not a figure of Western Europe, however, he sought to pose as its champion against Asiatic Bolshevism; nor did his melodramatic character respond to the Confucian ideal of a tidy, unobtrusive death. When he envisaged himself against an historical background, when his imagination was heated, and his vanity intoxicated, with flattery and success, and he rose from his modest supper of vegetable pie and distilled water to prance upon the table and identify himself with the great conquerors of the past, it was not as Alexander, or Caesar, or Napoleon that he wished to be celebrated, but as the re-embodiment of those angels of destruction—of Alaric, the sacker of Rome, of Attila, 'the scourge of God', of

[1] The facts given in this paragraph are given independently by Ohlendorf and Schellenberg. At Nuremberg both Speer and Fritzsche said that they understood the Werewolves to be controlled by Bormann —*ie* the Berlin group, who had usurped the name and tried to control the policy—although Fritzsche added that Bormann had under him an Obergruppenfuehrer whose name he had forgotten—*ie* Pruetzmann. In fact Pruetzmann was always responsible to Himmler, and remained on his personal staff to the end.

Genghiz Khan, the leader of the Golden Horde. 'I have not come into the world,' he declared, in one of these messianic moods, 'to make men better, but to make use of their weaknesses';[1] and in conformity with this nihilistic ideal, this absolute love of destruction, he would destroy, if not his enemies, then Germany and himself and all else that might be involved in the ruins. 'Even if we could not conquer,' he had said in 1934,[2] 'we should drag half the world into destruction with us, and leave no one to triumph over Germany. There will not be another 1918. We shall not surrender'; and again: 'We shall never capitulate, no, never! We may be destroyed, but if we are, we shall drag a world with us—a world in flames.'[3] Now, in his positive hatred of the German people, who had failed him in his megalomaniac designs, he returned to the same theme. The German people was not worthy of his great ideas; therefore let it perish utterly. 'If the German people was to be conquered in the struggle,' he told a meeting of Gauleiters in August 1944, 'then it had been too weak to face the test of history, and was fit only for destruction.'[4]

Such then was Hitler's answer to the challenge of defeat. In part, it was a personal answer, the vindictive gesture of a wounded pride; but in part it derived from another, more deliberate feature of his terrible philosophy. For Hitler believed in the *Myth*, as recommended by the irrationalist philosophers Sorel and Pareto whose precepts he so faithfully followed and so eloquently ratified.[5] Further, he despised, with an overwhelming contempt, the Kaiser and his ministers, 'the fools of 1914-18' who feature so largely in his limited vocabulary of

[1] Rauschning, *Hitler Speaks*, p. 274.   [2] *Ibid.*, p. 125.
[3] *Ibid.*, p. 15.   [4] Speer.
[5] Although it is improbable that Hitler had read either of these baleful philosophers, there are many striking similarities between their principles and his. Pareto's statement that the art of government lies in 'taking advantage of sentiments, not wasting energy in a futile effort to destroy them' (*Treatise on General Sociology*) is an exact parallel to the remark of Hitler just quoted; and Hitler's theory (*Mein Kampf*, p. 759) that a people or a class, that has once yielded to one threat, will go on yielding for ever, is exactly foreshadowed by Sorel. The Nazi elaboration of Sorel's theory of the Myth was claimed by Goebbels as one of his own decisive contributions to the movement (see Semler, *Goebbels*, pp. 56-8).

abuse. He despised them for many reasons; he despised them for many errors into which he also fell, such as undervaluing his enemies, and making war on two fronts,[1] and for many which he avoided, such as being too mild in their politics and too scrupulous in their methods of war; and he despised them in particular for their failure to understand the importance of the myth and the conditions of its growth and usefulness. In 1918 the Kaiser had surrendered; weakly despairing, he had thrown in his hand (such was the official Nazi version), without waiting for defeat. From such weakness, such despair, no flourishing myth could grow, whatever useful lies might be invented. Myths require a dramatic, an heroic end. Though its champions are overwhelmed, the idea must continue to live, that when the winter of defeat is over, and the cherishing airs return, it may put forth new flowers and blossom again in apparent continuity. Therefore on form, as the racegoers say, it had long been agreed by the experts (even when such speculations seemed remote and ridiculous) how Hitler and his apostles would face disaster. In the winter of 1944–5 the time for the corroboration of this theory was obviously near; and as in other dark hours, the prophet Goebbels came forth once more to corroborate it.

All his tricks had now been played out, and had failed, or their temporary success had contributed too little to make that last necessary difference. He had tried the glory of militarism, and failed. He had tried 'true socialism', and failed. He had tried the New Order, and failed. He had tried the advancing crusade against Bolshevism, and failed. He had tried the defence of Europe against the invading hordes of Asia, and that had failed too. As the days darkened, he had tried (as Speer said he should have tried) the appeal of blood, sweat, and tears. But propaganda is subject to the law of diminishing returns; what had worked in England in 1940 would not work in Germany in 1944, after the failure of so many incompatible promises; and that had failed too. Then he had tried the Frederican war. The German people were reminded how, in

---

[1] In *Mein Kampf* (p. 198) Hitler attacks the Kaiser's propagandists for representing the enemy as contemptible. His 'guarantees' that there would never be another war on two fronts needs no specification.

the eighteenth century, even the great Frederick had seemed doomed, when his allies fell away, and his enemies closed in, when the Russians took Berlin, and he was outnumbered on all sides and alone. Yet he had survived and triumphed in the end, thanks to his oriental endurance, his brilliant strategy, and the certain favour of Providence, which had sown dissension among his enemies. Since the Germans of 1944 were ruled by a leader of no less resource, the greatest strategical genius of all time, no less favoured by Providence (as events had recently shown), might not they too hope, if only they showed the same endurance, for a similar delivery? But even this appeal seemed inadequate in the winter of 1944–5. What then was left for the prophet to prophesy?

Goebbels was equal to the occasion. If all additional appeals had failed, if all supernumerary adherents had fallen away, at least there was still the original slogan of revolutionary Nazism, the slogan which had inspired the *déclassés* and the property-less, the outcasts and casualties of society who had made Nazism before the Junkers and generals, industrialists and civil servants had joined it, and which might yet inspire them again, now that these fair-weather allies could no longer be counted on. From Radio Berlin, and later from Radio Were-wolf, that slogan was heard again: the slogan of destruction; the authentic voice of Nazism uninhibited, unaltered by all the developments of the interim; the same voice which Rauschning had heard, with timid aristocratic dismay, ringing suddenly out among the teacups, the cream buns, the cuckoo-clocks and Bavarian bric-à-brac of the original Berchtesgaden. It was the doctrine of class war, of permanent revolution, of purpose-less but gleeful destruction of life and property and all those values of civilization which the German Nazi, though he some-times tries painfully to imitate them, fundamentally envies and detests. The trials of war, the horrors of bombardment, now acquired a new significance for the exultant Dr Goebbels: they were instruments not of fearful but of sanitary destruc-tion, and he welcomed them. 'The bomb-terror,' he gloated, 'spares the dwellings of neither the rich nor poor; before the labour offices of total war the last class barriers have had to go down.' 'Under the *débris* of our shattered cities,' echoed the

German Press, 'the last so-called achievements of the middle-class nineteenth century have been finally buried.' 'There is no end to revolution,' cried Radio Werewolf; 'a revolution is only doomed to failure if those who make it cease to be revolutionaries'; and it too welcomed the bombs which now fell nightly with ever more devastating effect on the industrial cities of Germany: 'together with the monuments of culture there crumble also the last obstacles to the fulfilment of our revolutionary task. Now that everything is in ruins, we are forced to rebuild Europe. In the past, private possessions tied us to a bourgeois restraint. Now the bombs, instead of killing all Europeans, have only smashed the prison walls which held them captive. . . . In trying to destroy Europe's future, the enemy has only succeeded in smashing its past; and with that, everything old and outworn has gone.' The virtue of Goebbels lay in his lucidity, the Latin clarity of his thought and style. The German language, especially in the mouths of its philoso-phers, is often cloudy and obscure; and such sentiments, uttered by Hegel or Spengler, Rosenberg or Streicher, would have been oracular but ambiguous, and might be misinter-preted. There is no such danger with the language of Goebbels. There is no mistaking his jubilation.

Meanwhile, what of Hitler himself? After the Generals' Plot of July 20th he had withdrawn from publicity—withdrawn, or been withdrawn, so effectively that many believed him dead, or imprisoned by the all-powerful Himmler. As nothing but silence answered these suggestions, rumour and exaggera-tion quickly extended their scope, and supplied the circum-stantial detail which so often passes for evidence. Resourceful journalists described, with the exact relish of Dante or Baed-eker, the medieval catacombs in which the deposed Fuehrer was now immured; or demonstrated, from the folds of his ears, that the Fuehrer portrayed in German photographs was a double, foisted upon the German people to conceal the death of their authentic master. In fact there is perhaps no period of Hitler's life with which we are more familiar, in its daily details, than the five months from October 1944 till the end of February 1945; over which period we possess the diary kept for him by his personal servant, Heinz Linge. This diary, picked up in September 1945 in the ruins of the Chancellery by a British officer, is in the form of a manuscript engagement-diary; but the reference to such unpredictable interruptions as air-raid alarms shows that the entries were made after, not before, the events they summarize. These are inscribed, hour by hour, on the left-hand page. The right-hand page, besides the regular signature of Linge, contains only the address of the Fuehrer's headquarters at the time—until November 20th '*Wolfschanze*',[1] at Rastenburg, where the Plot had occurred; thence till December 10th at Berlin; from December 11th till January 15th '*Adlershorst*',[2] at Bad Nauheim in the Taunus hills, whence Hitler directed the Ardennes offensive; and finally, from January 16th till the end at Berlin, in the Reich Chancellery, which he never left.

This dairy, though its entries are concise and factual, consisting only of interviews and meals and engagements, is nevertheless of value to the historian of Hitler. It shows the routine of his daily life, the nature of his court and visitors, the deviations of his health, and the increasing regularity of his engagements. Awakened daily at about noon, all his appointments have a corresponding eccentricity, and every day consists of a series of interviews with politicians and generals, adjutants and liaison officers, doctors and secretaries, punctuated only by belated meals, an occasional half hour stroll in the garden, and an evening nap, until his last reception, a non-political tea party between 2 and 3.30 in the morning, followed, some two hours later, by his retreat to bed. The strain which these eccentric hours put upon others can be imagined; for the interviews sometimes go on till 3.30 in the morning, and the other parties may not always have been able, like Hitler, to sleep through the following morning. In the last months they became even more eccentric; for by that time Hitler had reduced his hours of sleep to three.[3] But one man at least was equal to all such demands. The persistent Bormann determined never to lose sight of the master upon whom his whole power depended, or to allow another to monopolize that profitable

---

[1] Literally, 'Fort Wolf'.   [2] Literally, 'Eagle's nest'.
[3] Speer. Cf. Himmler's statement below, p. 132.

ear; and he adjusted his own hours according to the same outrageous timetable. He at least was always on call.

Apart from this diary there are, of course, many other sources of evidence on Hitler's personal life during these final months. One is again the indispensable Speer, who has described the gradual change which came over Hitler's habits and character during the war, and, in particular, after the Plot of July 20th 1944. It was not only the obvious corruption of power, which led him to resent criticism, to feed on flattery, and to surround himself with spineless toadies;[1] not only the growing conviction that he alone had the willpower to continue the struggle, he alone still believed in ultimate victory and his own divine mission, while all others had abandoned hope and would capitulate; it was a fundamental change in his manner of life, which these secondary developments did but illustrate and intensify. For Hitler (Speer insists) was by nature an artist, averse from those methodical hours, that unremitting labour, which is so clearly reflected in the diary of the last months. In the days of peace he had found, in the irregular habits, the filmgoing and fantasies, the delays and holidays, the truancies and picnics, the tours of inspection and weekends at Obersalzberg, the tea parties and social gatherings of fellow 'artists', that relief which the intolerable pressure of revolutionary politics demanded. Speer's account of Hitler's peacetime life is almost idyllic; for Speer had a vested interest in romanticizing the past. After all, he had shared that life, and in its personal haven had completely forgotten the price at which it had been bought, the cruelties and concentration camps upon which it was based, and the sanguinary politics which it supported, but which, to him, the happy technocrat, seemed irrelevant distractions. Nostalgically, he has described those more carefree days in which Hitler listened to criticism, laughed and gossiped with his associates, and, whenever the weight of regular politics became too oppressive, disappeared to

[1] The servility of Hitler's court makes a melancholy contrast to the ideals of *Mein Kampf* (p. 259), in which he denounces as 'gravediggers of the monarchy' the flatterers who surrounded the Kaiser, when an honest man would 'seriously admonish and seek to persuade even His Majesty, the wearer of the Crown himself'.

Obersalzberg with unpolitical friends and Eva Braun. There he would make up his mind on problems too vast to be considered in the hubbub of the Reich Chancellery, walking up and down in the Alpine summer, visiting small inns where he found (he said) 'the inner calm and assurance necessary to his world-shattering decisions'; there he occupied himself more intensively with artistic things, with architecture, and continual films; there he would recover from the exhaustion of politics: his eyes would brighten again, his reactions would quicken, his enthusiasm for making decisions would revive; there his conception of life would become almost bourgeois: he would behave as a hospitable Austrian paterfamilias, good-natured and jocular, friendly and affable with all. While Goering and others would cover themselves with 'tin-shops' of medals, he would exhibit a simplicity of manner and dress that brought him credit among his people and reconciled them to unpopular political decisions. "I suspect," says Speer "that he was not happy with his 'mission'; that he would rather have been an architect than a politician. He often clearly expressed his aversion from politics, and even more from military matters. He disclosed his intention of withdrawing after the war from state affairs, to build himself a large house in Linz,[1] and there to end his days. He insisted that he would then completely retire. He did not wish to embarrass his successor in any way. He would then be soon forgotten and left to himself. Possibly some of his former colleagues would visit him occasionally, but he would not count on that. Apart from Fraeulein Braun he would take no one with him; nor would anyone stand living with him of his own free will for any length of time. . . ." Such were Hitler's daydreams in 1939; and they are not reported by Speer only. On August 25th, 1939, Sir Nevile Henderson had an interview with Hitler in Berlin. 'Among various points mentioned by Herr Hitler,' reported the ambassador, 'were, that he was by nature an artist, not a politician, and that once the Polish question was settled, he would end his life as an artist and not as a war-monger.'[2]

A naïve judgment, pathetically naïve. It is surprising that

[1] Hitler always regarded Linz as his home town. Cf. below, pp. 104, 213.
[2] *Documents concerning German-Polish relations* (Cmd. 6106), p. 128.

the otherwise sagacious Speer could be so elementary a psychologist, and suppose that this aesthetic *cri-de-cœur* was of absolute, and not merely of relative significance. But it is a not infrequent error. How many historians have been subject to it, who have defended corrupt politicians, weak governors, and bloodthirsty tyrants by appealing to their domestic virtues, their artistic tastes, the amiable simplicity of their personal lives! It is the error common to those who, like Speer, suppose politics irrelevant, and, in so doing, insensibly judge politicians by unpolitical standards. In this at least Rauschning showed more judgment than Speer. Less interested in art and the artist, he at least was not deceived by this bourgeois *bonhomie*. Above the crunch of the cakes and the tinkle of the teacups he heard, if not the cry of the tortured in the prison camps, at least the bloodcurdling paean of universal destruction; and drew the consequences.

Though Speer's account of Hitler's life before the war is of only partial validity, it is nevertheless valid within the limits of its incidence; and the statements of fact are certainly true. But during the war, he explains, all this changed. When he became the great warlord, the greatest strategical genius of all time, Hitler's company changed, his hours of work became monotonously regular, the pressure of events gave him no release, he had no relaxations, no safety valves, for the harmless discharge of his pent-up dynamism. Defeat intensified the process. If the German people must cut down their pleasures, he must sympathetically cut down his; and his were not only pleasures but the necessary conditions of his political life. Then came distrust and its attendant neuroses; the corruption of power reinforced by the fear of treachery. There were no more films, no more visits to Obersalzberg. Hitler surrounded himself not with artists and friends, but with illiterate soldiers, whom, in the height of his vainglorious disdain, he despised not merely socially and politically, but militarily, too. Conversation, instead of being a relief, became confined to the tedious trivialities of the barracks and the mess. Nor were there any compensating advantages. It had once been the tradition of the German Army to allow free criticism from subordinate officers. As the Party increased its control, this criticism was steadily reduced; after July 20th, 1944, it ceased altogether. A universal suspicion suppressed all healthy conversation and multiplied the effects of every setback. More and more the once sociable Fuehrer became an isolated hermit, with all the psychological repressions inherent in that dismal condition. He was isolated from persons, isolated from events. Convinced that only he could lead the German people out of defeat to victory, and that his life was therefore of cardinal importance; and yet convinced that every man's hand was against him, and assassination awaited him around every corner; by a logical consequence, he seldom left the protection of his underground headquarters, or the banal society of his quack doctor, his secretaries, and the few spiritless generals who still pandered to his inspiration. He seldom visited the front, never knew the true extent of the disasters to his armies, his towns, his industries; never in the entire war did he visit a bombed city. He remained a frustrated recluse, restless and miserable. More and more he dreamed of an elegant retirement in Linz. While Germany was crumbling in ruins, he occupied himself with ever more elaborate architectural plans. He was not (as his enemies said) redesigning Buckingham Palace for his own use; he was envisaging a new opera house and a new picture gallery for Linz.[1] And as his contempt and distrust grew for the rest of mankind, so he thought more and more of Eva Braun, who was exempt from the otherwise universal vice of treachery. Only Eva Braun, he said, and his Alsatian dog Blondi, were faithful to him. He had only one friend, he repeated, who would remain loyal to him in the last decisive hour, and that was Eva Braun. "We would never believe it," says Speer; "but this time his intuition had not failed him."

The effects of such a life on Hitler's physical condition can easily be imagined. "Up till 1940," says Dr von Hasselbach, the most critical and reliable of his doctors,[2] "Hitler appeared to be much younger than he actually was. From that date he

[1] When I visited the Bunker in September 1945, Goebbel's room was still full of illustrated books on opera-house architecture.

[2] Von Hasselbach is thus described by his interrogators, and by Drs Giesing and Brandt (see below, pp. 106 foll., 110), who add that von Hasselbach was 'probably one of the few people associated with Hitler who did not fall under his spell'.

104

aged rapidly. From 1940 to 1943 he looked his age. After 1943 he appeared to have grown old." In his last days, says Speer, he was positively senile; and those were not yet the last days of all, the last days of April 1945, when all who saw him described him as a physical wreck. This rapid deterioration in Hitler's health has often been attributed to the effects of the bomb explosion of the July 20th, 1944; but this is wrong. The wounds which Hitler received on that occasion were trivial and temporary. The real damage to his health in the last months of his life proceeded from two causes: his manner of life, which has been described, and his doctors.

Whatever Hitler's psychological condition may have been —and on such a subject, and in so unique a character, it would be imprudent to speculate—there can be no doubt that his physical stamina was exceptionally strong. It could not have been otherwise, to have endured for so long, the tenancy of that violent personality. Before the war, his only recorded distemper was of the throat. In 1935, at the time of the'Anglo-German Naval Treaty, Hitler became alarmed at the condition of his voice, and sent for a specialist, Professor von Eicken, of the Charité Hospital in the Luisenstrasse in Berlin, who had previously attended one of his adjutants.[1] Von Eicken diagnosed a polyp on the vocal cords, and removed it; after which Hitler recovered, and apart from an occasional tingling in the ears, in consequence of general overstrain, and a tendency to stomach cramps, continued in good health until 1943. He believed indeed that he had a weak heart, and after 1938 avoided all forms of exercise. On a mountaintop above Berchtesgaden he had built a gazebo, the Kehlstein, whence he could overlook the fabulous Bavarian Alps, and conquered Austria, and the beautiful lake of Koenigsee. A lift, built in the entrails of the mountain, would take him and his visitors up to this eyrie; but Hitler soon ceased to make use of this expensive observation post. In that rarefied atmosphere, 5400 feet above sea-level, he felt a tightening of his chest, which he ascribed to the weakness of his heart; but his doctors found no evidence of such a condition, and satisfied themselves that these symptoms,

[1] The adjutant was Brueckner, and the incident the same which led to the appointment of Brandt.

like his epigastric pains and cramps, were of hysterical origin.

All this time Hitler was attended, in the main, by three doctors: Brandt, von Hasselbach, and Morell. Professor Karl Brandt was his principal surgeon, and had been with him since 1934. A fortunate accident had made the career of Brandt, and of other doctors too. Brandt belonged to the circle of notoriously Nazi doctors who surrounded Professor Magnus and had their Berlin headquarters at the clinic in the Ziegelstrasse. In August 1933 Brandt, then twenty-nine years old, was spending the summer in Upper Bavaria, when Hitler's niece and his adjutant Brueckner were injured in a serious motor accident at Reit-im-Winkel. Brandt was one of the doctors summoned to treat them; the impression he made was favourable, and next year he was invited by Brueckner to travel to Venice as personal surgeon to the Fuehrer. This was the beginning of a career at court. Brandt became official surgeon to Hitler, and his staff. But since this immobilized him for long periods, preventing him from the practice of surgery (for in fact Hitler never required his skill), Brandt introduced in turn two other members of Professor Magnus's circle to deputise for him at court—firstly Professor Haase, who retired soon afterwards to the Ziegelstrasse for reasons of health and will appear again at the close of this narrative, and secondly, as successor to Haase, Professor Hans Karl von Hasselbach. Brandt and von Hasselbach remained with Hitler until the great inter-medical battle of October 1944 which will shortly be related, Brandt being gradually promoted to the post of Reich Commissioner for Health and Sanitation; and their evidence is included in this summary of Hitler's health.

Professor Theodore Morell was Hitler's physician. If Brandt and his friends were not, technically, among the first flight of surgeons; if they owed their success to that element of chance which, after all, determines the majority of personal appointments; they were nevertheless not altogether disreputable. At least, under Brandt's treatment, Brueckner recovered from his motor accident; and if Hitler had been similarly injured, he would doubtless have received competent attention. But of Morell it is difficult to speak in the measured terms and discreet vocabulary proper to his profession. He was a quack. Those who saw him, after his internment by the American forces, a gross but deflated old man, of cringing manners, inarticulate speech, and the hygenic habits of a pig, could not conceive how a man so utterly devoid of self-respect could ever have been selected as a personal physician by anyone who had even a limited possibility of choice. But Hitler not only chose him; he kept him for nine years, in constant attendance, preferring him above all other doctors, and, in the end, surrendering his person, against unanimous advice, to the disastrous experiments of a charlatan. From 1936 to 1945, Morell, in his own words, was Hitler's 'constant companion'; and yet the health of his patient was to him only a secondary consideration. From all the evidence, it is perfectly clear that Morell's god was mammon. He was totally indifferent to science or truth. Rather than study the slow methods of patient research, he preferred to play with quick drugs and fancy nostrums; and when critics hinted at the inadequacy of his qualifications, he merely extended his claims in the empire of lies. He was, he maintained, the true discoverer of penicillin; but after he had devoted long years of singleminded research to its discovery, the ubiquitous British Secret Service had stolen the secret, and a British doctor had claimed the credit. Actually it was not necessary for Morell to make such defensive claims; for his position with Hitler depended upon his weaknesses, not his skill. Hitler liked magic, as he liked astrology and the assurances of somnambulism. "He had little respect for physicians," says one of that profession,[1] "and believed in a kind of mystic, medicine, which was akin to Christian Science." And so, when this ship's doctor, who had set up as a specialist in venereal disease among the artistic demi-monde of Berlin, came to Berchtesgaden as a necessary attendant on Hitler's photographer, Hoffmann, his fortune was soon made. And fortune does not mean the modest opulence of a successful practitioner. Morell's financial ambitions were far larger than that. He built factories and manufactured patent remedies. As court physician, he secured lucrative approval of his manufactures. Sometimes he had their purchase made compulsory throughout Germany; sometimes he secured a monopoly for his own brands. His vitamin chocolates

[1] Professor Gebhardt.

were a particularly successful venture. By an order from Hitler, Morell's 'Russia' lice-powder was made compulsory throughout the armed forces, and no priorities were allowed to interfere with the construction of factories for this important manufacture. 'Ultraseptyl', the sulphonamide produced by Morell's company in Budapest, was condemned by the pharmacological faculty of Leipzig University as harmful to the nerves, and worse than the corresponding German product. The report of the faculty was shown to Hitler, but without effect. Morell's proprietary product obtained the necessary political sanction, and priorities were granted to enable him to increase still further its production.

These drugs were not so lucratively dispersed among the German people without preliminary trial. The experiments were made on Hitler. An *almost* complete list of the drugs used by Morell upon Hitler, compiled from his own account (which is unlikely to exaggerate on such a topic) and excluding the morphia and hypnotics which were also used, contains the names of twenty-eight different mixtures of drugs, including the proprietary 'Ultraseptyl' condemned by the pharmacologists, various fake medicines, narcotics, stimulants, and aphrodisiacs. The way in which Morell made use of these drugs is thus described by Dr Brandt:

"Morell took more and more to treatment by injections, until in the end he was doing all his work by this method. For instance, he would give large doses of sulphonamides for slight colds, and gave them to everyone at Hitler's headquarters. Morell and I had many disputes about this. Morell then took to giving injections that had dextrose, hormones, vitamins, etc, so that the patient immediately felt better; and this type of treatment seemed to impress Hitler. Whenever he felt a cold coming on, he would have three to six injections daily, and thus prevent any real development of the infection. Therapeutically this was satisfactory. Then Morell used it as a prophylactic. If Hitler had to deliver a speech on a cold or rainy day, he would have injections the day before, the day of the speech, and the day after. The normal resistance of the body was thus gradually replaced by an artificial medium. When the war began, Hitler thought himself indispensable, and throughout the war received almost continual injections. During the last two years he was injected daily. When I asked Morell to name the drugs employed, he refused. Hitler came to depend more and more on these injections; his dependence became very obvious during the last year. With the exception of General Jodl, all the members of Hitler's staff were treated from time to time by Morell."

By the time Brandt was interned, he had good reason to hate Morell, and his opinion might therefore seem at first to be biased against him; but there can be no doubt of its accuracy. It is supported by every other doctor who had opportunities of knowing the facts; and the professional verdict of the faculty is supported by intelligent lay observers. Speaking of the mental overstrain to which Hitler subjected himself, Speer says: "I believe that anyone who does a great deal of intellectual work can understand this condition of mental over-exertion; but there can hardly be another person who has endured such an ever-increasing strain over so many years, and who has further found himself a physician who tried out completely new drugs on him, in order to keep him capable of work, and, at the same time, to carry out a unique medical experiment. It would be interesting to analyse Hitler's handwriting during the last months; it had the uncertainty of an old man. By his stubborn ways, his sustained outbursts of anger, he often reminded me of a senile man. This condition became permanent after 1944, and was only seldom interrupted." "For purely physical reasons," says the same authority elsewhere, "most other men would have broken down under the strain of such a life, and after an enforced relaxation would have regained the capacity for work; or else nature would have come to the rescue with an illness. But Hitler's physician, Morell, managed to cover up his exhaustion by means of artificial stimulants, a method which, ends by completely ruining the patient. Hitler became accustomed to these means of keeping up his endurance, and kept on demanding them. He admired Morell and his methods, and was in some sense dependent on him and his remedies."[1]

[1] This account given by Speer is almost identical, in its main points, with another account by Heinz Lorenz. Hitler's signature may be seen in his will (p. 252).

Under the combined pressure of such a life and such remedies, only a powerful constitution could have preserved Hitler's health from a much earlier collapse. In 1943 the first symptoms of physical alteration became apparent. Hitler's extremities began to tremble, especially the left arm and the left leg; his left foot dragged upon the ground; and he developed a stoop. The nature of this tremor was never satisfactorily explained. Some doctors thought that it might be due to Parkinson's disease;[1] but others supposed an hysterical origin, and no certainty could be achieved. At all events this tremor was not, as has often been stated, a consequence of the explosion of July 20th, 1944; it had already been obvious for some time, and the visible decline of the Fuehrer's health had even been the subject of an emotional birthday broadcast by Dr Goebbels, who, in April 1943, had drawn a pathetic picture of the now lined and haggard Fuehrer, 'the face of an Atlas, bearing the whole world on his shoulders'.[2] In fact, all the doctors are agreed that, after the shock of the explosion, the tremor, which had been becoming regularly worse, ceased altogether; but later it began again in aggravated form, and continued to grow worse until the end.

The events of July 20th, 1944, therefore, though they represent a military, political, and psychological crisis, had little physical significance in the life of Hitler. The first doctor to be summoned on that occasion had been Dr Erwin Giesing, ear, nose, and throat specialist at a nearby military hospital; and he was followed by Professor von Eicken, who had previously operated on Hitler. They found that the tympanic membranes of nearly all the officers present had been broken. Hitler's tympanic membranes were broken on both sides. He was also suffering from irritation in the labyrinths of the ears,

[1] This view was more widely held among those doctors who had no direct connection with Hitler (eg de Crinis; see below, p. 132); but it was not excluded as a possible interpretation by Brandt.

[2] This broadcast makes another contrast with *Mein Kampf*. There (p. 304) Hitler speaks with great contempt of the foolish propaganda which sought to gain support for the Kaiser by giving pathetic accounts of his long working hours and frugal meals. 'Nobody grudged him a square meal or the necessary amount of sleep . . . the legends helped him little and harmed him much.'

which cause a lack of balancing power; and a subcutaneous haemorrhage in the right arm.[1] He was sent to bed, and in about four weeks had completely recovered from the immediate effects of the explosion.

The cumulative effects of his overstrained life and Morell's treatment were not so easily cured. When Hitler resumed his working life at Rastenburg, it was a life of eccentric hours in an underground bunker in the damp, unhealthy climate of East Prussia. He never left the bunker, for his phobias were multiplying on him: he shunned the air, feared exercise, and suspected danger everywhere. Professor von Eicken, who had remained in regular attendance, urged him again and again to leave that insanitary dugout with its dank air and disturbing associations. It was still summer: a week or two in the Obersalzberg would cure him; but Hitler refused to go. Then Keitel added his representations; but although ultimately, in November, Hitler yielded to his pressure and returned to Berlin, it was after a long resistance. "I am staying in Rastenburg," Hitler would reply. "If I leave East Prussia, then East Prussia will fall. As long as I am here, it will be held." So he stayed on, a sick man, spending a few days in bed at intervals, but always getting up for the daily Staff conference, though his health was plainly low, and his voice, usually so loud, energetic, and passionate, had become weak and faint. In September, and again in October, von Eicken treated him for infection of the maxillary sinus; he also found that he was suffering from swollen glands in the neck. In October he removed another polyp from the vocal cords. During this time Hitler was also in pain from continual headaches and stomach cramps which Morell was treating with drugs. These stomach cramps were not new; he had suffered from them intermittently for some years. But now they had become serious, and Hitler was forced to return to bed for a fortnight.[2]

It is clear that in the autumn of 1944 the long-concealed effects of Hitler's declining health were becoming manifest; and the diary, which begins on October 14th, registers the

[1] It was observed that the photographs of Hitler greeting Mussolini after the Plot showed him shaking hands with his left hand.
[2] The facts in this paragraph come from Keitel and von Eicken.

coming and going of a continual series of doctors. Besides von Eicken and the daily Morell, there is Dr Weber, the heart specialist, and Professor Blaschke, the dentist, and several other medical men, whose visits continue until the end of November; then all is peace again, and an undisputed empire for Morell. Externally at least, and for a time, Hitler had weathered the crisis. When von Eicken revisited him, after a month's absence, on December 30th, in his headquarters at Bad Nauheim, Hitler seemed in good health once more; his voice was completely restored, and he seemed relatively strong and well. Nevertheless this period of illness had not passed without leaving its trace in the history of the court; for in it, as a direct consequence of Morell's treatment, occurred the great medical row.

The crisis occurred in September. Hitler's stomach cramps were then at their worst; and Dr Giesing, the ear, nose, and throat specialist who had been summoned after the Plot, had made an intetesting discovery.[1] He discovered that, in order to relieve these pains, Morell had, for at least two years, been giving Hitler a proprietary drug known as Dr Koester's Antigas Pills,[2] compounded of strychnine and belladonna. The dose which Hitler had been receiving was allegedly two to four pills with every meal, although the maximum dose which could safely be prescribed was said to be eight pills a day. Nor was this the worst. Morell did not himself administer the pills, but gave them, in gross, to Heinz Linge, Hitler's personal servant; Linge then gave them to his master as demanded, without medical supervision; and it was in Linge's drawer that Giesing had casually found these incriminating poisons. Shocked by his discovery, Giesing consulted Dr Brandt, the surgeon. Together they agreed that under Morell's treatment, Hitler was being slowly poisoned; and that this chronic poisoning was of itself quite enough to account not only for the stomach pains which it was designed to relieve, but also for the progressive

[1] Giesing was technically an ear, nose, and throat specialist, but he had experience in other fields also. His interrogators considered him to be a very competent doctor who had examined Hitler more thoroughly than his personal doctors.

[2] The prescription is given as Extr. Nux Vom.; extr. Bellad. a.a.o.5; extr. Gent. 1.a.

discoloration of Hitler's skin which had become noticeable. Brandt consulted further with his deputy, von Hasselbach, who agreed; and Brandt and Giesing then told Hitler that he was allowing his health to be ruined by systematic poisoning at the hands of Morell. But the time had passed when Hitler would listen to reasons and arguments. For a while there was an uncertain silence, while the deity remained wrapped in blue smoke; then the thunderbolt was launched. Brandt was suddenly dismissed from all his political offices and from the appointment which he had held for twelve years; von Hasselbach followed into the wilderness; and Giesing was summoned no more to the Fuehrer's headquarters. The fate of a fallen minister under an oriental tyrant is proverbially death; and if Brandt escaped this final punishment for his temerity, it was not through any remorse on the part of his enemies. On April 16th, 1945, when the final phase of the battle for Berlin was about to begin, and the doomed tyrant was crying for more blood before it was too late, Brandt found himself arrested on personal orders from Hitler and brought before a summary court. He was accused of having sent his wife to a place where she would fall into the hands of the advancing Americans. The court had received a personal letter from Hitler which charged Brandt with having lost faith in victory. He was condemned to death. "Your way of thinking is not our way of thinking," declared Artur Axmann, the spokesman of the court; "you will have to take the consequences"; and on Bormann's orders Brandt was removed to a condemned cell in Kiel. But events were now moving too fast for the Nazi leaders, and the procrastination of his friends saved Brandt until his capricious patron was dead. He was reserved to a more reasoned judgment, for more real crimes.[1]

The removal of Brandt and Hasselbach caused a vacancy

---

[1] Brandt's fall may not have been caused solely by the professional incident which precipitated it. Speer says that "for some incomprehensible reason" Bormann was a bitter and determined enemy of Brandt. Schellenberg thought that the whole affair was part of "a huge game of intrigue" in which Eva Braun and her sister were involved. [*Author's note*, 1956: For further light on these intrigues see A. Zoller, *Hitler Privat* (Düsseldorf, 1949), pp. 62–5; *The Bormann Letters* (1954) *passim*.]

for a surgeon at Hitler's court. To fill this vacancy Hitler applied to the faithful Himmler. In the days of universal treachery there were few others whom he could trust. Could the Reichsfuehrer SS recommend an absolutely reliable man? On this important matter Himmler decided to take the best professional advice. He therefore summoned his own doctor, Professor Karl Gebhardt.

Professor Gebhardt had been an intimate friend of Himmler since their early days, and there is a surprising unanimity of opinion about him. He was universally regarded as Himmler's evil genius. Schellenberg calls him 'detestable'. Ohlendorf, another of Himmler's subordinates and himself no squeamish character (at Nuremberg he confessed to the mass-murder of ninety thousand Jews), describes him as a corrupt and selfish intriguer, animated solely by personal expediency. Others knew him as an unscrupulous dabbler in politics, concealing his intrigues behind the innocent cloak of medicine. As a doctor he carried out experimental operations on Polish girls in the concentration camp at Auschwitz, and was rewarded by Himmler with the post of President of the German Red Cross. Speer's experience of him was curious. When suffering from a long illness in 1944, Speer accepted from Himmler the medical services of Gebhardt; but his health did not respond to the treatment, and his friends, being suspicious, called in another doctor, Professor Koch of the Berlin Charité Hospital, to observe Gebhardt's method. Professor Koch declared that Gebhardt's method was designed to aggravate rather than cure the ailment. Doctors disagree, and the incident may have been insignificant; but Gebhardt's reputation was enough to ensure the most sinister interpretation, and from that time Speer reduced his relations with Himmler to the minimum. Such was the appropriate adviser whom Himmler now consulted; such the sponsor who recommended his own most promising pupil, Ludwig Stumpfegger, a competent orthopaedic surgeon who had worked at his clinic at Hohen-lychen and specialized in the regeneration of bones.

Whatever motives may have inspired Himmler and Gebhardt to send Stumpfegger to East Prussia as Hitler's new surgeon—and those who knew Gebhardt could not believe that he lacked a selfish purpose—they certainly gained nothing thereby. Possibly they sought nothing; for Himmler at least was too naïve to conceive of any elaborate plans. At all events, Stumpfegger had no intention of continuing to serve those whose usefulness was over; and once arrived at the Fuehrer's headquarters, he became conspicuous for his unconditional and apparently genuine loyalty to Hitler. A faithful giant (for he was of huge stature), he bowed in unfeigned adoration before the god into whose presence he had at last been admitted, and frequently spoke with contempt of the sponsor who had shown him the way thither. It was on October 31st that Stumpfegger first appeared at Hitler's headquarters. After that, his visits gradually became frequent. In the diary there is recorded, almost daily, the word *Spaziergang*—Hitler's single form of ventilation, his stroll round the garden of his headquarters. Rarely is anyone recorded as accompanying him on these occasions; the only companions ever mentioned are Himmler, Goering, Albert Bormann (an adjutant of Hitler, brother of Martin Bormann), and Stumpfegger. In the last days Stumpfegger moved to Berlin with Hitler. When others, including Morell, left or were dismissed, he remained. Asked whether he really supposed that Germany could still win the war, he answered, with the naïve conviction of the true believer, that though military ignorant, he did not suppose—he knew. The intense conviction in the Fuehrer's eyes was his guarantee. Those walks in the garden were not the walks of a patient with his doctor—to the end Hitler never needed a surgeon; they were the communion of the Messiah with his disciple, of the divinity with his chosen priest.

It goes without saying that Stumpfegger never fell into the sin of Brandt. He never quarrelled with Morell. He kept to his surgical duties, which entailed no disputes with the now all-powerful physician. Morell's control over Hitler's person for the last six months of his life was unchallenged. He even succeeded in capping the dismissal of Brandt with the dismissal of Hitler's photographer Hoffmann, whose convenient malady had been the beginning of his success, but whose presence now only served to remind him of the humiliations of patronage. With all the former doctors removed, his former patron dismissed, and the new doctor obedient to his will, Morell could look forward comfortably, if only the war would allow it, to the last and most spectacular of his medical monopolies.

Thus, in his last days, though he suffered from no organic disease, Hitler had become, according to universal testimony, a physical wreck. Ceaseless work, the loss of all freedom, the frustration of all his hopes. Morell's drugs, and perhaps more than all these, the violence of his temperament when bitterness and disappointment had multiplied around him, had reduced that once powerful conqueror to a trembling spectre. All witnesses of the final days agree when they describe his emaciated face, his grey complexion, his stooping body, his shaking hands and foot, his hoarse and quavering voice, and the film of exhaustion that covered his eyes. They agree about certain less clearly physical symptoms too: his universal suspicion, his incessant rages, his alternation of optimism and despair. But two characteristics of his former temper he still possessed. The fascination of those eyes, which had bewitched so many seemingly sober men—which had exhausted Speer, and baffled Rauschning, and seduced Stumpfegger, and convinced an industrialist that he had direct telepathic communication with the Almighty[1]—had not deserted them. It was useless for his enemies to complain that they were really repellent. 'They are neither deep nor blue,' protested Rauschning; 'his look is staring or dead, and lacks the brilliance and sparkle of genuine animation';[2] nevertheless, in spite of his explanations and evasions, Rauschning had to admit, what Speer freely confesses and thousands of less critical Germans (and not only Germans) too eloquently witness, that Hitler had the eyes of a hypnotist which seduced the wits and affections of all who yielded to their power. Even his doctors, and the most critical of them, admit the fascination of those dull, blue-grey eyes which compensated for all coarseness in his other features; 'pictures',

---

[1] The industrialist was Wilhelm Keppler, mentioned above, p. 72 n.[1]. Keppler was sent by Hitler as one of his representatives to the World Economic Conference in London in 1933. Asked about Hitler by an English acquaintance, he replied, "Der Fuehrer hat eine Antenne direkt zum lieben Gott."   [2] *Hitler Speaks*, p. 23.

they say, 'cannot reproduce the suggestive power of his face'. This personal magnetism remained with him to the end; and only by reference to it can we explain the extraordinary obedience which he still commanded in the last week of his life, when all the machinery of force and persuasion had disappeared, the failure and cost of his disastrous rule was apparent, and only his personality remained.

Secondly, Hitler's lust for blood was unabated, perhaps even increased, by time and defeat. Though he was physically afraid of the sight of blood, the thought of it excited and intoxicated him, just as destruction in all its forms seems to have appealed to the inherent nihilism of his spirit. In his early conversations (we learn from Rauschning), when he spoke of the revolution by which the Nazis would attain power, 'he lingered with special interest over the chances of a bloody destruction of Marxist resistance in the streets'; for he conceived that historical greatness was not to be achieved without the spilling of blood.[1] Nor did it matter to him whose blood was shed; for it was the spectacle, the imaginary contemplation of rivers of human blood that inspired him, not the thought of victory and its practical use. 'Nature is cruel, therefore we too may be cruel,' he said in 1934, when discussing the Jews and the Slavs; 'if I can send the flower of the German nation into the hell of war, without the smallest pity for the spilling of precious German blood, then surely I have a right to remove millions of an inferior race that breeds like vermin!'[2] *Without the smallest pity* . . . As a logical syllogism, the proposition is perhaps defective; but as a psychological illustration it needs no improvement.

Throughout the war Hitler continually gave evidence of this lust for blood, this physical delight in the intellectual contemplation of slaughter for its own sake. The generals, hardened automata, notorious as impersonal men of blood and iron, were shocked at such positive emotions, and have given numerous instances of it. During the Polish campaign, Halder maintained that the storming of Warsaw was unnecessary; it would fall of itself, since the Polish Army no longer existed;

[1] *Hitler Speaks*, p. 26.
[2] *Ibid.*, p. 140.

117

but Hitler insisted that Warsaw must be destroyed. His artist's temper aroused, he described the delicious scenes which he demanded—the sky darkened, a million tons of shells raining down on the city, and the people drowned in blood; 'then his eyes popped out of his head, and he became quite a different person. He was suddenly seized by a lust for blood.' Another general[1] has described how Hitler received the news that his personal SS division, the *Leibstandarte Adolf Hitler*, had been decimated in Russia. Apologetically, General Reichenau sought to explain that German losses had unfortunately been high. Hitler cut him short. "Losses can never be too high!" he exclaimed triumphantly; "they sow the seeds of future greatness." We have seen how, after the Plot of July 20th, the mere mention of the great Blood Purge of 1934 set him off into one of his famous tantrums. Satisfaction never abated this terrible appetite for blood, which like his appetite for material destruction, seemed rather to grow when the price was to be paid not in inferior currency but in good Aryan coin. In his last days, in the days of Radio Werewolf and suicidal strategy, Hitler seems like some cannibal god, rejoicing in the ruin of his own temples. Almost his last orders were for execution: prisoners were to be slaughtered, his old surgeon was to be murdered, his own brother-in-law was executed, all traitors, without further specification, were to die. Like an ancient hero, Hitler wished to be sent with human sacrifices to his grave; and the burning of his own body, which had never ceased to be the centre and totem of the Nazi state, was the logical and symbolical conclusion of the Revolution of Destruction.

[1] General Heim.

CHAPTER THREE

THE COURT IN DEFEAT

THE PROSPECT of universal destruction may be exhilarating to some aesthetic souls, especially to those who do not intend to survive it and are therefore free to admire, as a spectacle, the apocalyptic setting of their own funeral. But those who must live on in the charred remainder of the world have less time for such purely spiritual experience. It is therefore not surprising that there were many in Germany who looked with dismay upon this orgy of deliberate destruction, and resolved, as far as they had any power to do so, to frustrate it. One such was Karl Kaufmann, Gauleiter of Hamburg. Having seen his city, the greatest port, and one of the most ancient and prosperous towns in Germany, shattered from the air, he was resolved not to see it still further ruined either by British shells or by Nazi dynamite. Another was Kaufmann's closest friend, perhaps the ablest and most interesting of all the Nazi Government, Albert Speer.

Speer has already been often mentioned, often quoted, in this narrative. He has not been quoted uncritically, or because it is easier to quote than to compete with him. Many other Nazi politicians have employed the aching leisure of their confinement to compile their personal autobiographies and apologias, and to enunciate those large cosmic propositions so dear to the German mind. Speer has been quoted because his observations do but give literary, and sometimes lapidary form to the conclusions already reached from the study of many less personal, and therefore, at first sight, less fallible records. It is not necessary, for instance, indeed it is inadvisable, to quote the careful autobiography of Schellenberg; for the judgments and opinions of Himmler's expert on foreign affairs illustrate nothing except the jejunity of his intellect, the provincialism of his horizon. And the autobiography of Count Lutz Schwerin von Krosigk, though he had been a minister for thirteen years, will deserve quotation not for the sagacity, but for the imbecility of his observations. But Speer deserves quotation in his own right. His conclusions are never naïve, never parochial; they seem always honest; they are often profound. If he seems sometimes to have fallen too deeply under the spell of the tyrant whom he served, at least he is the only servant whose judgment was not corrupted by attendance on that dreadful master; at least he retained the capacity to examine himself, and the honesty to declare both his errors and his convictions. In the last days of Nazism he was not afraid to tell Hitler of his own acts of defiance; and in Allied captivity he was not afraid to admit, after his searching analysis of Hitler's character and history, the residue of loyalty which he could not altogether shed.

The whole political career of Speer is extraordinary, if 'extraordinary' is not too obvious a word to use for any of the events of Nazi Germany. It is strange enough that such a man should have risen in the corrupted *entourage* of Hitler; and that having risen he should have survived, a single, solitary, disapproving figure in that ambuscade of vigilant and vindictive conspirators. That having never held any political or administrative position, he should suddenly, at the age of thirty-six, and in a time of crisis, be entrusted with the entire control of all armament production and co-ordination of production, of the building and maintenance of communications, and the direction and reformation of industry, is perhaps less surprising in the arbitrary world which we are contemplating; but that he should succeed, and succeed regularly, in this gigantic task, is indeed almost incredible; and that after such a triumph in such a world he should retain not merely an objective but an intellectual outlook on his experience, is a mystery past facile interpretation. For Speer began his career as an architect. In 1934, at the age of twenty-nine, he was building manager in the Reich Chancellery, a subordinate official working under Hitler's architect, Professor Troost. Himself an artist, Hitler took an interest in his architects, and after a few conversations he included Speer in his intimate circle, invited him to lunch, and took a close interest in him. From that moment Speer's future was assured. Hitler had 'intuitively' chosen him, as he had chosen Ribbentrop, the champagne salesman, to be an ambassador and foreign minister, and Rosenberg, the Baltic mystagogue, to govern the conquered East. But Speer was a more felicitous choice than these. It is true he succumbed, like all the others, to the mesmeric influence of his employer; like them he could not withstand the mysterious intensity of those dull, glaucous eyes, the messianic egotism of that harsh, oracular voice. "They were all under his spell," he explains, "blindly obedient to him, and with no will of their own—whatever the medical term for this phenomenon may be. I noticed, during my activities as architect, that to be in his presence for any length of time, made me tired exhausted, and *void*. Capacity for independent work was paralysed." It is true, too, that his architectural achievements were perhaps of questionable elegance—the vast new Reich Chancellery, for instance, which he was ordered to complete in haste, in time for the reception of President Hacha of Czechoslovakia and Prince Paul of Yugoslavia, that these tributary kings might tremble before the geometric magnificence of the new Pharaoh. But at least, unlike the Third Reich, they were structurally sound. Even now, like the ruins of Memphis, the relics of that vainglorious edifice are the most substantial memorial in the great cemetery of central Berlin.

For in truth (and herein probably lies the secret of his survival) Speer was not an artist, not a politician. He had no common interests or ambitions with the rest of the court. He observed their antics, but did not compete in their field; and since he was obviously a personal friend and immediate dependant of Hitler—perhaps the only personal friend he had —they found it safest to leave him alone in his unsympathetic isolation. Speer was a technocrat and nourished a technocrat's philosophy. To the technocrat, as to the Marxist, politics are irrelevant. To him the prosperity, the future of a people depends not upon the personalities who happen to hold political office, nor upon the institutions in which their relations are formalized—these are irrelevant phenomena of no ultimate significance—but upon the technical instruments whereby society is maintained, on the roads and the railways, the canals and bridges, the services and factories wherein a nation invests its labour, and whence it draws its wealth. This is a very convenient philosophy; and it is true that in certain times (so long, that is, as they can be taken for granted) politics can be ignored. For nearly two years after he had succeeded Todt as Armaments Minister, Speer found that he could take politics for granted, merely observing the antics of the politicians from his favoured seat in the royal box, while he concentrated his activities and interests upon the communications and factories which he so completely understood. Then he was disillusioned. When Hitler and Goebbels raised the slogan of 'Scorched Earth', and called upon the German people to destroy their towns and factories, to blow up their dams and bridges, to sacrifice their railways and rollingstock for the sake of a myth and a Wagnerian Twilight, then at last the fallacy of his philosophy became apparent to Speer. Politics do matter; politicians can affect the destiny of nations. The crisis of his life occurred.

The choice was not easy. For eleven years, supported by that convenient philosophy, Speer had enjoyed the sunshine of Hitler's favour. He had grown rich and powerful under the shadow of a tyrant whose tyranny (he had convinced himself), since it did not interfere with his own impersonal ambitions, was irrrelevant to him. He had been fascinated by the personality and flattered by the attentions of his master; but he remained (if we can forgive his initial error of yielding to the totalitarian embrace) intellectually uncorrupted. His impersonal ideals remained valid; and when Hitler declared himself their enemy, Speer prepared to sacrifice not his ideals, but Hitler, together with all the associations of patronage and friendship and personal influence engendered by this long relationship. Naturally he chose to deceive himself. Having collaborated over so long a period, he could not admit (like the exiled Rauschning) that this nihilism was always implicit, and often explicit, in Nazi philosophy. He preferred to suppose a sudden change, the arbitrary reorientation of a despot corrupted by the exorbitancy of unchallenged power. Hitler's path, he said, had become suddenly random and erratic, and was leading to terrible consequence. "He was deliberately attempting to let the people perish with himself. He no longer knew any moral boundaries; a man to whom the end of his own life meant the end of everything." A more critical observer would have realized that Hitler never knew any moral boundaries; after all, he had often said so.

Between his public duty and his private relationship, Speer did not hesitate. "From then on," he says, "—and not only within my official jurisdiction—I had to plan, initiate, and execute many acts which were directed against Hitler's policy, or against himself." While Hitler, with increasing radicalism, demanded the destruction of Europe, Speer, with increasing zeal, sought to nullify his orders. He was himself charged with the destruction of industrial installations; he ordered their preservation. To every order of industrial suicide which emanated from the Fuehrer's headquarters, or the Party Chancery, or Radio Berlin, Speer issued, through his own channels, a countermanding order. By his great authority and his continual journeys throughout Germany, he everywhere stayed the hand of the destroyer, and persuaded his agents, his subordinates, and his sympathizers that if communications and factories must be surrendered to the enemy, they should be surrendered intact. The mines and factories of Belgium and northern France, the canals of Holland, the nickel mines of Finland, the ore of the Balkans, the oilfields of Hungary, were all protected by his authority; and when the New Year came, and the Allied armies penetrated into Germany itself, Hitler and his single personal friend continued the same silent but bitter struggle over the body of Germany.

It was in February 1945 that Speer's intellectual dilemma became most acute. The situation was now clearly hopeless; but despair only intensified the nihilism of the Party. General Guderian, Chief of Army General Staff since the July Plot, himself told Ribbentrop that the war was lost. Ribbentrop reported the words to Hitler, and Hitler summoned both Guderian and Speer and told them that such words were treason; in future neither rank nor position would save such traitors from death, or their relatives from arrest. At the same time Goebbels, maddened by the great air raid on Dresden, demanded the repudiation of the Geneva Convention, the massacre of forty thousand Allied airmen, and the use of two new and terrible poison gases, *Tabun* and *Sarin*. On his side, Speer walked more openly in the way of treason. He decided at last to intervene even in politics, which he had so long thought it possible to ignore.

Speer's plan was nothing less than the removal by assassination of the entire political directorate of the Reich. Seven months ago such a project would have been inconceivable to him; he had neither known nor approved of the Generals' Plot; but since then his whole world had changed, and the chosen disciple had caught up with the most inveterate enemies of the Fuehrer. Hitler was now in Berlin, in the Reich Chancellery. There it was his custom to discuss policy with his immediate associates—Goebbels, Bormann, Burgdorf and Ley[1]—in his underground Bunker, which no one, not even they, could now approach without being searched for hidden explosives. But Speer's plan did not entail the introduction of visible weapons. The Bunker was ventilated by means of an air-conditioning plant, of which the external funnel projected into the Chancellery garden. As an architect Speer was familiar with its construction, and he completed his knowledge by consultation with the chief engineer of the Chancellery. He discovered that if poison gas were introduced into the funnel at the time of one of Hitler's conferences, it would very quickly be distributed throughout the Bunker; and thus, in a few minutes, the whole disastrous coterie would be destroyed. Into this plan Speer initiated a few trusted collaborators, and the preparations for its execution went ahead; but it was never executed. When his preparations were complete, Speer visited the Chancellery garden, only to find that by a recent and personal order of the Fuehrer a protective chimney, some twelve feet high, had been

---

[1] *Reichsleiter* Robert Ley, chief of the German Labour Front, is chiefly remembered as the sponsor of the 'Strength Through Joy' movement. He seems to have aspired to a millennium of unlimited fun for the proletariat; but his own habitual inebriety rendered the public expression of his views often indistinct. He represented no political interest, being merely a personal sycophant of Hitler, who on March 28th, put him in charge of an abortive partisan group, the *Freikorps Adolf Hitler*. Ley did not stay in Berlin. He was captured in South Germany by American forces and contrived to commit suicide while awaiting trial at Nuremberg.

built round the funnel, and the plan was no longer feasible. Thus, for the second time in seven months, Hitler escaped assassination.[1]

Nevertheless it was not merely a technical hitch which saved Hitler from the hand of Speer; for in one of the few reluctant statements which he has made on this evidently distasteful subject, he has described another incident which also contributed to his failure. About this time Speer visited the German Front on the Rhine, and there, one night, sat with a party of German miners in a dugout. In the darkness, only occasionally relieved by a trench light, he was unrecognized; he listened silently to the conversation of the miners around him, and from it he drew a new political conclusion. These miners, he was convinced, represented the ordinary German soldier or worker; and they, it seemed clear to him, still believed in Hitler as they believed in no one else. They believed that he, and only he, both understood the working class from which he had risen, and the mystery of politics which had been concealed from the rest of the German race, and that he would therefore be able, as no one else, to work the miracle of their salvation from this forlorn predicament. Chastened by what he had heard and seen, Speer reconsidered his design. If he were to remove Hitler, he would remove the grand saboteur of German industry and communications; but he would also deprive the German people of the one political leader in whom, apparently, they still believed; in whom they reposed, by habitual abnegation, their common will; and whose orders they would still, in this penultimate moment, obey. Once again Speer realized the importance of politics, the alternative to his simple technocratic philosophy. His plan for destroying Hitler and his court was cancelled and never revived; and Speer joined that great and discouraging company of Germans, the conspirators who have failed.

Which of these two factors, the technical fault or the political lesson, really determined Speer's failure as an assassin, is a question of little importance, to which he himself has given

[1] The details of Speer's plot have been independently confirmed by Dietrich Stahl, head of the Main Committee for Munitions (*Hauptausschuss Munition*) in Speer's ministry.

no clear answer;[1] but one fact emerges clearly from this curious history. No intellectual conversion can be entirely without an emotional backwash; and the apparent decisiveness of Speer's breach with Hitler, which at first sight contrasts so strongly with the infinite hesitations of Himmler, must not obscure the difficulty with which he made it, the psychological crisis which it entailed. How serious these were is clear from his subsequent history—the history of a mind still divided between political antagonism and personal allegiance.

On March 18th, in spite of Hitler's explicit veto, Speer wrote to him declaring that militarily and economically the war was lost; if the nation was not to be lost also, it was essential that some material basis be preserved upon which the life of the people, however primitively, might be continued. It was a manifesto against the declared policy of destruction; and Hitler's answer was emphatic. Sending for Speer, he told him: "If the war is to be lost, the nation will also perish. This fate is inevitable. There is no need to consider the basis even of a most primitive existence any longer. On the contrary it is better to destroy even that, and to destroy it ourselves. The nation has proved itself weak, and the future belongs solely to the stronger Eastern nation. Besides, those who remain after the battle are of little value; for the good have fallen." That day new orders of destruction were issued by Hitler and Bormann: the fight was to be continued 'without consideration of the German people'; eight officers who had failed to destroy a bridge were shot by Hitler's order, and the fact was published in the bulletin of the Armed Forces; and Speer's authority over industry was suspended.

Nevertheless Speer continued his activity, which no longer rested upon formal appointments. He ordered the concealment of high explosive and reduced its manufacture, so that existing stocks might be wasted; and he issued machine-pistols to his works managers, to use against Gauleiters who might insist

[1] In his earlier statement, Speer ascribed his failure to his experience on the Western Front; at Nuremberg he referred only to the technical hitch. In general he has given less emphasis to his personal dependence on Hitler in his statements at Nuremberg than in his earlier version; but this does not make them inconsistent, or suggest that one version is untrue.

upon destruction. He sent out orders in the name of the Combined General Staff; and where his own channels failed, he used those of the High Command or the Reich railways. The suspension of his authority had made no difference, and on March 29th he found himself summoned by Hitler once again.

Hitler accused him of publicly stating that the war was lost and ordered him publicly to assert the opposite. Speer replied, "The war is lost." Hitler gave him twenty-four hours in which to consider the matter; and at the end of this time Speer returned with a letter defending his views.[1] Hitler refused to receive the letter and ordered Speer to go away on permanent leave. Speer refused; it was his duty, he said, to remain at his post. Thereupon a strange scene of reconciliation took place between the Angel of Destruction and his recalcitrant but unpunished disciple. "I declared to him," said Speer "that even so he could rely upon me in the future"; and by that simple, lying formula Speer found himself restored to authority, which he used, as before, to circumvent the purpose of its bestowal. The duality of Speer's behaviour that is apparent in these episodes, will be clear again in the course of this narrative. It will appear in his last visit to the Bunker and his frank confession to Hitler on April 23rd. It is clear also from the words with which he concludes his own account of Hitler's personality. "Although inwardly I had broken with him by that time," he says, "it has been difficult for me even now to write this study. I feel it to be my duty to help in exploring his faults, which were the origin of his disastrous influence, as tragic for Germany as for the rest of the world. Even if sometimes I have had to speak in blunt terms, I should not like to be numbered among those who malign him in order to exonerate themselves."

Meanwhile it was not only Speer who had passed through an intellectual crisis in his attitude towards the Fuehrer, although 'intellectual' is perhaps not quite the word to use in

---

[1] This letter, in which Speer describes to Hitler their conversation of March 18th, is extant and was used as evidence at Nuremberg. It is a remarkable document, showing the extraordinary freedom which Speer (and no one else) could use in his relations with Hitler. The account of that meeting printed above is taken from this letter.

describing so incredibly simple a character as Himmler. For Himmler also had begun to notice the inconsequence, the eccentricity, the peevishness of Hitler's behaviour. He had not discovered it himself, of course; but once it had been pointed out to him (and eager conspirators were always willing to point it out), he had to admit that he no longer received those clear, explicit, and intelligible directives which had once enabled him to conceal, under the brisk efficiency of his executive action, the chronic indecision of his mind. The God had gone out of his world; what then was the high-priest to do? His litanies, his sacraments, his endless human sacrifices all seemed vain and meaningless now. He required another God. It is true he had found another God, in Heaven, thanks to the miracles of the past year; but that God was somewhat remote, and his advice somewhat too general to be of much practical assistance in the extraordinarily complicated political and military situation of contemporary Germany. He needed a more earthly god; and the personal tragedy of Himmler in these last months is that he could not find one; he could only find a missionary who was persuasive enough to dissolve his belief in the old revelation, but could never quite convince him of the validity of the new. This missionary was Walter Schellenberg.

In his first task of constructing a vast, efficient, totalitarian intelligence service, Schellenberg had already failed, and failed completely. It is not altogether fair to blame him for his failure; for the task was now quite impossible. In such a jungle of conflicting egoisms as 'totalitarian' Germany all planning, especially Schellenberg's planning, was an academic exercise. But in his second, more limited plan, the plan to build up Himmler into the rival, the successor, and if necessary the destroyer of Hitler, who would negotiate peace with the West and become the saviour of Germany, he was having, or at least he persuaded himself that he was having more success. For nearly a year now he had not sought to conceal from Himmler the extent and exorbitancy of his plans; and convinced of his own subtlety, his brilliant perception of trends and nuances, on which the Chinese game of diplomacy, and the feminine game of seduction depend, he probably believed that Himmler both understood, and accepted, more of his ideas than could ever penetrate that slow, unagile mind. It is true Schellenberg had not dared to inform Himmler of the hopes which some of the wilder July conspirators had entertained of him; but he had dropped judicious references to Fraeulein Hanfstaengl of Munich, who had conceived a plan of evacuating Hitler by force to Obersalzberg, there to reign as nominal but impotent head of the state, while all the acts of government were carried out on the orders of Himmler. This suggestion had been ignored by Himmler, but Schellenberg was ready with another. In Hamburg he had discovered a promising astrologer called Wulf, a student of poisons, Sanskrit, and other interesting subjects. Wulf's prophecies, as seen by Schellenberg in retrospect, seemed remarkably accurate. He had prophesied that Hitler would survive a great danger on July 20th, 1944; that he would be ill in November 1944; and that he would die a mysterious death before May 7th, 1945. His prophecies concerning Himmler were equally remarkable, though discreetly enveloped in diplomatic silence. Schellenberg found that in politics Wulf was sound; he introduced him to Himmler as a counterweight to the unsound Kaltenbrunner; and this introduction was so successful that before the end of the Third Reich, according to Schellenberg, "Himmler seldom took any steps without first consulting his horoscope." No less valuable to Schellenberg was Himmler's Finnish masseur, Kersten. Himmler, in Schellenberg's opinion, suffered from cancer of the bowel; at any rate he suffered, and only Kersten could relieve the pain. Gradually Himmler became as dependent on Kersten's massage as Hitler upon Morell's drugs. Thus indispensable, Kersten soon found that he could say things to Himmler which even Schellenberg dared not; and Schellenberg, who also relied on Kersten's massage, found that his politics were sound too. From that time Kersten became another agent in Schellenberg's conspiracy; and Schellenberg congratulated himself on still further proof of his own subtlety.

Thus, little by little, by judicious hints and careful indiscretions, referring sometimes to minute particulars, sometimes to large generalities, and always stopping by the way to admire his own virtuosity, Schellenberg succeeded, or thought that he had succeeded, in fretting away that essential chain of unconditional loyalty upon which the whole of Himmler's personality hung, by which its whole balance was adjusted, its inherent instability concealed; and at the same time, in the niche of Himmler's private worship, from which the idol of Hitler was thus gradually crumbling away, Schellenberg substituted, slowly and tentatively and against stubborn and despairing resistance from the worshipper, a new and even more inappropriate image: the image of Himmler himself, crowned as the second Fuehrer, the second incarnation of the spirit of Aryan Germany. With what tenacity Schellenberg pressed, with what obstinacy Himmler resisted, is clear from the long, complacent, insensitive account which Schellenberg himself has given of his endless manœuvres. In February 1945, when Himmler, discredited as a general, broken in spirit, suffered a 'physical and spiritual collapse' and retired to Professor Gebhardt's clinic at Hohenlychen, it was little rest he found there. How could Schellenberg leave him alone with the detested Gebhardt? At once he arrived at Hohenlychen with a fresh batch of prophecies from the astrologer Wulf, and the familiar theme was reopened. When Count Folke Bernadotte, representing the Swedish Red Crosss, came to Berlin, with what self-admired diplomacy did Schellenberg arrange interviews with the reluctant Himmler so that not even Ribbentrop or Kaltenbrunner could complain! They were abortive interviews, it is true, for Bernadotte would not approach the Allies on his own initiative and Himmler could not bring himself to act independently of Hitler. 'You may think it sentimental, even absurd,' he protested, 'but I have sworn loyalty to Adolf Hitler, and as a soldier and a German I cannot deny my oath';[1] but Schellenberg did not despair of altering that. There is an almost brutal relish in the words with

[1] Folke Bernadotte, *The Fall of the Curtain*, p. 20. Count Bernadotte had altogether four interviews with Himmler, on February 19th, April 2nd, April 21st, and April 23rd–24th. The two last will be described later. It was at the interview of April 2nd that Himmler gave his interesting but overdrawn account of the Nazi leaders: Hitler almost entirely occupied in studying architectural plans for rebuilding German cities; Goering taking cocaine, dressing up in a toga, and painting his fingernails red.

which he praises the pertinacity of his assaults upon Himmler's agonized doubts. "I owe all I am to Hitler," Himmler would plead, "how can I betray him?"; "I have built up the SS on the basis of loyalty; I cannot now abandon that basic principle." But the subtle temper was ready with a hundred methods by which basic principles could be justifiably abandoned. Himmler protested that his health was failing, "and indeed," says Schellenberg "he was the image of a torn soul, the picture of unrest and discontent." But Schellenberg was unaffected by the spectacle of mental torture in the man he seems (incredible though we find it) to have genuinely liked and admired. "I struggled with him," he says unfeelingly, "like a devil struggling for a soul."

It was already the spring of 1945 when the decisive moment came, and Schellenberg resolved to put aside prevarication, to abandon infertile hints, and to admit to Himmler the full implications of his project. He had hesitated for long, for Himmler was still surrounded by other, more sinister advisers: by Kaltenbrunner, the Austrian thug who controlled Himmler's central office, and therefore (in theory) Schellenberg himself, and whose head was now swollen by the personal favour of Hitler; by Skorzeny, the Viennese terrorist, who had rescued Mussolini and kidnapped the son of the Regent of Hungary, and who was now in charge, under Himmler, of all the terrorist bands in the Reich; and by Fegelein, the ignorant horse-fancier who was now Himmler's representative at the Fuehrer's headquarters and had become an intimate member of Hitler's family circle, as close and regular in his attendance as Bormann and Burgdorf. These were the 'Southern' party, the diehards who advocated resistance, who hated compromise and frothed in loud ignorance about a glorious *Goetterdaemmerung* in the Alps, while the 'Northerners' like Speer and Schellenberg preferred to think in terms of political compromise. Nevertheless Schellenberg now felt strong enough to take the risk. "So you are demanding that I depose the Fuehrer?" asked Himmler. "Yes," replied Schellenberg. The issue was now clear, and the conversations continued on a new level.

"In the course of these conversations," says Schellenberg,

"Himmler often spoke of Hitler's declining health. To my rejoinder, How then was he still able to exert such influence?, Himmler replied that his energy was undiminished, although the completely unnatural life he led, turning night into day and sleeping only a few hours, his continuous activity, and his constant outbursts of fury completely exhausted his *entourage* and created an unbearable atmosphere. I often suggested that perhaps the Plot of July 20th had after all injured Hitler's health, in particular his head. Himmler thought this possible. He mentioned especially the constant stoop, the pale visage, the increased trembling of Hitler's left arm, and the operation on his ear, which took place in November, obviously a result of the concussion he had received."

These statements of Himmler, not strictly accurate, as can be seen, opened a new line of argument to the resourceful Schellenberg. At the beginning of April, he applied to his friend Professor de Crinis, director of the Psychological Department of the Charité, for information about Hitler's health. De Crinis was not one of the doctors who had actually attended Hitler, but in medical circles he had doubtless heard of the conjectures of those who had. "In my opinion," he replied, "Hitler's completely crippled movements, which I have observed in news films, are the visible signs of Parkinson's disease." At the mention of that exciting name Schellenberg's spirits rose. He arranged a meeting between Himmler and de Crinis, to which Himmler brought the Reich Health Leader, Conti—perhaps the completest charlatan of all the Nazi doctors. De Crinis expounded again his notions of Hitler's condition and the symptoms of Parkinson's disease; and the Reichsfuehrer, he afterwards reported, 'listened with great interest and considerable understanding.'

Several days later on April 13th, Himmler summoned Schellenberg to his headquarters in the old Ziethen castle in Wustrow, and there, for an hour and a half, they walked together in the flowering woods. "Schellenberg," said Himmler, "I believe nothing can be done with Hitler. Do you think de Crinis is right?" Schellenberg replied that he had not seen Hitler for two years, "but from everything I have seen of his actions recently, I am inclined to think that the last moment for you to act has come." They digressed to matters of detail: the Jewish question; new contacts abroad; new negotiations in Schellenberg's ever more delicate diplomacy.

"Himmler was in great mental distress. Even openly he had been almost completely abandoned by the Fuehrer; for Hitler had ordered the *Leibstandarte Adolf Hitler* to remove their armbands as a dishonouring punishment.[1] He said that except perhaps Standartenfuehrer Dr Brandt,[2] I was the only man he could completely trust. What should he do? He could not kill Hitler, could not poison him or arrest him in the Chancellery, or the whole military machine would come to a standstill. I explained that all this was of no importance. There were only two possibilities. Either he could go to Hitler, tell him openly of the events of the last two years, and persuade him to resign. . . . 'Quite impossible!' retorted Himmler, 'he would fall into one of his rages, and shoot me out of hand!' 'Then you must protect yourself against this,' I said. 'You have enough high SS leaders who can carry out a surprise arrest; or if there is no other way, the doctors must intervene.'"

To these suggestions Himmler made no answer. He was prepared to contemplate, in the abstract, such drastic measures; but Schellenberg had not yet so changed his attitude of mind that he would actually decide upon a course of action, far less

[1] This refers to one of Hitler's most outrageous acts of spite towards his army. The *Leibstandarte Adolf Hitler* was a division of the *Waffen SS* and at this time was fighting on the upper Danube with the 6th SS Panzer Army, under the command of Hitler's gangster-favourite Sepp Dietrich. The *LAH* was ordered to attack according to Hitler's strategical plans, but owing to an error in the weather forecast the attack was timed to take place on a day of torrential rain. Hitler's plan was nevertheless regarded as sacred; the attack was made; and a disastrous massacre was the consequence. When this failure was reported to Hitler, he was furious with the *LAH*, and ordered them to remove their armbands as a punishment. The indignant soldiers tore off their orders and decorations, and sent them to Hitler, through Himmler, in a tin chamber pot. They also sent the arm, complete with armband, of one of their dead comrades. This order of Hitler was never rescinded, and the soldiers never forgave Himmler and Sepp Dietrich, who, though equally insulted by the gesture, had been unable to prevent it.

[2] *ie* Dr Rudolf Brandt, Himmler's secretary, not to be confused with Dr Karl Brandt, formerly Hitler's surgeon.

embark on one. When the walk was over, all that Himmler would say was that he would like to bring together, with one of his own representatives, Professor de Crinis, Professor Morell, Dr Stumpfegger, and Bormann. Nothing could better illustrate the unreality of Himmler's ideas, or the essential naïvety of Schellenberg in thinking that Himmler could ever be a conspirator. Morell and Bormann lived entirely by Hitler. Their power rested on no political independence, no private armies, no personal indispensability. As for Stumpfegger, though Himmler may have thought that he was still loyal to his old patrons at Hohenlychen, in fact he was already burning incense at the new shrine in the Reich Chancellery. These men were not going to declare Hitler incapable and enable Himmler to put him quietly aside. In fact de Crinis did do as he was told. He consulted Stumpfegger about Hitler's health. But Stumpfegger could not agree that the Fuehrer was suffering from Parkinson's disease; and although de Crinis offered to make up some medicines which, Stumpfegger agreed, might do the Fuehrer some good, Stumpfegger unfortunately never sent round to collect them. Indeed, why should he? He was a surgeon, not a physician; and after the experience of Brandt he was much too wise to interfere in the business of Morell.

Frustrated once again, Schellenberg now remembered another collaborator who might come to his help and persuade Himmler to act. He arranged for Himmler to meet, on April 19th, Count Lutz Schwerin von Krosigk, Hitler's minister of finance. But before descending down the scale of ineptitude to Count Schwerin von Krosigk, the narrative must return to Berlin.

For Hitler was now back in Berlin, facing the last desperate battle of the war. From Bad Nauheim, in December, he had directed his last counterattack in the west, the Ardennes offensive; it had failed, and the Western Allies were now across the Rhine. He had turned east and massed divisions for a counterattack against the Russians on the Danube; it had failed, and the Russians were now over the Oder and on the upper Elbe. Now, in his underground bunker beneath the Reich Chancellery, he was directing the final operations. All his staff, all his court knew inwardly that the war was lost; some of them had known it for years; but he continued to believe in his star, in Providence, and in his own indispensability. He was more indispensable than ever now, for there was now no successor. The decree appointing Goering as his successor was still valid, but Goering was completely out of favour and almost forgotten.[1] Bormann's monopoly of the internal affairs of the Reich and Himmler's control of the SS suggested their claims, but no formal announcement consecrated their aspirations. The military leaders were of course out of the question since July 20th; only compliant toadies had survived the suspicion that now attached to their whole order. In a discussion with his secretaries in March 1945 Hitler admitted that in the matter of the succession he had failed utterly. Hess, he said, had gone mad; Goering, thanks to his style of life and the failure of the Luftwaffe, had been rejected by the German people; as for Himmler, who seemed the obvious third choice, whose very title of Reichsfuehrer was supposed by many to denote the predestined successor to the crown—he, said Hitler, would never do: he was on bad terms with the Party (that is, with Bormann), 'and anyway useless, since he is so completely inartistic.' He did not know whom he could choose and in consequence he chose no one. At this time Hitler of course did not know that Himmler was preparing to deny him, and that Speer had already denied him; but he felt the atmosphere of treachery everywhere. Fortunately he also had the company of those two creatures whom he believed to be exempt from that spreading infection—Blondi and Eva Braun.

"For all writers of history," says Speer, "Eva Braun is going to be a disappointment"; and for readers of history too. She had none of the colourful qualities of the conventional tyrant's mistress. She was neither a Theodora, nor a Pompadour, nor a Lola Montez. But then neither was Hitler a typical

[1] In January 1945, Lammers (head of the Reich Chancery) asked Bormann whether Hitler might be willing to reconsider the question of the succession, since Goering had fallen into disrepute. Bormann replied, 'If the question had not already been settled, I do not think the Fuehrer would now nominate the Reich Marshal; but I do not think he will change the appointment he has once made. Let us drop the matter.' (Statement by Lammers.)

tyrant. Behind his impassioned rages, his enormous ambitions, his gigantic self-confidence, there lay not the indulgent ease of a voluptuary, but the trivial tastes, the conventional domesticity, of the petty-bourgeois. One cannot forget the cream buns. It was to this permanent, if submerged element in his character that Eva Braun appealed; and because she appealed to the triviality not the extravagancy of his nature, she is herself uninteresting. Indeed, the most interesting fact about her is probably the well-kept secrecy of her existence; for their friendship had lasted at least twelve years, and both parties were dead before the knowledge of it was extended beyond their immediate circle. A conspiracy of silence surrounded her life; the servants were forbidden to speak to her; and her picture was expurgated from photographs of the Fuehrer before they could be published or circulated.

Eva Braun's introduction to Hitler had been effected, like Morell's through the photographer Hoffmann, in whose business she worked. Pretty rather than beautiful, with a fresh colour and slightly high cheekbones, unobtrusive, uninterfering, anxious to please, she soon achieved an ascendancy over Hitler, supplying that ideal of restfulness which was so lacking to his political life, but for which his bourgeois soul so hankered. In her company Hitler found the rest which elsewhere he never sought; and she in turn, by providing a domestic retreat, and never seeking to influence him in external, political matters, lubricated the routine of his harsh, distempered life. Good at ski-ing and mountain climbing, fond of dancing (which she had studied professionally), passing for erudite among that ignorant clique, eager to discuss books and pictures, and to help Hitler, in his purchase of *objets d'art* she fitted well into the Alpine, 'artistic' world of Berchtesgaden to which, for the most part, she was confined; for it was only in the last two years of his life that Hitler allowed her to come to Berlin. In his affection for her Hitler never wavered; she had no rival;[1] the blowsy Nordic actresses whom Goebbels

[1] Not even the mysterious Olga, whose name was discovered on the door of the room 'next to Hitler's private apartment' in the temporary headquarters of the OKW at Ohrdruf in Thuringia. When Ohrdruf was captured, imaginative journalists speculated eloquently about Olga,

introduced to the Chancellery for the sake of publicity never interested him. In general indeed, Hitler seems to have been frightened of women; he was afraid they would interfere in politics, and he dreaded 'petticoat politics'—although the politics of an absolute court are not very different. In this matter Eva Braun was safe. She confined her attentions to the intervals of politics, presiding over the teacups and keeping the politicians away during the few hours of relaxation. All praised her moderation. In spite of all her temptations and opportunities, she exploited none of them, which makes her even duller. Though she disliked Bormann, she never sought to influence Hitler against him; and Hitler would not have tolerated it if she had. In his turn Hitler fussed over her, over her health and her habits and her safety. She was not allowed to fly, or to drive a car faster than forty miles an hour.

Of their more intimate relations nothing is known. "They slept in different beds," says the odious Dr Morell, "nevertheless, I believe . . ." But the mere beliefs of Dr Morell are irrelevant. Hitler enjoyed in their relationship what he considered its idealism; 'many years of true friendship' was how he described it in his will; and in order not to mar it by conversation on such base but necessary subjects as cash, he established her independence by granting her, with Hoffmann, a monopoly of the sale of his photographs. Nevertheless there were undoubtedly inhibitions about her status. The servants, who referred to her always as 'E. B.', dropped their voices when they mentioned her; and even now, when the whole affair is of merely historical interest, continue to do so. For over twelve years she had no admitted status: she was neither wife nor acknowledged mistress; and this ambiguity of her position induced, or increased, in her the symptoms of an inferiority complex, showing itself in the appearance of haughtiness and conceit. It was probably from this cause, too, that other unattractive features derived; for her letters show signs of mental and psychological immaturity, of schoolgirl melodrama. When

her style of beauty, her influence on Hitler, and the nature of her meditations on the balcony of her room. Unfortunately she never existed. 'Olga' was simply the code name for the signals office at Ohrdruf; nor was Ohrdruf ever visited by Hitler.

Hitler was absent, or when she did not see him often enough, she would strike rhetorical attitudes and threaten suicide. But these are matters of taste, in which, perhaps, he himself did not set a perfect example.

Since Hitler undoubtedly loved her, one cannot avoid asking why he kept her for so long in this undefined and evidently embarrassing position. Though the details of their relationship will probably always remain an enigma the easiest answer may perhaps be correct. If their relations were, or were meant to be understood as platonic, then the position of either wife or mistress would have been meaningless and compromising. Certainly a platonic relationship would have been most appropriate to the German Messiah, the revolutionary spirit who seemed, and must seem, to transcend all human limitations. If this answer is correct the marriage which ultimately took place on the eve of their death is of purely symbolic significance; without some definition of her status, Eva Braun had no better right to share in the ritual death of the Fuehrer than his secretaries, or Fraeulein Manzialy, the vegetarian cook, who shared Hitler's meals with him in her absence. But that final act Eva Braun was determined not to miss. As the battle approached Berlin, Hitler had sent her away to Munich; but she would not stay there. On April 15th, when the capital was already preparing for a siege, she arrived unbidden at the Reich Chancellery. Hitler ordered her to leave, but she would not go. She had come for her wedding, and her ceremonial death.

Of the political atmosphere in Berlin in these last days we happen to possess a document of unusual and ironical interest. It is the diary of Count Lutz Schwerin von Krosigk, the friend in whom the indefatigable Schellenberg now misplaced his hopes. Schwerin von Krosigk, like Schellenberg, was one of those conscientiously cultured Germans who, by their efforts to identify themselves with western civilization, only show how completely they misunderstand it. Schwerin von Krosigk had used every opportunity of understanding the West; he had even been a Rhodes scholar at Oxford. But he had acquired none of its values. Though he spoke its language, he neither thought its thoughts nor acted its actions. Just as Schellenberg deplored the Nordic nonsense and gaseous metaphysics in which the true German felt at home, and carefully warned Himmler, when talking to educated Swedes, "not to speak of the *Karma* between the two peoples, nor of *Weltanschauung, etc,*" but would himself solemnly vaporize about "what I like to call the cosmic outcome of the event"; so Schwerin von Krosigk, for all his careful education, was continually striking operatic attitudes, and losing himself in cloudy German rhetoric. Like Schellenberg, he was also completely unrealistic. Indeed, the two form a perfect pair, the Tweedledum and Tweedledee of pretentious German silliness. The truth is that, as some sage philosopher has observed, one cannot touch pitch and be undefiled; and both Schellenberg and Schwerin von Krosigk were long-standing members of the Nazi administration. Their belief that they could preserve their independence within it, could influence it for good, and could be accepted as themselves anti-Nazi or at least non-Nazi, only showed the extent of their blindness. All Nazis misunderstood foreign politics; it was left to the Schellenbergs and Schwerin von Krosigks to misunderstand Nazi politics as well. It was perhaps because he misunderstood them to thoroughly that Schwerin von Krosigk was able to survive among them for so long. Certainly he showed a genius for survival. He had been a minister before the Nazis came to power in 1933; he was a minister throughout the Nazi era; the new government recommended to Doenitz in Hitler's political testament still includes his name; a place was reserved for him in the shadow government projected by Himmler; and though this project never materialized, Schwerin von Krosigk had his consolation. When Doenitz set up his administration, though he refused to be bound by Hitler's will, and rejected every other name contained in it, he appointed as his foreign minister (it was his only appointment) Count Schwerin von Krosigk.

Schwerin von Krosigk kept his diary for two periods in this long but inconspicuous political career: in the winter of 1932–33, when the Nazis were climbing to power, and in April 1945, when they were collapsing in ruin. He kept it (he has stated) not, as might have been expected, to acquaint posterity with the events of those historic times, but 'so that my descendants may know what kind of a man it was who was a member of the Reich cabinet during the years of Germany's greatest rise and deepest decline'. If posterity concludes that Schwerin von Krosigk was a ninny, he has only himself to blame for that deliberate revelation.

The second part of the diary begins on April 15th, 1945, but goes back a few days to describe an important incident. Goebbels told Schwerin von Krosigk how he had recently been reading aloud to the Fuehrer, to solace him in his universal discomfiture. He was reading from his favourite book, Carlyle's *History of Frederick the Great*; and the chapter he was reading described 'how the great king himself no longer saw any way out of his difficulties, no longer had any plan; how all his generals and ministers were convinced that his downfall was at hand; how the enemy was already counting Prussia as destroyed; how the future hung dark before him, and in his last letter to his minister, Count Finckenstein,[1] he gave himself one last respite: if there was no change by February 15th, he would give it up and take poison. "Brave king!" says Carlyle, "wait yet a little while, and the days of your suffering will be over. Already the sun of your good fortune stands behind the clouds, and soon will rise upon you." On February 12th the Czarina died; the Miracle of the House of Brandenburg had come to pass.' At this touching tale, said Goebbels, "tears stood in the Fuehrer's eyes." They discussed the matter to and fro, and in the course of the discussion sent for two horoscopes that were carefully kept in one of Himmler's research departments: the horoscope of the Fuehrer, drawn up on January 30th, 1933, and the horoscope of the Republic, dated September 9th, 1918. These sacred documents were fetched and examined, and 'an astonishing fact' was discovered, which might well have repaid an earlier scrutiny. 'Both horoscopes had unanimously predicted the outbreak of war in 1939, the victories till 1941, and then the series of defeats culminating in the worst disasters in the early months of 1945, especially the first half of April. Then there was to be an overwhelming victory for us in the second half of April, stagnation till August,

[1] Schwerin von Krosigk has not quoted either Carlyle or the facts correctly. The minister to whom Frederick wrote was in fact Count d'Argenson.

and in August peace. After the peace there would be a difficult time for Germany for three years; but from 1948 she would rise to greatness again. Next day Goebbels sent me the horoscopes. I could not fathom everything in them; but in the subjoined interpretation, newly drawn up, I found it all; and now I am eagerly awaiting the second half of April.'

Such were the incidents which enlivened the dreary hours of waiting in the underground Bunker of the Reich Chancellery. The horoscopes, which had so accurately prophesied the past, were less reliable for the future, and Schwerin von Krosigk waited in vain for the resounding victory which was to brighten the second half of April; but the reading from Carlyle had a sequel which deserves to be recorded.

A few days later, after a long and heavy air raid on Berlin, Schwerin von Krosigk was sitting up after midnight, drinking wine with some friends, when he learned that the last powder factory in Germany had been evacuated by order of the General Staff. The end must now be near, his friends agreed; 'without ammunition even the bravest soldiers cannot fight'. 'Would this really be the end,' asks the rhetorical diarist, 'which my reason had so long seen as inevitable, but which my spirit had striven so hard not to see? At that moment the telephone rang; the state secretary wished to speak to me. What could he want at so late an hour? He only uttered one short sentence: "Roosevelt is dead." We felt the wings of the Angel of History rustle through the room. Could this be the long-desired change of fortune?' Next morning Schwerin von Krosigk called Goebbels on the telephone to congratulate him on this signal event—and not only to congratulate, but to advise. For Schwerin von Krosigk, like Schellenberg, was a very subtle man; he always saw the fine shades, the slight nuances, imperceptible to less sensitive observers; and he was afraid that, unadvised by him, the somewhat crude German Press might miss its golden opportunity. He suggested to Goebbels that the new President should not be abused, nor yet too obviously praised, but that the differences between him and Roosevelt should be judiciously emphasized. Goebbels indicated politely that the Ministry had already considered these points, and that the necessary instructions had been given. Then Goebbels described how yesterday he had been at General Busse's headquarters at Kuestrin, and how in the evening he had sat with the officers of Busse's staff and 'had developed his thesis that, for reasons of Historical Necessity and Justice, a change of fortune was inevitable, like the Miracle of the House of Brandenburg in the Seven Years War. One of the staff officers had somewhat sceptically and ironically asked, What Czarina will die this time? That, Goebbels had replied, he could not say; but Fate still held many possibilities in her hand. Then he had driven home, and had heard the news of Roosevelt's death. Immediately, he had telephoned to Busse, and said, "The Czarina is dead". Busse had told him that this made a great impression on his soldiers; now they saw another chance. Goebbels believed that this news would awaken a new spirit of hope in the whole German people; they would surely see in it the power of Historical Necessity and Justice. . . . I [says the sententious Count] interrupted, "Say rather, of God". . . .'

Schwerin von Krosigk is so fond of rhetoric and apostrophe, so free with abstract nouns, and so prone to hear the wings of the Angel of History rustling about him, that his account may seem overdrawn; but we happen to have indirect confirmation from another quite independent source: from one of the secretaries in the Propaganda Ministry.[1] 'I well remember Friday, April 13th,' she says. 'Every week Goebbels paid a visit to the Eastern Front to address the troops, taking them supplies of cigarettes, cognac, and books. On this day he had been to Kuestrin. . . . While he was on his way back to Berlin by motorcar, we received the news of the death of President Roosevelt. Goebbels, as usual, returned very late at night. A very heavy bombardment was going on and the Chancellery and the Adlon Hotel were burning. We met Goebbels on the steps of the Propaganda Ministry. A reporter said to him, "Herr Reichsminister, Roosevelt is dead". Goebbels jumped up out of his car and stood for a moment as if transfixed. I shall never forget the look on his face, which we could see in the light of Berlin blazing. "Now," he said, "bring out our best

[1] Frau Inge Haberzettel, who worked in the same room with Goebbels' secretary, Fraeulein Hildebrandt. I am indebted to Mr Leslie Randall, correspondent of the *Evening Standard*, for this report.

champagne and let us have a telephone talk with the Fuehrer."
We went into his study, and champagne was served. Goebbels
spoke to Hitler on his private line, and said, "My Fuehrer,
I congratulate you! Roosevelt is dead. It is written in the stars
that the second half of April will be the turning-point for us.
This is Friday, April the 13th. It is the turning-point!" Hitler
said something to him, and then Goebbels put down the
receiver. He was in an ecstasy.'[1]

To us it seems incredible that in these last days of the
Third Reich its leaders should have thought that the stars, or
a stroke of subtlety, could save them; nevertheless all the
evidence is clear that they never understood the real certainty
of their ruin. Isolated for twelve years behind a Chinese wall of
political and intellectual self-sufficiency, they had long ceased
to understand, if they had ever understood, the politics, the
ideas, the habits of mind of other nations. Not one of the
German leaders could appreciate that whatever political or
diplomatic differences might be concealed beneath the surface
of the Grand Alliance, all the members of it were determined
that these should not interfere with the defeat of Germany,
and that no diplomatic or other arrangement was conceivable
until the Nazi Government was destroyed. We read with
incredulity of the elaborate unreality of Schellenberg, of the
naïve consolations of Schwerin von Krosigk, of the astrological
assurances of Goebbels and Himmler. At this time, when the
armies of East and West had almost cut Germany in two,
Goebbels was still saying that the inevitable breach between the
Russians and the Anglo-Americans was so near (presumably

---

[1] Both Steengracht, an official in the German Foreign Office, who
gave evidence for Ribbentrop at Nuremberg, and Speer have also
mentioned Goebbels' exhilaration on hearing of the death of Roosevelt,
of which another full account, confirming the details given here, is to
be found in Semler's diary (Semler, *Goebbels*, pp. 191–2). It should be
added that Goebbels himself almost certainly did not believe in the
astrology which he exploited. 'Crazy times call for crazy measures'
was his comment to Semler on another such occasion (*ibid*. p. 124).
Nor was it only the Nazis who relied on the stars to preserve the Third
Reich: the opposition also relied on them to overthrow the Nazis. See
the opinions of Senatspraesident Kameke in the diary of Ulrich von
Hassell (*Vom andern D utschland*, pp. 53, 107, 140, 152). It is a pity
that the science of astrology should have failed *all* its devotees.

for reasons of Historical Necessity and Justice) that the German Government need only wait in Berlin and let it mature. But the most striking, most conclusive proof of the fools' paradise in which these men were living is the eagerness with which these doomed marionettes were still competing for the dwindling fragments of power. The succession to Hitler was still undetermined, still legally vested in Goering. By now, one would have thought, it was an uncoveted heritage. Not at all. Himmler still took it for granted that it would be his, though he still flinched from Schellenberg's suggestion that he should hasten its devolution. Bormann still schemed at the centre of affairs, distilling his subtle poison in his master's ear and ruining, whenever he could, his rivals. Goebbels was now intriguing for the post of Foreign Minister in the place of Ribbentrop.[1] Only Ribbentrop was unconcerned in these feverish intrigues; for Ribbentrop had now no party, no supporters, with whom to combine in the incalculable politics of the court. All the others, bitter rivals, in all else were agreed upon one thing: Ribbentrop must go. It was the cry alike of Goering and Himmler, of Goebbels and Bormann, of Speer and Schellenberg and Schwerin von Krosigk. Not long ago they had sung it in harmonious chorus to Hitler himself; but Hitler had replied that they misjudged Ribbentrop's ability: he was 'a second Bismarck' and could not be spared; and Ribbentrop's dearest wish, at this important juncture, was at last gratified: a picture was published in the Press showing the Foreign Minister at the Front.[2]

Throughout these days of intrigue and conspiracy, Schellenberg and Schwerin von Krosigk, having once met,[3] were cementing their alliance. Each was favourably well impressed with the other. Schellenberg found the Count well-informed about foreign and especially English affairs; the Count found Schellenberg 'young, very able, and sympathetic'. They had several conversations together. They agreed that some attempt

[1] Schwerin von Krosigk. Cf. Semler, *Goebbels*, pp. 119–23.
[2] Speer; Schwerin von Krosigk; and cf. Bernadotte, *The Fall of the Curtain*, p. 18, who also indicates that in the spring of 1945 Ribbentrop apparently 'still had Hitler's ear and enjoyed his support'.
[3] Through the intermediacy of Schellenberg's subordinate, Ottfried Dewitz.

must be made to open negotiations with the West. Together they deplored Ribbentrop. On a theoretical level only one difficulty obstructed their aspirations. Schwerin von Krosigk insisted that any foreign powers with which they might negotiate must of course understand that although the other Nazi leaders would at once be jettisoned, Hitler and Himmler were indispensable and must stay; they were the only guarantees against chaos. Unfortunately, foreigners seemed to regard Hitler and Himmler as the most objectionable of all. . . . Gently Schellenberg prepared his ground. It was true, he admitted, that Himmler's name had unfortunate associations abroad. He was blamed for many things which were done under his name but not under his orders (this gentle phrase referred doubtless to Belsen and Buchenwald). But Schellenberg was doing his best to remedy this misunderstanding. For a long time he had been seeking, by subtle means, to influence the Foreign Press in his favour. . . . Would Schwerin von Krosigk agree to meet Himmler? There was a difficulty of course—the two had quarrelled earlier in the year; but Schellenberg could smooth that over. Of Hitler Schellenberg said nothing. He had no interest in sweetening that reputation.

On April 19th the formalities had been arranged and Himmler and Schwerin von Krosigk had a long conversation together at the Count's house. The Count had been well briefed by Schellenberg. He urged upon Himmler the necessity of negotiation with the West; for the German people could only be asked to continue its heroic resistance if the respite thus gained were used to find a solution. But how could such negotiations be carried on? asked Himmler. Schwerin von Krosigk was full of resource. There were numerous possibilities, he explained. First there was the Pope. The Roman Catholics in America were a large, compact bloc, while the Protestants were divided into multiple, ineffective sects. If the Pope were to be got at . . . Then there was Dr Burckhardt, head of the European Red Cross, and Dr Salazar in Portugal, and all kinds of useful business men and travelling professors. And then there was always the impending breach between East and West. But what of Hitler? objected Himmler. That was indeed a difficult problem, Schwerin von Krosigk admitted, a

145

psychological riddle. "However high-flying his plans may be, the Fuehrer is after all a man, standing with both feet on the ground; he can see the position in black and white; surely he has no illusions? What then, I ask myself, is he waiting for?" Himmler fidgeted uneasily. The Fuehrer had some plan, he said vaguely, and was doubtless right; he himself was also convinced that all would be well in the end. It was not a rational belief, he agreed; it was an instinctive conviction. Did Schwerin von Krosigk realize that Himmler was no longer an uninstructed heathen, but believed in God and Providence? So he told him the story of the miracles that had converted him—of the Fuehrer's escape of July 20th, 1944, and of the thaw on the Oder. Thus Schwerin von Krosigk had fared no better than Schellenberg in his conversations with Himmler. He had no sooner drawn towards the crux of the problem than Himmler had slid away under vague irrelevant generalities, and the conversation ended leaving everything exactly as before.

When Himmler and Schwerin von Krosigk had finished, they joined Schellenberg and the Count's friend Seldte[1] outside. These two had also been discussing the same problem, but, as usual, had travelled a little further than their superiors. They had decided that Himmler should take over the power of the state and force Hitler, on his birthday (that was, tomorrow), to broadcast a manifesto to the German people, announcing the end of the single party and the People's Courts, and promising elections. When Himmler emerged, Seldte appealed to him to use his influence with the Fuehrer and to negotiate for peace. It was no longer a personal matter, he protested; 'the biological substance of the German people' was at stake. There could be no doubt of the origin of those words; it was one of Schellenberg's favourite phrases. In the car, as they returned from Schwerin von Krosigk's house, Schellenberg again took up his familiar theme. He also urged upon Himmler the virtues of Schwerin von Krosigk—the only man, he assured him, fit to be Foreign Minister in Himmler's government.

[1] Seldte was formerly leader of the *Stahlhelm*. Like Schwerin von Krosigk, he was a skilful survivor, having been *Reichsarbeitminister* since 1933.

Thus through Schwerin von Krosigk and Seldte, as through Kersten and Wulf, Schellenberg ceaselessly urged Himmler to detach himself from Hitler, to depose Hitler, if necessary to murder Hitler, and to open negotiations with the West. Naturally a sanguine man, confident of his skill and ignorant of reality, with each new effort he believed that he was nearing his goal. But the evidence is clear against him. Himmler was as obstinately undecided as ever, suspended between loyalty and doubt. That night, at midnight, he sent for champagne to toast the Fuehrer; for it was now the Fuehrer's birthday. When Schellenberg heard the order, he left the house. He could not participate in such a ceremony. He set out on his way to Harzwalde, the estate of his ally Kersten, there to continue his desperate, incessant machinations.

CHAPTER FOUR

CRISIS AND DECISION

20th–24th April

APRIL 20TH WAS Hitler's birthday; and Germans were reminded of the fact by a broadcast speech from Goebbels, calling upon them to trust blindly in the Fuehrer and the stars who together would lead them out of their present difficulties. On that day Hitler had planned to leave Berlin for Obersalzberg, thence, from the fabulous mountain cave of Barbarossa, to direct the battles for the south. Ten days ago, he had sent his servants before him to prepare the house for his reception.[1] But in those ten days disaster had followed disaster. "All through the week," says Schwerin von Krosigk, "there was nothing but a succession of Job's messengers." Germany was now almost cut in two; only a narrow corridor of land divided the Americans, already over the Elbe, from the Russians, already over the Oder and Neisse and threatening both Dresden and Berlin. In the north, the British were in the outskirts of Bremen and Hamburg; in the south, the French were on the upper Danube, the Russians in Vienna. In Italy, the armies of Field-Marshal Alexander had captured Bologna and were pouring into the valley of the Po. And in the heart of the Reich, General Patton was thrusting south through Bavaria, the cradle of the Nazi movement, towards the Alps, its intended grave.

Hitler's headquarters were in the Reich Chancellery, the vast mausoleum which he had built to house his pride and awe his tributary kings. The huge rooms, with their vast slabs of porphyry and marble, their ponderous doors and multiple candelabra, were now disused. Bombed out and burnt, they had been abandoned as offices and were only manned as a command post. But underneath the old Chancellery and the garden, fifty feet below the ground, a bunker had been built

[1] Statement by Artur Kannenberg.

during the war. It could be reached from within the Chancellery, by stairs leading down through the butler's pantry. At the foot of these stairs was a narrow space enclosed by three airtight, watertight bulkheads. One of these bulkheads closed the passage to the butler's pantry, or 'Kannenberg-alley'[1] as it was called (Artur Kannenberg was Hitler's butler); the second led to an outer stair with access to the garden of the Foreign Office; the third led into the Bunker.[2] The Bunker was in two parts. The first part consisted of twelve rooms, none larger than a large cupboard, six on each side of a central passage. These were lumber rooms and servants' quarters, and included the *Diaetkueche* or vegetarian kitchen where Hitler's meals were prepared. At the end of the central passage, which was now used as a general dining-place for the shelterers, a curved stair led downwards to a still deeper and slightly larger bunker. This was the *Fuehrerbunker*, Hitler's own bunker, the stage on which the last act of the Nazi melodrama was played out. Contracted within these narrow limits, it could at least preserve the essential dramatic unities of Boileau.

The Fuehrerbunker consisted of eighteen rooms, all of them small, cramped, and uncomfortable, and a central passage. There could be no greater contrast than that between the Egyptian vastity of the rooms of the new Chancellery, which trembling ambassadors had taken, as it seemed, a fragment of eternity to cross, and these miserable underground hutches in which the diminished court now paid its less elaborate but still servile homage. The central passage was divided in two by a partition. On the near side of the partition, it was used as a general sitting-room, and the rooms to which it gave access were utilitarian offices, the lavatories and guardroom, the emergency telephone exchange and the powerhouse. Beyond the partition was the holy of holies. There the central passage became the conference room in which Hitler presided over the daily staff conferences. A door on the left led into a suite of six rooms, the private apartments of Hitler and Eva Braun. Eva Braun had a bed-sitting-room, a bathroom, and a dressing-room; Hitler a bedroom and a study. The sixth was an ante-room.

[1] *Kannenberggang.*
[2] For a plan of the Bunker see page 180.

Two other doors on the left led into a small 'map room', used for small conferences, and a narrow cupboard known as the 'Dog bunker',[1] and now used as a rest room for the personal detectives who guarded the Fuehrer. At the end of this Dog bunker a ladder gave access to an unfinished concrete observation tower above the ground. On the right of the passage were the rooms occupied by Hitler's two doctors, Morell and Stumpfegger, and Stumpfegger's first-aid room. At the beginning of April, Hitler had ordered Stumpfegger to set up a dressing station in the Chancellery, for the casualties of the fighting, and Stumpfegger had fetched his surgical equipment from his old hospital at Hohenlychen. This dressing station was not in the Bunker, but under the new Chancellery; the surgery in the Fuehrerbunker was his personal store.

At the end of the passage, a door led into a small ante-room, used as a cloakroom; and thence four flights of concrete steps led up again into the Chancellery garden. This was the emergency exit.

Apart from the Fuehrerbunker, there were other underground bunkers within the complex of the government buildings. There was the bunker of the Party Chancellery, where Bormann and his staff lived, with the service officers and SS guards, and a third bunker which housed SS Brigadefuehrer Mohnke, the commandant of the Chancellery, and his staff; while Goebbels and his staff sheltered in the cellars of the Propaganda Ministry. From all these bunkers, officers and officials came daily to the Fuehrerbunker for the continuous conferences that took place in the narrow central passage. Jodl and Keitel also came thither from their headquarters at Zossen or Potsdam, with the new chief of the Army General Staff. For General Guderian no longer held this post. Like his predecessors, he had been unable to acquiesce in the Fuehrer's inspired strategy, and on March 30th, after a series of violent scenes, he had accepted Hitler's 'advice' to resign on account of his weak heart. In his place Hitler had appointed General Hans Krebs. Krebs had long been military attaché in Moscow. Able but time-serving, 'a smooth, surviving type', as Speer called him, a toady of Hitler and an intimate friend of Bor-

[1] *Hundebunker.*

150

mann, he professed undeviating national-socialism, and will last appear as its emissary of surrender to his Russian friends. To this subterranean bunker, then, on April 20th, came some usual and some unusual visitors, bringing their formal, and for the most part insincere congratulations on the Fuehrer's birthday. From noon onwards they came and went, and the day was taken up by receptions, speeches, and conferences. In spite of the catastrophic situation, they found the Fuehrer still confident; the Russians, he still believed, were going to suffer their bloodiest defeat of all before Berlin. In the Chancellery garden he received a delegation of boys from the Hitler Youth, under their leader Artur Axmann, and in the presence of Himmler, Goering, and Goebbels (but no soldiers were there to overshadow these young warriors) he thanked and decorated them for their efforts in this now decisive battle. Then he withdrew to his small conference room and received, singly, and in turn, Doenitz, Keitel, Jodl. The rest were then lined up in his presence, and he shook hands and spoke with all. To Keitel he was particularly affable. "I will never forget you," he said; "I will never forget that you saved me on the occasion of the Plot, and that you got me out of Rastenburg.[1] Those were the right decisions, and the right actions, for the times." Among others present on this last ceremonial occasion were Bormann, Ribbentrop, and Speer.

After the receptions came the conference. The great question before the conference concerned the imminent threat to the geographical unity of the Reich. In a few days, perhaps hours, the last land route to the south would have been cut. Would Hitler, or would he not, move his headquarters to the south, whither all the service headquarters and ministries had gone or were going? His advisers were unanimous that the Russian ring around the city would ultimately close; that once caught in it, there would be no escape; that the only alternative was to withdraw to the south, to Obersalzberg; and that such a withdrawal must be made now, while the road remained open, or perhaps never. Goering and Keitel, Himmler and Bormann, Goebbels, Krebs, and Burgdorf all entreated Hitler to leave

[1] On July 20th, 1944, Hitler had fallen into Keitel's arms (see above, p. 79; and cf. p. 111).

the doomed city; but Hitler would neither agree nor disagree. The most he would do was to implement the decision reached ten days earlier against such a situation as had now arisen. Then it had been decided that if the Allied armies should cut the Reich in half, two separate commands should be set up in the two disconnected areas. In the north, Grand Admiral Doenitz, in the south Field-Marshal Kesselring should command all the German forces, unless Hitler himself chose to move his headquarters to one or other of the two theatres. Now Hitler decided to confer upon Doenitz full military powers in the north; but in regard to the south he still made no appointment. It was not that he distrusted Kesselring, or knew the truth— that even this favourite Field-Marshal had now abandoned hope, and was meditating unconditional surrender.[1] Hitler simply had not yet made up his mind. Sooner or later he would decide—or rather, as he put it, he would leave it to Providence to decide. For Hitler's indecisions were not, like Himmler's, a permanent state of mind; they were a preliminary to decision; and once he had declared his decision, it was as impossible for any other man to alter it, as it would have been futile to have sought to hasten it. How he would decide, no one as yet could tell. When the conference was over, Bormann assured his secretary that in a day, or at most two days, Hitler and the rest of his staff would leave Berlin. Others were less certain. Colonel Nicolaus von Below, Hitler's air force adjutant, who had worked with him for eight years, was convinced that now he would never leave.

After the conference, the visitors left the Bunker, and a long convoy of lorries and airplanes led the general exodus from Berlin to Obersalzberg. Among those to leave were the high commanders of the Luftwaffe. They left with relief. In Obersalzberg at least they would be free from the endless insults, the impossible orders, the violent recriminations with which Hitler had recently received their every failure. "One

---

[1] The unconditional surrender of all German armies in Italy was actually negotiated by Kesselring's successor in Italy, General Vietinghoff, and SS General Wolff; but the first steps had been taken by Kesselring before his transfer. Kesselring and Schoerner were generally regarded as 'Hitler's field-marshals'.

or two Luftwaffe officers should be shot!" he would shout at some self-exculpating general; "then we would have a change!" "The entire Luftwaffe staff should be hanged!" he would scream down the telephone at the trembling General Koller, and bang the receiver on the hook. For the Luftwaffe had failed, failed utterly; and nothing now could reverse the consequences of its failure. With it, there left Berlin the author both of the Luftwaffe and of its failure, Hermann Goering. He took his leave of the Fuehrer on the evening of April 20th. It was an icy farewell. They never met again. Behind him Goering left two of his senior officers, to maintain contact with the Fuehrer's headquarters: General Koller, his chief of staff, and General Christian, his chief of operations.[1] General Christian, a young and successful officer, had risen rapidly in the new and once favourite service; as his second wife, he had married Hitler's secretary, Fraeulein Gerda Daranowski; and he was now one of the domestic circle at court. General Koller was less young, less effective, and less favoured. On him would fall the accumulated insults, the continuous threats of the Fuehrer, which he, being a conscientious, nervous, and rather fussy old gentleman, would ceaselessly but fruitlessly deplore. Nevertheless he is of value in the reconstruction of this complicated story: for he was keeping a diary.

Another who left the Bunker on the night following Hitler's birthday conference was Albert Speer. For many weeks now Speer had been developing his plans for saving German industry, German plant, and German communications from the destructive policy of the Party. Everywhere his most trusted technicians, his industrialists and works managers, had been ordered to let the front roll over them; to stay at their posts and then, when the tide was past, to preserve and reconstruct what they could under Allied control.[2] When Speer came to Berlin on April 20th, it was not solely to congratulate Hitler on his birthday. It was to argue his cause, the sole cause that

---

[1] Christian's correct title was *Chef Luftwaffenfuehrungsstab*. Both Koller and Christian have supplied information on the events in which they participated.

[2] Speer's account of his policy is confirmed by Koller and by Karl Kaufmann, Gauleiter of Hamburg.

now preoccupied him, the cause of saving not the German Government, or the German Army, or the Nazi Party, but the material inheritance of the German people. A week ago he had written a speech, which he intended to broadcast, on a suitable occasion, to the German nation. Now that the war was clearly drawing to its end, he dreaded the wilful holocaust with which the Party might signalize its downfall. In this speech, therefore, he announced that the war was lost and ordered the German people to hand over intact to the Allies all plant and factories, all concentration camps and prison camps, with their inmates. All demolition, all activity by the Werewolves, was to cease. A few days later, his speech still undelivered, Speer had visited the armies east of Berlin and had proposed to the generals that, when the time came for their retreat, they should bypass Berlin on the north and south, without fighting for the city, thus reducing the destruction and leaving Hitler to his fate; for he was now convinced that his only public loyalty was to the German people, and the sooner Hitler died the better. At the same time Speer suggested that, in course of their retreat, they should seize Radio Werewolf at Koenigswuster-hausen. From that station, appropriately, Speer would broad-cast his speech. The generals had agreed to these proposals. Now, on April 20th, he had come to Berlin to dissuade Goebbels from his declared intention of destroying some hundred bridges in the Berlin area; an act of destruction which would have paralysed the delivery of food to the city for a long time to come. Goebbels ultimately yielded to his argument, and agreed that the *Volkssturm* should fight outside, not inside the city. The decision was reported by Krebs to Hitler, and confirmed by him.

Successful in this, Speer now left for Hamburg. His plan for broadcasting from Radio Werewolf now seemed less feasible, and he was preparing an alternative scheme. At Hamburg he met his friend Kaufmann, the Gauleiter. Together they made arrangements for the preservation of the plant and bridges of Hamburg. Then Speer told Kaufmann about the speech, the text of which was still in his pocket. Kaufmann approved of both the plan and the text; and together they agreed that Speer should have the speech recorded at Hamburg radio station. In the underground studio of the radio station

Speer uneasily delivered this treasonable oration before two unknown officials. Before beginning, he told them to consider it as they listened, and at the end to decide whether the record should be kept or destroyed. They listened impassively, and at the end, since they made no objection, Speer took the record and deposited it with Kaufmann. It was to be broadcast, he explained, if anything happened to him—if the Werewolves, whom he feared, should murder him, or if Hitler, hearing of it, should order his death. In any case, it was to be broadcast on Hitler's death. For even now, Speer was inhibited by some shreds of personal loyalty to the tyrant whose disastrous policy he was resisting, but whose long patronage he could not forget. Even now, he could not bring himself to oppose, in politics, the one man in whom, as he believed, the German people still put its trust.[1] Speer's speech was directed not against Hitler personally, but against the still unknown Nazi who would attempt to carry on Hitler's policy of destruction after Hitler had fallen in Berlin. Nor was this the full extent of Speer's inhibition. Soon it will be time to describe an even more curious episode in this history of divided loyalties.

After the conference of April 20th, Himmler also left the Fuehrerbunker. Late in the evening he reached his headquarters at Ziethen castle, and there, awaiting him, found the persistent Schellenberg. Schellenberg had a message for him. While Himmler had been in Berlin, he had been at Harzwalde, negotiating with his friends of the World Jewish Organization about the Jewish question. There he had been telephoned from the Swedish Legation. Count Bernadotte was leaving Germany at half past six tomorrow morning. Schellenberg had acted at once. Count Bernadotte was now at Hohenlychen, spending the night, and Himmler was to meet him for breakfast there at six o'clock.

Promptly at six o'clock, Himmler and Schellenberg arrived at Hohenlychen and breakfasted with Count Bernadotte. Schellenberg was full of hope. Now at last, he thought,

[1] I have taken this account from Speer's earliest statement on the subject. At Nuremberg, a year later, Speer's version was slightly different: he then ascribed the provision that the speech should only be broadcast after Hitler's death to the demand of the recording officials, who were constrained by their oath of loyalty to Hitler.

Himmler would admit the logical consequence of his behaviour; would break the invisible chain of loyalty that still bound him to Hitler and interfered with his freedom to follow the advice of Schellenberg; would accept the opportunity, the last opportunity, that had thus spontaneously presented itself; and would speak to Bernadotte not, as in his two previous interviews, as a subordinate official, limited by his instructions, but as *de facto* Fuehrer of Germany, prepared to offer terms to the West. But Himmler did none of these things. He merely discussed certain technical details—the release of certain Polish women from Ravensbrueck concentration camp; and even to this he had insisted on securing Hitler's approval by representing it as an anti-Russian gesture. After half an hour Bernadotte took his leave, and the opportunity had been missed for the third and perhaps last time. Schellenberg accompanied Bernadotte for part of the way. He piqued himself on reading the secret thoughts of others, and always found that they coincided with his own wishes. "Himmler secretly hoped," he says, "that I would again request the Count to fly to General Eisenhower on his own initiative and thus prepare the way for direct negotiations between Eisenhower and Himmler." But Bernadotte saw the facts and possibilities more clearly than Schellenberg. Nothing but a direct and explicit mandate from Himmler would cause him to interfere in these high matters. "The Reichsfuehrer is no longer in touch with reality," he said, as they motored together on the road to Waren. "I can help him no more. He should have taken the affairs of the Reich into his own hands after my first visit." When Schellenberg returned to Hohenlychen, he found Himmler paralysed with indecision, tormented by doubt. "Schellenberg," he said, "I dread the future"; and the irrepressible Schellenberg at once retorted that that should encourage him to act. Himmler made no reply. He was 'a torn soul'.

It was not in this cloud-cuckoo-land that the affairs of Germany were being, or would be, decided. All this time the evacuation of ministries from Berlin was continuing; but Hitler remained in his bunker, undecided, at least until he had made one further effort to throw the Russians back from the city.

On April 21st, Hitler, who in all these days personally directed the movements of every battalion, ordered a final, all-out attack by the troops in Berlin. It was the Steiner attack, under the command of an SS general, Obergruppenfuehrer Steiner; it was to be launched in the southern suburbs of the city; and every man, every tank, every airplane was to be diverted to take part in it. "Any commanding officer who keeps men back," Hitler shouted, "will forfeit his life within five hours." "You will guarantee with your head," he told Koller, "that absolutely every man is employed."

So Hitler ordered; but his orders bore no relation now to any reality. He was moving imaginary battalions, making academic plans, disposing non-existent formations. The Steiner attack was the last, most symbolic instance of Hitler's personal strategy; it never took place.

The facts emerged at the staff conference of April 22nd. All through the morning, a series of telephone calls from the Fuehrerbunker had never ceased to demand whether the attack had been launched. At one time a telephone message from Himmler reported that it had; at another a report from the Luftwaffe stated that it had not. At three o'clock in the afternoon, there was still no news. Then the conference began. Bormann, Burgdorf, Keitel, Jodl, and Krebs were there, and Herrgesell and Hagen, the two stenographers. Doenitz was not; during the night he had moved, with his staff, to his new headquarters at Ploen in Schleswig-Holstein, leaving only a liaison officer, Admiral Voss, in the Bunker. Voss, with the other liaison officers, Hewel and Fegelein, and adjutants and others, remained on the profane side of the partition, ready to join the conference on demand. General Koller, Goering's chief of staff, was not there. He was preoccupied with command work; 'and anyway', he records plaintively, 'I should never have been able to tolerate being insulted all day long.' He had therefore arranged for General Christian to deputize for him.

The conference opened with the usual expositions of the military situation by Krebs and Jodl. As usual they were un-favourable, but not hopeless. Then came the news of the Steiner attack. It had not materialized. Nothing had happened. In spite of elaborate plans, in spite of ferocious threats, the

Luftwaffe had not gone into action. No orders had been received from Steiner. And then, following on these negative tidings came reports of positive calamities. While troops had been withdrawn to support Steiner in the south, the Russians had broken into the suburbs in the north, and their armoured spearheads were now within the city of Berlin.

Then came the storm, which made the conference of April 22nd famous and decisive in the history of Hitler's last days. It has been variously described, both by the principals who witnessed it, and by the trembling adjutants and secretaries who waited on the far side of the partition and pumped the participants when they emerged, exhausted, after a three-hour session. Their narratives are confused and fragmentary, for emotion, on this notable occasion, interfered with the memories of all; but on the main points there is agreement.[1] Hitler flew into a rage. He shrieked that he had been deserted; he railed at the Army; he denounced all traitors; he spoke of universal treason, failure, corruption, and lies; and then, exhausted, he declared that the end had come. At last, and for the first time, he despaired of his mission. All was over; the Third Reich was a failure, and its author had nothing left to do but to die. His doubts were now resolved. He would not go to the south. Anyone else who wished might go, but he would stay in Berlin and there meet the end when it came.

The generals, the politicians, everyone protested. They reminded him of the sacrifices of the past, which had not been in vain. They pointed out that the Army Groups of Schoerner and Kesselring were still intact. They assured him that there was no reason for despair; and again they urged him to leave for Obersalzberg now, before it was too late. Fegelein telephoned Himmler, Voss telephoned Doenitz; and Himmler and Doenitz entreated him to think again, promising to send all naval and SS troops at their disposal to the relief of Berlin. Ribbentrop called the Bunker and sent a message to the

[1] The principal sources for the conference of April 22nd are: Keitel, Jodl (reported by Koller), Christian, Freytag von Loringhoven, Lorenz, Herrgesell, von Below, and Fraeulein Krueger. Their opportunities of knowledge vary, and their accounts are not always consistent; but I am satisfied that the relevant points, as given in the above account, are correct.

Fuehrer; he had great hopes, he said, of a diplomatic coup which would set all aright; but Hitler refused to hear him. Even the second Bismarck was now, at last, failing to convince. Hitler repeated that he would stay in Berlin; he would personally take over the defence of the city; and he ordered an announcement to be made to the people of Berlin, telling them that the Fuehrer was in Berlin, that the Fuehrer would not leave Berlin, and that the Fuehrer would defend Berlin to the very last. Next day the news was relayed to the world. Berlin and Prague, said the German radio, were the inviolable twin citadels of the Reich, and in Berlin Hitler and Goebbels, the Fuehrer and the Gauleiter, would remain to the end.

With that the full conference ended, and the astonished participants withdrew to the outer bunker, where the adjutants and secretaries were waiting. They could not conceal their emotions of indignation and gloom. Everyone seemed to have lost his bearings. 'When they came from the conference-room,' says one of the secretaries,[1] 'they were all distraught, saying that the end had come.' 'So much has broken up within me,' exclaimed General Christian, who had witnessed the scene, 'that I still cannot grasp it. The atmosphere in the Bunker has made a deep impression on me—an impression I cannot begin to explain.'[2] Even Krebs admitted cautiously to his adjutant that the Fuehrer had become violently excited and had thrown unworthy reproaches at the high command.[3]

Meanwhile the drama was not over; in the Fuehrer's private quarters it was continuing before a narrower group of witnesses. Hitler sent for Goebbels, and then for Frau Goebbels and the children. Hitherto Goebbels and his family had lived in their own house, or in the Propaganda Ministry; henceforth their home was to be in the Fuehrerbunker. Frau Goebbels and the six children would live in the further of the two bunkers, Goebbels himself would have a room in the

[1] Fraeulein Krueger.
[2] Christian, quoted by Koller. Christian's account, given under interrogation some months later, was still confused.
[3] Freytag von Loringhoven.

private part of the Fuehrerbunker. They all sat together and discussed the future. Goebbels said that he too would stay in Berlin and commit suicide there; his wife, resisting the remonstrances of Hitler, declared that she would do the same; and they would give poison to the children. After this, Hitler sent for his papers and sorted them out, personally selecting the documents which must be destroyed. The selected papers were then taken out into the garden by one of his adjutants, Julius Schaub, and burned.

After this scene, as if he had not sufficiently emphasized his decision, Hitler called Keitel and Bormann back to him and said, simply, "I will never leave Berlin—*never!*" Again there were protestations, again expressions of astonishment; but Hitler was unmoved. He sent for someone from the Press Division and asked whether his announcement had yet been made in the streets of Berlin. Then he pointed his finger at Keitel and said, "You are ordered by me to leave tomorrow for Berchtesgaden." Keitel protested that he would not go except in the Fuehrer's company. Hitler sent for Jodl and told him that he too must go to the south; and he told Bormann to leave the room.

The scene which followed was the climax among the extraordinary events of that day; for it was a scene which entailed dramatic consequences. Only Jodl and Keitel witnessed it; but though the words in which they describe it differ, the sense, in all important particulars, is the same, and there is no reason to doubt their circumstantial versions. Hitler repeated his resolve to take over the defence of Berlin which others had failed to secure; when it fell, he said, he would shoot himself at the last moment. He could not fight, he explained; for physically he was a broken man; and neither alive nor dead would he fall into enemy hands. Jodl and Keitel sought vainly to dissuade him; they offered to divert troops from the west, to abandon western Germany to the British and Americans, and thus at least to save Berlin from the Russians. They protested that three-quarters of the armed forces were in the south, and if the Combined General Staff, with its operational command, were to go south too, how could he possibly direct it from Berlin? If negotiations were necessary,[1] it was thence that they must be made. Still Hitler would not listen. "I have taken up a fixed position," he said; "I cannot change it." There was no need of further orders, for the whole Reich was falling apart. There was nothing further to be done. It was the end. They begged him for orders; at least if he had himself abandoned hope, let him remember that he was Supreme Commander of the armed forces. His generals awaited his commands; what were they to do? "It is simply impossible, after you have been directing and leading us for so long, that you should suddenly send your staff away and expect them to lead themselves!" Hitler repeated that he had no orders to give; and then, in the words which had such far-reaching consequences, he added that if they wished for orders, let them apply to the Reich Marshal. "There isn't a single German soldier," they protested, "who would fight under the Reich Marshal!" "There is no question of fighting now," Hitler replied; "there's nothing left to fight with. If it's a question of negotiating, Goering can do that better than I."[2]

After these pregnant words, Hitler discussed with Keitel the manner in which Berlin might yet be relieved. The 12th Army, commanded by General Wenck, Hitler's personal creation, was now on the Elbe, south-west of Berlin; it must disengage itself and fight its way in the direction of Potsdam to rescue Berlin, the Chancellery, and the Fuehrer. Keitel offered to go at once to Wenck with this message, but Hitler insisted that he must stay and take a meal first; for it was now eight o'clock in the evening. He sent for his servants and ordered food to be brought, and himself sat by and watched while Keitel ate. He was now perfectly quiet again; his nervous

[1] There seems no doubt that at this time Hitler spoke of the possibility of negotiation. The versions of Jodl (given verbatim to Koller within a few hours of the incident) and of Keitel (given under interrogation several months later) both explicitly refer to the possible necessity of negotiation, and Goering's qualifications for such a task; and cf. Hitler's remarks to Speer on April 23rd (quoted below, p. 177).

[2] These words are quoted from Jodl's account. Keitel's version contains the same explicit statement that orders should be sought from Goering, adding later: 'I think he also said, "Well, Goering is much better at these things: he can deal much better with the other side"— or words to that effect.'

fit seemed completely past, and he became once more the kindly, simple host of Obersalzberg, taking personal care to see that sandwiches were put up for the Field-Marshal's journey, and half a bottle of cognac, and chocolate, and all the accessories of a picnic.

Then, while Krebs had orders to remain in the Bunker as the Fuehrer's military adviser, Keitel and Jodl left together, Keitel to visit Wenck, Jodl to the new headquarters of the Combined General Staff at Krampnitz.[1] Keitel was the compliant puppet, Jodl the overdriven brain, through which Hitler had exercised his control over the armed forces. Now apparently he had abandoned it. They went for part of the way together. "There is only one thing I can say to Wenck," said Keitel, as they sat in the car, "and that is, the fight for Berlin is on, and the fate of the Fuehrer is at stake." What Jodl replied to this loyal phrase, if he replied at all, we do not know; but his views at least were different. He at least shared the opinion of the more orthodox, more independent generals, who had been less affected by the melodrama than by the military irregularity of Hitler's behaviour. Toadies though they were, the mere servile rump of a thrice-purged institution, there were still some of them who remembered that Hitler was supposed to be a soldier; that a soldier's duty is to give orders and to take responsibilities; and that in this their Supreme Commander had failed, preferring to act like an overwrought *prima donna*. The threatened suicide, the gestures of despair, seemed to them a cowardly dereliction; it made no favourable impression on those cold, practical hearts; and they withdrew to their new headquarters filled with secret contempt, to plan the strategy which their self-appointed warlord had thus rhetorically resigned.

Meanwhile the news of this dramatic conference was having

[1] Although the main service departments had been and were being evacuated to Bavaria, and all departments would have gone thither had Hitler himself agreed to go, Hitler's refusal compelled Keitel and Jodl to keep a skeleton staff of the OKW in the north, where it could be in touch with him. The headquarters of this staff were first at Krampnitz, in the western suburbs of Berlin, then at Fuerstenberg, near Mecklenberg. Ultimately it joined Doenitz's staff in Ploen, and moved with it to his final capital in Flensberg.

other repercussions elsewhere. At Hohenlychen, whither he had moved his headquarters at midday, Himmler had received the astonishing news from Fegelein. With him at the time were two of his subordinates: Professor Gebhardt, his 'evil genius', whom yesterday he had proposed as head of the German Red Cross,[1] and Obergruppenfuehrer Gottlob Berger, head of the SS Head Office,[2] and Himmler's Prisoner of War Administration,[3] already about to leave for Bavaria (it was one of Schellenberg's schemes) to counteract the influence of the sinister Kaltenbrunner.

"Everyone is mad in Berlin!" Himmler exclaimed to Berger when he had heard Fegelein's news. "The Fuehrer is raging, saying that the armed forces have deceived him all along and that now the SS is leaving him in the lurch.[4] I still have my Escort Battalion here, six hundred men, mostly wounded or convalescent; what am I to do?"

Berger was a Swabian, a simple, elementary character, full of honest good nature, indefinite garrulity, and unsophisticated emotion. The political subtleties, the psychological refinements of Schellenberg meant nothing to him. He had no sympathy with a soul in doubt, no understanding of the conflicting pressures, the divergent loyalties, to which Himmler had so long been subjected. To him it was an uncomplicated moral matter, and he spoke with the clear, unhesitant voice of the undivided man. "You go straight to Berlin, Herr Reichs-fuehrer, and your Escort Battalion with you, of course. You have no right to an Escort Battalion here, at a time when the Fuehrer intends to stay in the Reich Chancellery. . . ." "The words failed me," he says, "to voice my disgust; I was at the end of my tether. I said, 'I am going to Berlin, and it is your duty to go too.' "[5]

[1] In place of Professor Grawitz, who had committed suicide in Berlin.
[2] *SS Hauptamt*. The office was in the Douglasstrasse.
[3] *Kriegsgefangenenwesen.*
[4] A reference to the failure of Steiner and Sepp Dietrich, both SS generals.
[5] Berger's accounts of his activities in these days are all characterized by indistinct and sometimes inconsistent loquacity. They have been carefully checked against statements of Gebhardt and Grothmann; but the accounts of his conversations with Himmler and Hitler, which rest on his testimony alone, are given with some reservations.

Himmler would gladly have agreed—and yet he remembered Schellenberg. What would Schellenberg say if he went to Berlin now? Of all things Schellenberg most dreaded Himmler's visits to Hitler, and the reawakening, in that devoted character, of the never wholly exorcised spirit of loyalty. He had tried to dissuade Himmler from visiting Berlin even on Hitler's birthday. This time he was not there to dissuade. After lunch he had stayed behind, alone with Himmler, and had heard words which gave delight to his optimistic spirit. "I almost think, Schellenberg, that you are right," Himmler had said; "I must act in one way or another." It was not a very definite pronouncement, but it was enough for Schellenberg. He had obtained leave to pay one more visit to Count Bernadotte, now on the Danish frontier, and to inform him of Himmler's readiness to begin negotiations; and full of confidence, he had stepped into his car and driven to the north-east. Within a few hours Fegelein was telephoning from the Bunker urging Himmler to come and persuade the Fuehrer to leave, and Berger was assuring him, in unhesitant, imperative tones, that it was his duty to go. Himmler could not make up his mind. He was once more a torn soul.

Himmler telephoned again to the Bunker. He spoke to Hitler himself and urged him to leave; but in vain. He spoke to Fegelein again, and listened to his entreaties. In the end they reached a compromise. Himmler would drive half way to Berlin, to Nauen, and Fegelein would drive out to Nauen, and there they would discuss the matter. At dusk he left Hohenlychen by car, accompanied by his adjutant, Grothmann. Gebhardt followed in another car; for he had reasons of his own for visiting Berlin. He wished to be confirmed by Hitler as head of the Red Cross; and that afternoon he had had a telephone conversation with his former pupil, Dr Stumpfegger.

The party drove to the crossroads at Nauen, and there Himmler waited for Fegelein. He waited for an hour, nearly two hours, and still Fegelein had not come. Then Gebhardt asked if he might go on alone to the Bunker. Himmler agreed, and since Fegelein had not arrived to take it, and he himself was afraid to go on to Berlin, he entrusted to Gebhardt the message which he wished to send to the Fuehrer: the offer of his Escort Battalion to fight in defence of the Chancellery. It was about eleven o'clock that night when Gebhardt arrived in the Bunker. He learned from Stumpfegger the details of the momentous conference, and then was admitted to the Fuehrer's presence and delivered his messages. First, as agreed with Stumpfegger, he offered to evacuate the women and children from the Chancellery—Eva Braun, the secretaries, Frau Goebbels and her children. Hitler replied that all these had decided, of their own free will, to stay with him. Then Gebhardt delivered Himmler's offer of his Escort Battalion. Hitler accepted it, and showed on the map the position which he wished it to hold in the Tiergarten. Finally Hitler confirmed Gebhardt's appointment as head of the German Red Cross. The interview lasted twenty minutes; then Gebhardt turned to go. Before leaving, he asked whether Hitler wished to send any message to Himmler. "Give him my regards," said Hitler; and Gebhardt withdrew.

Scarcely had Gebhardt left Hitler's presence when another visitor arrived. It was Berger, who had been summoned by telephone to report to Hitler before leaving for the south. He had immediately motored to Berlin. When he arrived, Russian shells were falling near the Chancellery. Berger reported to the Bunker, but Hitler was in conference and he had to wait. Now he was admitted. He found a few Army officers still there. Hitler, he says, was finished, a broken man. They spoke about Berger's mission, about the disloyalty that was universally springing up in the south, and which would have to be investigated and suppressed. Then they spoke of Hitler's decision to remain in Berlin. Hitler explained that Himmler had made a long speech to him on the telephone, seeking to dissuade him; it was senseless, he had said, to remain; why would he not go to the south, to the still defensible Alpine Redoubt? But Berger, if his own account is to be believed, encouraged Hitler to stay. To the simple all things are simple; and to his elementary, boy-scout nature the duty of the Fuehrer was as clear as the duty of the Reichsfuehrer had been. "I told him," he says, "that it was out of the question; he couldn't betray the German people. It was quite simple to put a bullet through one's head, or to take one of those pills or tubes that are issued, which work instantaneously. One couldn't desert the people, after they had held out so loyally and so long. . . ." *Loyally and long* . . . that was not what Hitler thought of the German people in this hour. "All this time," says Berger, "the Fuehrer had never uttered a word; then suddenly he shrieked, 'Everyone has deceived me! no one has told me the truth! the armed forces have lied to me!'—all in that vein. He went on and on in a loud voice. Then his face went bluish-purple. I thought he was going to have a stroke any minute. I had the impression that he had had a stroke already, on his left side—but of course they kept one in the dark. His arm, which a fortnight before used to jerk, was suddenly still, and he never put his left foot to the ground properly. He didn't rest his left hand properly, either, as he used to do; he only rested his right hand on the table."

At the end of the interview they discussed the *Prominenten*, the well-connected British and American prisoners of war who were being held as hostages. These prisoners had been in camp in western Germany; but as the Allied armies moved forward, they had been separated from their fellow prisoners and removed to Bavaria, where they would come under Berger's control. They also discussed the outbreak of separatism in Austria and Bavaria. When Berger left, Hitler, who had been sitting at the table, rose to his feet. His whole body was trembling. "His hand was shaking, his leg was shaking and his head was shaking; and all that he kept saying was 'Shoot them all! shoot them all!' or something like that." But whether it was the prisoners or the separatists that were to be shot does not transpire from the incoherent narrative of Berger.

It was one o'clock in the morning when Berger left Berlin, under the fire of the Russian batteries, to fly to Bavaria in Himmler's four-engined plane. Others were leaving too. "Any man who wants may go!" Hitler had said; "I stay here." All that night, parties were leaving Berlin for Obersalzberg; it was the last stage of the great exodus. Hitler's adjutant Schaub, his naval adjutant Admiral von Puttkamer, his two stenographers, Herrgesell and Hagen, two of his four secretaries,

Fraeulein Schroeder and Fraeulein Wolf, and many others. Among them was the odious physician, Professor Morell. "I don't need drugs to see me through," were Hitler's last words to him, and he too went out to the aerodrome. From the Party Chancellery too, three omnibuses had taken, or were taking, the fugitives. Only Martin Bormann stayed, with his assistant SS Standartenfuehrer Zander, and his secretary Fraeulein Krueger. He had not wished to stay; he still had political ambitions; to his undramatic spirit the prospect of a glorious *Goetterdaemmerung* made no appeal, and he had joined his voice to those of the generals who had urged Hitler to leave. But since Hitler had decided otherwise, he would not even now leave the sole source and centre of his authority; and he stayed.

Another who left the Chancellery that night was General Koller. Koller had been sitting at his command post when the telephone had rung, and General Christian, in an excited voice, had told him that 'events of historical importance' were taking place in the Bunker; but when Christian had arrived himself to amplify this bald summary, his account had been emotional and confused, and Koller went at once in search of Jodl for a more explicit version of this important episode. He found him at Krampnitz. Jodl told him all, and Koller wrung his hands in dismay over the deplorable details. "When the Mayor of Leipzig shot himself and his family, the Fuehrer said it was 'senseless, a cowardly evasion of responsibility'; now he's doing exactly the same himself." Jodl agreed. "Was there any chance that the Fuehrer might change his mind?" asked Koller. "None at all," replied Jodl. But the incident most significant to Koller, as Jodl told him the story, was Hitler's phrase about leaving everything to the Reich Marshal. The Reich Marshal was now in Obersalzberg, and Koller was his representative in Berlin. It was plainly his duty to fly at once to Obersalzberg and inform Goering of these tremendous developments; "he would be justified in reprimanding me severely if I failed to do this, and it cannot be explained in a radiogram at all". Jodl agreed. At half past three on the morning of April 23rd, Koller flew from Gatow to Munich, and a new sub-plot in the drama began.

At noon on April 23rd, Koller reported to Goering at Obersalzberg. Word for word, he repeated his conversation with Jodl. Goering's eyes popped as the astonishing details were recounted to him. He collected a group of adjutants and advisers around him, and sent for Reich Minister Lammers, head of the Reich Chancellery and official expert in Nazi legalities. Lammers had once possessed a power equal to that of Bormann, and the two had co-operated closely in the quest of further authority; but Bormann had gradually elbowed his partner out, and now Lammers was a comparatively insignificant figure. Goering felt himself in a very delicate position. By decree, he was Hitler's successor; now, according to Koller's account, Hitler had resigned and devolved his powers upon him. The legal position was quite clear. Goering sent for a tin box, and from it extracted the text of Hitler's decree of June 1941. All agreed that the meaning was unmistakeable. But what of Bormann? All knew that it was Bormann's dearest wish to eliminate Goering from the succession to that post which, it now seemed, would soon be vacant. At present, since there was no other suitable candidate, Goering's right had not been altered; but any indiscretion might be fatal. He picked his way carefully among the possible traps. Might not the Fuehrer have issued other orders since 1941, he asked, which would have invalidated this decree? "No," replied Lammers. "If the Fuehrer had ever issued any other orders, they would certainly have come to my notice." Senatspraesident Mueller, Bormann's personal assistant, was present at the conference, but apparently raised no difficulties. Goering asked all in turn for their opinion. They were unanimous. Supposing Koller's statement to be correct, Goering was by law obliged to take over the inheritance. Goering then proposed that he should send a telegram to Hitler, and supplementary telegrams to Keitel, Ribbentrop, and von Below,[1] seeking approval for such an interpretation. All agreed; or at least, if Lammers, Mueller, and SS Obersturmbannfuehrer Dr Frank, leader of the SS in Obersalzberg, did not agree, it was by reservation, not expression of their opinion.

[1] As Hitler's Luftwaffe adjutant, von Below would naturally handle service relations between Hitler and Goering.

There was now no communication with the north except by wireless. Goering himself began to draft the telegrams, but his style was too voluble for that parsimonious medium and alternative versions were supplied by Koller and Goering's adjutant, Colonel von Brauchitsch. Goering demanded the inclusion of the phrase 'of all powers at home and abroad'; for he was determined, once in power, to open immediate negotiations with the West, and even declared himself ready to fly personally to General Eisenhower. After all, that was precisely why Hitler had handed over to him: 'if it is a question of negotiating, Goering can do that better than I'. He also demanded a deadline for reply; otherwise, if communications were cut off, he might have to wait indefinitely; and events would not wait. Perhaps Hitler was already dead. The final version seemed admirably phrased:

MY FUEHRER!—In view of your decision to remain at your post in the fortress of Berlin, do you agree that I take over, at once, the total leadership of the Reich, with full freedom of action at home and abroad, as your deputy, in accordance with your decree of June 29th 1941? If no reply is received by ten o'clock tonight, I shall take it for granted that you have lost your freedom of action, and shall consider the conditions of your decree as fulfilled, and shall act for the best interests of our country and our people. You know what I feel for you in this gravest hour of my life. Words fail me to express myself. May God protect you, and speed you quickly here in spite of all. Your loyal—
HERMANN GOERING.

Suitable telegrams, explanatory, supplementary, and conciliatory, were sent to Keitel, Ribbentrop, and von Below.

The same evening, another meeting was taking place at Luebeck between Himmler, Schellenberg, and Count Bernadotte. The important events which had taken place in the Bunker were unknown to both Schellenberg and Bernadotte; but Himmler knew of them, and they had had a great effect on his hitherto divided mind. They had solved, or seemed to have solved, his problem. For years Himmler had had no problem, and his cumbrous mind had never needed to think. The principle of loyalty, on which his whole life, his whole success, his whole system was based, had spared him from any introspective or intellectual difficulty. To that principle he remained, in spite of many ambiguities and vacillations and inadvertencies, ultimately true; and thanks to that principle, his life had been as simple and uncomplicated as his naïve faith in the metaphysical Nordic balderdash of the Nazi religion. Protected by that magic armour, he had known neither thought nor doubt; he had believed and acted. He had worshipped the Aryan deities, contemplated the Aryan truth, and partaken of the Aryan sacraments. He had extirpated heresy, and in the name of orthodoxy had sent millions, unthinkingly, even benignly, to the torture chamber and the gas van. Imagination cannot comprehend the sum total of the human suffering, or even of the mere deaths, which had proceeded from the authority of that single true believer, whose wife remembers him only as a somewhat insignificant person but a good breadwinner, and whom his subordinates, hating each other with a bitter detestation, united to admire as a paternal governor; and who himself never seems to have considered, far less examined or relished or regretted, the consequences of his authority. Then Schellenberg had come, and little by little, by suggestion and insinuation, by persistence and persuasion, by flattery and protestation, he had sapped the strength of that fundamental principle; and Himmler, lacking it, from a terrible, impersonal priest of Moloch, had become a weak, vacillating, purposeless human being, incapable of thought or action, always looking nostalgically back to the lost rule from which his life had drawn its significance.

Such was Himmler's condition in the middle of April, when Schellenberg was urging him to assume the Fuehrerdom of Germany and make peace with the West. If Himmler were Fuehrer, he would indeed act as Schellenberg bade him; but he was not; Hitler was still alive; and the shreds of loyalty which Himmler still cherished made all Schellenberg's earnest and persuasive counsels vain. It was psychologically impossible for Himmler to eliminate, or even to ignore Hitler. Even if it had been possible, there were further difficulties. If Himmler deposed or ignored Hitler, how could he be sure that he would be obeyed? From the German people, as Speer had realized, Hitler, so long as he lived, was the one man who could command unconditional obedience. It was a spell wherewith the whole German people had been bewitched, and Himmler and Speer among them. Indeed, their problem was essentially the same. Both had come to believe, by different processes, that Hitler's continued rule was disastrous; both had, or thought they had, alternative policies; but neither was prepared fully to implement his policy as long as Hitler was alive, the sole source of inspiration, the sole focus of devotion, the sole centre of power and authority. Neither Speer nor Himmler could act against Hitler, or independently of him. To carry out their policy they had only one course—to wait until God, or chance, or time should remove the terrible figure whom they themselves could not touch; and while they waited, events were moving and their policies were becoming daily less possible of fulfilment.

Then came the conference of April 22nd. For Himmler it was of decisive importance. He had heard all the details from Gebhardt and Fegelein when all three met for breakfast at Hohenlychen next morning; and when he set out for Luebeck in the afternoon, his mind and conscience were clear as they had never been since the day when he had walked through the woods of Wustrow with Schellenberg. Hitler had declared his intention of staying in Berlin and dying in its ruins. Himmler knew enough of Hitler to be sure that he would not change his mind. In a day or two Berlin would fall, and Hitler would be dead without the interposition of any sacrilegious hand. For two days Himmler could indulge his loyalty—he had already sent half of his Escort Battalion to fight in defence of the Fuehrer and the Chancellery.[1] Then, when all was over, he would be free to become, as Schellenberg persuaded him, the negotiator of peace, the saviour of Germany.

The meeting took place in the Swedish consulate in Luebeck. It has been described independently by both Schellenberg and

[1] It had been sent under the command of SS Obersturmbann-fuehrer Persch, Fegelein having arrived too late to lead it.

Bernadotte. The electric light had been cut, and they sat in candlelight. They had scarcely taken their seats when an air raid sent them to the cellars. After midnight they returned. For the first time in all these days of negotiation and vacillation, Himmler spoke clearly. "The Fuehrer's great life," he said, "is drawing to its close." Possibly he was already dead; if not, he would certainly be dead within the next few days. He had gone to Berlin to perish with its inhabitants, and it would be only a matter of days before Berlin would fall. Hitherto, he went on, he had agreed with Bernadotte in his heart but had been unable to break his oath to the Fuehrer. Now it was different. He empowered Bernadotte to communicate to the Western Allies, through the Swedish Government, his offer of surrender. In the East he would not surrender; there the Germans would continue to fight until the Western Allies had advanced to relieve them. Thus the entire northern sector would escape senseless destruction. Himmler also promised that Danish and Norwegian internees should be transferred to Sweden; and he wrote a personal letter for Bernadotte to take to the Swedish Government as proof of his offer. The interview was over in an hour, and Bernadotte left to return at once to Stockholm. His greatest problem solved, Himmler now began once more to turn his mind to the details of procedure; what name he should choose for the new political party which his government should represent, and whether he should bow or shake hands when introduced to General Eisenhower.[1]

Thus Hitler's staff conference of April 22nd, which created a problem for Goering, brought a solution to the long doubts of Himmler; but Schellenberg—for the faith of the optimist feeds on trifles—could not deny himself the comfort of one additional theory. To him, knowing nothing of the conference, Himmler's words were capable of another meaning. When Himmler said that Hitler would be dead in a matter of days, Schellenberg at once remembered his own suggestions; how

[1] Count Bernadotte (*The Fall of the Curtain*, p. 55) ascribes both to Himmler and (before Himmler's arrival) to Schellenberg the statement that Hitler could only last a few days and that Himmler was prepared to offer surrender. This must be a slip of memory. Schellenberg had no means of knowing, and says himself that he first heard the words from Himmler in Bernadotte's presence.

he had urged Himmler to make use of physicians and poisoned drugs; how he had elaborated the astrological predictions of Wulf in that direction, and discussed with de Crinis the symptoms of Parkinson's disease. He convinced himself, and remained long convinced, that Himmler had made secret arrangements for the murder of Hitler and was waiting daily for news of their success; and to help himself in that conviction, he conveniently forgot to record in his account of the interview, what Bernadotte has explicitly given in his—Himmler's own clear explanation: that Hitler was staying in Berlin deliberately to share its imminent fate.

On the very same night, while Goering was awaiting a reply to his telegram in Obersalzberg and Himmler was offering his capitulation to Bernadotte in Luebeck, yet a third significant meeting was taking place in Berlin. Albert Speer was paying his last visit to the Fuehrer whom, like Goering and Himmler, he was seeking both to supersede and to obey. On April 23rd, in Hamburg, having heard that Hitler had decided to remain in the capital, he decided that personal loyalty required him to go to Berlin and take his leave. His political acts of disobedience were done, and could not be undone. His speech, though undelivered, was recorded, and in safe hands in Hamburg; Hitler would soon be dead, and the occasion for its delivery was imminent; since it could be delivered whether Speer was alive or dead, he had now no further political function to perform. He therefore decided to go to Berlin and explain to Hitler the decision which he had made in his 'conflict between personal loyalty and public duty'. What would happen to him in consequence of such a confession, Speer did not know. He assumed that he would be arrested, probably shot; but it was immaterial to him, for his work was finished and he was ready to accept the consequences of the breach which it had entailed in his otherwise undiminished personal loyalty.

It was now no longer possible to reach Berlin by road. Speer motored as far as Rechlin, and then flew in a training plane to Gatow, the western aerodrome of Berlin. At Gatow he met General Christian, who had just left the Fuehrerbunker for the last time. Then he flew on into the city in a Fieseler

Storch, and landed on the East-West Axis—the great boulevard which leads up to the centre of Berlin—close to the Brandenburger Tor. He went straight to the Bunker. Hitler was there, with the remainder of his court: Bormann, Goebbels, Ribbentrop, Krebs, von Below, his personal adjutants, and Eva Braun. Speer gave Hitler a full account of his recent activities; Hitler listened, and seemed to Speer to be 'deeply moved' by his candour. At the end he did nothing. Speer was not arrested, not shot. The incident was closed.

Why Hitler, who, in these days of universal suspicion, was shrieking for blood—the blood of hostages and prisoners, of German officers and his own servants—was thus unexpectedly lenient to the transgressing Speer is a question which may admit of many answers. Dr von Hasselbach has observed, in his professional examination of Hitler, that he 'could hate fiercely in some fields, while forgiving almost anything to those he loved'; and perhaps this is an illustration of this general characteristic. Certainly Hitler entertained a strong affection for Speer, who came from his favoured 'artistic' world, and whom he had himself chosen, intuitively, for one of the most difficult and testing tasks in Germany. That Speer had succeeded, and always succeeded, in this gigantic task was an additional reason for satisfaction; it showed that Hitler's intuition was sometimes justified by results—he did not always choose Rosenbergs and Ribbentrops. Hitler referred to Speer, with his customary indifference to the subtler distinctions of language, as 'the greatest genius of all time'. But there is perhaps another explanation also. On April 23rd, when Speer visited him, Hitler was in a state of unnatural calm: the calm after the storm. All who saw him on that day have borne witness to this relaxation, this inner peace, which had followed the tempestuous scenes of the day before.[1] It was a long time, says Speer, since he had seen him so composed, so human. For more than a year his behaviour had been harsh and strained, the result (Speer believed) of his obstinate belief, against all advice and all evidence, that Germany would win the war. Now that he had at last abandoned that impossible conviction, the tension of his spirit was relaxed, and he looked upon the

[1] Christian and Keitel confirm Speer's observations in this respect.

world with more dispassionate, philosophical eyes, awaiting death (he said) as a release from a hard life full of difficulties. In this serene mood, he was perhaps uninterested in a disobedience which, since Speer had come voluntarily to confess it, seemed formal only and implied no fundamental disloyalty; and Speer escaped from the lion's den unexpectedly free. Nevertheless, in a few days Hitler would recover from this unnatural calm. Bormann had long been seeking to persuade him that Speer was betraying him; Speer's own confession had confirmed, in part, these suggestions. In his last days Hitler complained that Speer, like all the rest, was deserting him;[1] and in his political testament the name of Speer was silently dropped from the new Nazi Government. Even now, Hitler's calm was not such as to extend beyond Speer, who was soon to witness the very different treatment of a less voluntary disobedience.

Speer remained in the Bunker for eight hours, while Allied planes bombed the city of Berlin, and the Propaganda Ministry went up in flames. He spoke with Eva Braun, who told him of Hitler's collapse on the day before and of Bormann's intrigues against his rivals. He also took part in two other conversations with Hitler.

The first concerned Hitler's decision to stay in Berlin. Though he had declared his fixed intention to stay, and it had been announced to Berlin and to the world, Bormann and Ribbentrop still sought to dissuade him. Perhaps they thought that a decision taken in a period of mental storm might be altered in the calm which had followed it. If so, they were wrong. Goebbels and Eva Braun supported him in his decision to stay; Goebbels even urged him, as he had so often urged the German people, not to be so 'defeatist' about the outcome of the battle. Bormann appealed to Speer for his support; but Speer would not give it. Instead he opposed the policy of flight. If the defence of Berlin should fail, he told Hitler, then the end would clearly have come; and it would be more dignified to meet it here, in the Reich capital, than in his 'weekend bungalow' at Obersalzberg. His advice was perhaps as irrelevant as the protestations of Bormann. Hitler had already

[1] Axmann.

175

made up his mind; and no occasion has ever been recorded when he changed it. Firmly and quietly he reasserted his decision; and he repeated to Speer, what he had already described to Keitel and Jodl, the manner in which he intended to die. He would not go out of the Bunker, he said, to die fighting among the barricades, lest he should be wounded and captured by the Russians. He would shoot himself in the Bunker. Nor would even his dead body fall into the hands of the enemy, who would use it for propaganda. He had made all arrangements for it to be burned away.

The second conversation concerned the telegram from Goering which had arrived in the course of the afternoon.

For four years Bormann had waited for an opportunity to ruin Goering; but none had arisen. Now the time was short. Any day now Hitler might be dead, and then, by law, unless the law was altered, Goering would be his successor, and Bormann's day of power would be past. For in the universal unreality of German politics, Bormann, like Himmler and Schellenberg and Goering and Schwerin von Krosigk, still believed that there would be power to inherit and to exercise after Hitler's death. Now, at the last moment, such an opportunity had come; and it had come at the most favourable time, when no personal explanations were any longer possible, no rival views could be heard. By his telegram Goering had played into Bormann's hands at a time when Bormann, as never before, monopolized the ear of Hitler. It is true that Goering had sought to provide against such an event by sending parallel telegrams to Keitel, Ribbentrop, and von Below; but Keitel and Jodl had by now left the Bunker for the last time and were at their new headquarters, and Ribbentrop would not intervene to save Goering. The telegram to von Below asked him to see that the telegram to the Fuehrer was properly delivered, and to use his influence to persuade Hitler, if possible, to fly to the south. This telegram was taken from von Below by Bormann, and never returned.[1] Bormann was determined to play this hand alone.

How Bormann had handled the incident can be deduced from the explanation later given by Hitler to Goering's suc-

[1] von Below.

cessor, Ritter von Greim.[1] Unerringly, Bormann had directed Hitler's attention to the passage in which Goering had demanded a reply by ten o'clock. It was an ultimatum, he had said; and he had also reminded Hitler that six months ago Goering had been suspected of seeking to open negotiations with the Allies. Clearly he now wished to usurp power in order to resume them. Hitler's suspicions, never more than half asleep, had been easily awakened. A telegram had therefore been sent to Goering assuring him that Hitler still possessed full freedom of action, and forbidding any independent move. Now, in Speer's presence, the next stage was considered: the fate of Goering. "Hitler was highly enraged," says Speer, "and expressed himself very strongly about Goering. He said that he had known for some time that Goering had failed, that he was corrupt, and a drug-addict . . ."; "and yet," he commented, "he can negotiate the capitulation," adding as an afterthought, "not that it matters who does that." "His contempt for the German people," says Speer, "was expressed in the manner of this remark." In the end Hitler would not agree that Goering should be shot; but he agreed that he should be dismissed from all offices and from his right of succession. He told Bormann to draft a telegram accordingly. Bormann withdrew, and returned with the proposed text. Hitler authorized it, and it was sent. It informed Goering that his action represented high treason to National Socialism and to the Fuehrer; that the penalty for this was death; but that Goering would be excused this extreme penalty, in view of his earlier services to the Party, provided he resigned at once from all his offices. He was to answer yes or no. At the same time, a telegram was sent by Bormann to the SS leaders in Obersalzberg, Obersturmbannfuehrer Frank and Obersturmfuehrer Bredow, ordering them to arrest Goering for high treason. His staff and advisers, including Koller and Lammers, were to be arrested or confined to their houses. "You will answer for this with your lives."[2] The orders were obeyed. Shortly after

[1] Quoted by Koller, *s.d.* May 8th, 1945, and confirmed by Hanna Reitsch (cf. below, p. 187).

[2] This telegram was seen and quoted by Karnau; the text, as given by him, has been recognized and pronounced authentic by Zander.

midnight the entire party at Obersalzberg was arrested. Next day it was announced from Berlin that Goering had resigned from all offices for reasons of health. Bormann had triumphed. The question of the succession was now open again.

But why, we ask, did Bormann succeed so easily? Why did Hitler yield so readily to his obvious designs? Had not Hitler himself authorized Goering to assume authority, and to use it for negotiation? At first we wonder whether perhaps Hitler's words on that momentous occasion have not been wrongly reported. But the evidence is too strong for such a method of escape. The crucial words, as taken down verbatim by Koller from Jodl that very night, were reasserted by Jodl five days later,[1] and after six months were independently confirmed in all substantial points by Keitel. Had Hitler then forgotten them, or did he refuse to remember them? Or did he attach a different meaning to the words which the hearers had too literally interpreted? The truth may lie anywhere among these alternatives.

Words at all times have two possible functions: sometimes they convey ideas, and sometimes they merely express moods. When a man says, in a moment of desperation, that he wishes he were dead, he does not always mean to be literally understood; and it is possible that in that sudden outburst of despair Hitler's words, which were interpreted as a statement of his intentions, were in fact merely a liberation of his feelings—or at least were afterwards so regarded by him, if he remembered them; for it is immaterial, in such circumstances, whether he failed to remember or refused to admit what he had said. Nor is this the only instance in which he afterwards disregarded the utterances of that night. For during that stormy afternoon he had also renounced control of the armed forces. In spite of all the protests of Keitel and Jodl, he had insisted that they should direct the strategy of the war themselves, and it was in answer to their protests at such a suggestion that he had referred them to the Reich Marshal. And yet, four days later, without ever explicitly announcing that he had resumed control, Hitler was issuing orders as if he had never abandoned it. When

[1] Koller, *s.d.* April 27th, 1945. 'Jodl again confirms the accuracy of everything he told me that night' (*ie* April 22nd–23rd).

Goering, at Nuremberg, sought to rehabilitate himself in Nazi eyes as the loyal paladin of the movement, it was clearly not without some justification that he represented his dismissal as the unfortunate consequence of a technical error. What he did not explain was why that technical error was knowingly exploited, universally welcomed, and never corrected. The occasion of Goering's fall was supplied by his incautious telegram; but the reason was more fundamental than that. It was the ruin of the Luftwaffe.[1]

At four o'clock next morning, April 24th, Speer left Hitler's Bunker for the last time. Ribbentrop had already left and did not return. Jodl and Keitel had visited it for the last time on April 23rd; and Field-Marshal Schoerner had also been and gone. For two days Hitler had steadfastly resisted all those who had sought to dissuade him from his fixed purpose of staying in Berlin; now the time was running short, for the Russian armies were closing around the city and soon it would be impossible to leave, at least by land. Nevertheless, a few last efforts of dissuasion were still made. On April 24th a telegram from Schoerner urged him to leave Berlin and join the Army Group, as yet undefeated, in the mountains of Bohemia; but Hitler replied once more that he would defend Berlin, or die there.[2] That evening Gauleiter Wegener, whom Doenitz had made responsible for civil affairs in the northern area, aghast at the magnitude of his problems, sought alleviation in a change of policy in Berlin. He telephoned to the Bunker: would not the Fuehrer sanction a surrender in the West to reinforce the East and avoid a double devastation? He was crying for the moon. Hitler did not want to avoid devastation; devastation was just what he wanted—the more the better—to illuminate his Viking funeral. 'It was terrible to hear,' records Schwerin von Krosigk, now with Doenitz in the north, 'that no counsel, no reasoned arguments, no reference to the fearful sufferings of our poor people, can break through those walls which the Fuehrer has erected around his convictions, and behind which he allows nobody to see. Can it be that there is really nothing

[1] Almost every Luftwaffe officer has agreed that Goering was personally responsible for the failure of the Luftwaffe.

[2] Lorenz.

there—only the gigantic obstinacy of a deluded spirit, sacrificing all to its self-worshipping Ego?' The former Rhodes scholar did not attempt to answer this question; no doubt he was satisfied that the posing of it alone would impress posterity with his philosophical profundity.

Thus by April 24th Hitler had in turn rejected every attempt to alter the decision which, after his customary vacillation, he had firmly reached. Thereafter there was no purpose in further attempts; for next day the Russians had completely encircled Berlin and only a dangerous communication by air was possible. The period of crisis and decision was over; the siege of the Bunker had begun.

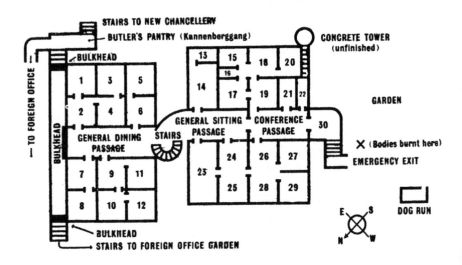

PLAN OF HITLER'S BUNKER

1–4	*Diaetkueche* (kitchen, etc.)	19	Anteroom to Hitler's suite
5–6	Lumber rooms	20	Hitler's bedroom
7–8	Servants' quarters	21	'Map room' or conference room
9–12	Frau Goebbels' and children's rooms	22	'Dog-bunker' or guards' room
		23	Power house (Diesel engine)
13	Electric light switchboard	24	Telephone and guard room
14	WCs	25	Emergency telephone exchange
15	Private bathroom	26	Drawing room
16	Eva Braun's dressing-room	27	Goebbels' bedroom (previously Morell's)
17	Eva Braun's bed-sitting room	28–29	Stumpfegger's rooms
18	Hitler's study	30	Anteroom and cloakroom

CHAPTER FIVE

THE SIEGE OF THE BUNKER

25th–28th April

WITH THE departure of Speer on April 24th, the last of the casual visitors to the Bunker had gone, and from that time on, apart from two interesting pilgrims from the outer world, the *dramatis personae* of the tragi-comedy remained constant. They were also few. In the Fuehrerbunker were Hitler and Eva Braun; Goebbels (who occupied the rooms abandoned by Dr Morell) with his wife and children and his adjutant, Hauptsturmfuehrer Schwaegermann; Dr Stumpfegger; Sturmbannfuehrer Heinz Linge, Hitler's personal attendant; Sturmbannfuehrer Otto Guensche, his SS adjutant and faithful shadow; his two remaining secretaries, Frau Christian and Frau Junge; and Fraeulein Manzialy, his vegetarian cook. Apart from these, there were others who lived in the other bunkers, and came as occasion drew them to the Fuehrerbunker. Most regular in their attendance were of course Martin Bormann, with his assistant SS Standartenfuehrer Zander and his secretary Fraeulein Krueger; General Krebs, with his adjutant Major Freytag von Loringhoven and his aide-de-camp Rittmeister Boldt; General Burgdorf, with his assistants Colonel von Below, Lieut Colonel Weiss, and Major Johannmeier; General Weidling, the commandant of the city; Hitler's two pilots, Gruppenfuehrer Baur and Standartenfuehrer Beetz; Brigadefuehrer Mohnke, the commandant of the Chancellery; Artur Axmann, leader of the Hitler Youth, who were defending positions in the city;[1] Werner Naumann, Goebbels' assistant in the Propaganda Ministry; Heinz Lorenz,

---

[1] There were about 1000 *Hitler Jugend* fighting in Berlin. Their main task was to hold the Wannsee bridges against the arrival of Wenck's relieving army. Axmann's command post was at 86 Kaiserdamm until April 26th, and from then until April 30th in the cellar of the Party Chancellery at 64 Wilhelmstrasse.

of the Press Service, who delivered news to the Bunker; Brigadefuehrer Rattenhuber, head of the detective force which watched over the Fuehrer's safety, and Standartenfuehrer Hoegl, his deputy; the officers of the SS Bodyguard; and the liaison-officers Admiral Voss, Gruppenfuehrer Fegelein, and Ambassador Walter Hewel, who represented Doenitz, Himmler, and Ribbentrop. Eleven of these have been captured and interrogated by British or American authorities;[1] and their statements, supplemented by the evidence of less prominent persons, of guards and drivers, clerks and batmen, a casual visitor and a tailor, and checked against documents, diaries, and captured telegrams, have shed what light now illuminates the dark period of Hitler's last week of life.

It is an unsteady light. It could not be otherwise. Though some of the documents are contemporary, the full investigation was not begun till five months had passed, when memories were already beginning to fade, and imagination and conjecture to fill the gaps. On some matters they had never been strong—particularly dates and times. This can hardly surprise us as we envisage the life that was led in those doomed, subterranean bunkers, amid perpetual shelling and bombing, often in total darkness, in which all count of the hours was lost; when meals took place at wayward hours, and the boundaries of night and day had been forgotten. Nevertheless, there are a few certain incidents, a few established facts and dated documents upon which, with careful analysis, the otherwise uncertain sequence of events can be confidently suspended. The coming and going of Ritter von Greim, the telegrams to Doenitz, the news of Himmler's treachery, the signing of Hitler's will, the suicide of Hitler and Eva Braun, the mass escape from the Bunker—these are events which can be ascribed with certainty to days and hours; and the other events whose occasions rest on the fallible testimony of bewildered men, though they cannot be minutely dated or firmly guaranteed, can at least be related

[1] *Viz* Schwaegermann, Frau Christian, Frau Junge, Zander, Fraeulein Krueger, Freytag von Loringhoven, Boldt, Below, Johannmeier, Axmann, Lorenz. Subordinate witnesses are the chauffeur Erich Kempka, the guards Karnau, Mansfeld, and Poppen, the batman Matthiesing, the casual visitor Baroness von Varo, and the tailor Mueller. For full list of sources see *Note on Sources*.

to each other, and to those fixed moments in a probable sequence and interdependency.

Apart from these eleven resident witnesses who have fallen into our hands, we must refer to the two outsiders, whose three-day sojourn in the Bunker was perhaps the most interesting episode in those dull days of siege. On April 24th, a telegram from the Fuehrerbunker arrived in Munich ordering Colonel-General Ritter von Greim[1] to report to the Reich Chancellery. A second telegram required the presence of General Koller, whose message to Goering had precipitated the crisis, and who had now been released from his imprisonment in Obersalzberg, under SS supervision. Koller refused to go. It was meaningless he said, suicidal. Wireless communication with the north had been cut, and no one could learn which aerodromes were fit for landing; he did not intend to fly straight into Russian hands. He had a good excuse, for he had an appointment next day; his health was broken; his morale was low; everything he had heard of life in the Bunker suggested that they were all mad anyway; and he replied that for reasons of health he was unable to come. No such considerations òccurred to Ritter von Greim. Greim was a Luftwaffe officer with a distinguished record; he was also a Nazi, whose acceptance of the Nazi system, even at this hour, is attested by his shrill, insensitive utterances. That night he planned to fly immediately to Rechlin, but his plane was damaged on the ground in an air raid. Next day he turned up at Obersalzberg to visit Koller. The Allies had just raided Obersalzberg from the air, and the place, according to those who saw it in the morning, looked like a landscape on the moon. Hitler's Berghof was half destroyed, Bormann's house destroyed, Goering's house almost entirely gone. General Koller, as usual, was wringing his hands, writing exculpatory reports to the Fuehrer, to the Reich Marshal, to everyone, seeking to explain that the whole incident arose from some misunderstanding and that Goering was guiltless. His

[1] Ritter von Greim was in command of Luftflotte 6, with head-quarters in Munich, Oberfoehring-Freimann. Greim committed suicide after capture on June 24th, 1945; but contemporary evidence from him is included in the diaries of Koller and Schwerin von Krosigk, the interrogation of General Christian, and the statement of Hanna Reitsch.

explanations were in vain. "Greim was more angry with the Reich Marshal than ever before. He condemned him sharply for not staying with the Fuehrer in the Bunker, and was just as savage about his behaviour on April 23rd, which he calls treason. He told me," says Koller, "that I ought not to defend the Reich Marshal." But Koller defended him: "I can understand why he didn't stay in the Bunker. He hadn't a single friend there. He was surrounded by enemies, who instead of helping him, had fought against him and the Luftwaffe in the most malevolent and insidious way for months—one might say, for the last two years. Moreover, what would happen to Germany if all those who were responsible for the conduct of affairs were to lock themselves up in bunkers? It isn't for me to defend the Reich Marshal—he has too many faults for that. He has made my life almost impossible—has treated me abominably, has threatened me with court-martial and death for no reason at all, and has threatened to shoot General Staff officers in front of the assembled General Staff. In spite of all this, I cannot change the facts which happened on April 22nd and 23rd. The Reich Marshal has done nothing that can be called treason."

Koller's protestations were futile; but they have their interest. To Greim, to Christian, to von Below, to the leaders of the Combined General Staff, to Hitler himself,[1] Koller continued to explain the real cause of the incidents which had precipitated the fall of Goering; but neither the condemnation nor the punishment was reversed. Rather, both were accentuated; for in the last days Bormann ordered Goering's execution, and Hitler, in his will, formally denounced him and expelled him from the Party. Clearly the truth was of no interest to those who had condemned him. What they wanted was not justice in this particular incident, but judgment on his whole career; and having secured that judgment, they were no longer interested in the technical details by which it had been secured.

[1] Koller sent a full written report to Hitler by hand of Greim, and Greim reported its delivery. Nevertheless Hitler continued to rail at Goering to the end, and when Greim and Reitsch met Koller at Zell-am-See on May 8th, 1945, they 'attacked the Reich Marshal with coarse insults'. Greim threatened to have Goering shot, and Reitsch begged Koller not to defend him.

On the night of April 25th–26th, Ritter von Greim flew to Rechlin. He was piloted by another exotic character, who accompanied him throughout his last adventures—the celebrated test pilot, Hanna Reitsch.

Hanna Reitsch's account of her last visit to Hitler's Bunker has often been published.[1] It is a dramatic, indeed rhetorical account; since rhetoric tends to discolour facts, its contents can sometimes be doubted and occasionally disproved; and Hanna Reitsch has herself recently disowned it, at least in part and in form. Nevertheless enough of it remains undisputed to serve as corroborative evidence of certain incidents.[2] The authorship of its more lurid passages may be in doubt, but these faults of style and detail are easily detached; and though the motives which inspired Hanna Reitsch to that last visit may be uncertain, one element of her personality remains clear: her courage. The journeys which she made with Greim to and from Berlin were as hazardous and exciting as any that she can have made as a test pilot.

Arriving at Rechlin in the early morning of April 25th–26th, Greim and Reitsch had intended to fly on into Berlin in a helicopter which could land in the gardens of the Reich Chancellery or the streets of the city. They found that only one helicopter was available, and it had been damaged that day. But the sergeant-pilot was there who had piloted Speer on his last visit to the Bunker, and since he had had that experience once, he was ordered to repeat it, and to take Greim into Berlin by the same route. The plane was a Focke Wulf 190; it had room for one passenger only, behind the pilot's seat; but Hanna Reitsch was determined not to miss this last stage of the journey; and since Greim agreed to take her, and she was small, she was stuffed into the tail of the plane through a small emergency opening. Forty fighter planes accompanied them as they hedge-hopped through continuous Russian air attacks towards Gatow, the only Berlin aerodrome still in

[1] In *News Chronicle* December 28th, 29th, and 31st, 1945; *Cornhill Magazine* (Winter, 1946); William L. Shirer, *End of a Berlin Diary*; and several American and German papers.

[2] No use has been made of Hanna Reitsch's interrogation report without explicit indication. For a full discussion of the evidence of this report see Introduction to Second Edition (1950).

German hands. They reached Gatow with only a few shots in the wings; but many of the escorting fighter planes had been lost.

From Gatow Greim tried to telephone to the Chancellery, but it was impossible. Finding a training plane on the aerodrome, he therefore decided to fly into the city, and land on the street within walking distance of the Chancellery. The remainder of the German fighter planes engaged the Russians while Greim took off from the airfield. He was now himself at the controls, and Reitsch was with him as a passenger. They flew at treetop-level towards the Brandenburger Tor.

Below them, in the Grunewald, street fighting was in progress. Within a few minutes heavy Russian fire tore the bottom out of the plane and shattered Greim's right foot. Reitsch leaned over his shoulder to take the controls, and by dodging and squirming close to the ground, brought the plane to rest on the East-West Axis. A passing car was commandeered and Greim was taken to the Chancellery, receiving first-aid on the way. In the Bunker he was taken to Stumpfegger's surgery, and Stumpfegger dressed his injured foot. It was now between six and seven o'clock in the evening of April 26th.

Hitler came into the surgery and welcomed Greim. His face, says Reitsch, showed gratitude for his coming. Even a soldier, he said, had a right to disobey orders which seemed futile and hopeless. He asked Greim if he knew why he had been summoned. Greim did not know. "Because Hermann Goering has betrayed both me and his Fatherland," Hitler explained. "Behind my back he has established connections with the enemy. His action was a mark of cowardice! And against my orders he has sent me a disrespectful telegram, saying that I once named him as my successor, and that now, since I can no longer rule from Berlin, he is ready to rule from Berchtesgaden in my place. He closes the telegram by saying that if he had no answer from me by 9.30 that night,[1] he would take my assent for granted!"

As Hitler spoke, there were tears in his eyes. His head sagged; his face was white; and when he handed Goering's fatal telegram to Greim to read, it fluttered with the trembling of his hands. While Greim read, Hitler watched, breathing

[1] Actually 10 pm.

hard, in short, convulsive puffs. The muscles in his face twitched. Suddenly he screamed:

"An ultimatum! a crass ultimatum! Nothing now remains! nothing is spared me! no loyalty is kept, no honour observed; there is no bitterness, no betrayal that has not been heaped upon me; and now this! It is the end. No injury has been left undone!"[1]

After a pause, Hitler recovered his composure, and told Greim that he had summoned him to declare him Commander-in-Chief of the Luftwaffe, with the rank of Field-Marshal, in succession to Goering. It was for this formality alone that the lives of German airmen, and badly needed machines, had been sacrificed to bring Greim into the Bunker. A telegram would have been sufficient; but Hitler preferred this dramatic, if expensive method, which incidentally imprisoned Greim for three days, bedridden and useless in the Bunker. Day after day planes were sent from Rechlin to bring him out to his new headquarters, now that he had received his commission—for although Greim and Reitsch begged to be allowed to stay in Berlin and atone with their lives for the honour of the Luftwaffe (whatever that may mean), Hitler insisted that they must return; but every plane in turn was shot down by the Russians before it reached Berlin.[2]

That night, Hitler summoned Hanna Reitsch to his own room. His face was lined, and his eyes were glazed by a constant film of moisture. He told her that the cause now seemed hopeless, unless, as he still hoped (and his confidence grew as he mentioned the hope), Wenck's army could advance to relieve the city from the south-west. But if not—if the Russians took

[1] The more vivid passages of this narrative have since been disowned by Frl. Reitsch, but she confirms the general sense. So does Koller, quoting Greim.

[2] The fact that every plane was shot down emerges from a careful reading of Reitsch's narrative, and is explicitly stated by General Christian. Reitsch's statement that a plane which succeeded in landing in Berlin on April 27th was sent back empty since Greim and Reitsch wished to stay in Berlin is inconsistent with the statements of both Christian and Koller, who were responsible for sending such planes. Koller quotes a telephone conversation with Greim on April 27th in which Greim asked for planes to be sent to fetch him away.

the city—then he and Eva Braun had made all plans to commit suicide and to have their bodies consumed by fire; and he gave Hanna Reitsch phials of poison for herself and Greim, to be used in that emergency. There was a melodramatic scene, such as seems to have happened so regularly in the life, or at least in the story, of Hanna Reitsch.

That night Russian shells began to fall on the Chancellery itself, and the inhabitants of the Bunker sat up in various postures of fear and bravado while the vast and solid-seeming superstructure cracked and crashed above their heads. Hanna Reitsch spent most of the night watching at the bedside of Ritter von Greim, and in preparing for their common suicide if the Russians should break in in the morning. They had agreed that they would swallow the poison which Hitler had given them, and then quickly, before it had taken effect, pull the pins from heavy hand-grenades close to their bodies. Thus in one movement they would die of poison and their corpses be blown to pieces. It was not only Hitler and Eva Braun who would go out of the world with a bang.

Meanwhile the unfortunate General Koller was not being allowed to stay in sense and safety at Obersalzberg. His excellent excuses of health, reason, and duty were ignored. In the afternoon of April 26th, he was informed, by Bormann's representative in Berchtesgaden, that whatever the state of his health, he must fly to Berlin and report to the Fuehrer; it was the Fuehrer's personal order. Even a soldier, it seemed, had not the right to disobey orders which seemed futile and hopeless. Koller wrung his hands, telephoned hither and thither, and soliloquized eloquently but indecisively in his diary. How was he to know that the order came from the Fuehrer? How could anyone tell who had signed a telegram? And why had an order from the Fuehrer come through Bormann's office, and not through the Luftwaffe's own representative with the Fuehrer? It was very curious. He thought of the unfortunate Goering, the malevolence of Bormann, and the inadequate protection of mere innocence. But then the whole situation in the Bunker was somewhat curious; in that looking-glass world the Fuehrer's actions were bound to be a little queer; and it certainly seemed, from an order which had arrived in

Munich for General Winter, that Hitler had resumed that full authority over the armed forces which, on April 22nd, he had seemed to renounce. Koller decided after all to fly to Berlin. He had caused one muddle by too original an interpretation, and now he would risk his life rather than trust his judgment. He said goodbye to his family, resisted the dissuasions of his orderly officers, and prepared to go. 'The officers of the staff pulled long faces,' he records; 'they said afterwards that they wouldn't have given a brass farthing for my life, and had believed that Bormann would get rid of me. That would have been easy to do in encircled Berlin. No one need know of it.' In the early hours of the morning Koller landed at Rechlin, prepared to fly on into the city and to land, like Speer and Greim, on the East-West Axis. The accounts he received at Rechlin were discouraging. Since last night, he was told, it was impossible to fly to Berlin. Columns of smoke were rising from the doomed city; all airfields were closed, even Gatow; and a chain of defensive fires blazed along all approaches to the East-West Axis. All agreed that the last plane had visited Berlin; Ritter von Greim and Hanna Reitsch were there for good.

At the headquarters of the Combined General Staff at Fuerstenberg, Koller alternately listened to such gloomy tales, and sought consolation in the distressing matter of the Reich Marshal. He consulted Jodl; Jodl was sympathetic but inconclusive. He consulted Keitel, but Keitel pleaded pressure of work and slid away. He found Himmler, and applied to him for enlightenment. "A bad business," said Himmler ambiguously, and disappeared, expressing a polite hope of conversation at some later time. Then Doenitz arrived for the briefing, and Koller turned to him. "The Grand Admiral said that he was convinced the Reich Marshal's motives had been of the best; but then he cut the conversation short, saying that he must go to lunch. He also said that he wanted to speak to me later, but he left very suddenly." It was all very queer, thought Koller. He had expected these important events to be the main topic of discourse and speculation; "but I got the impression that no one wanted to talk about the affair of the Reich Marshal or about the seriousness of the situation. It had always seemed to me that these people were living on a different planet, and were afraid to open their mouths."

In perplexity of spirit, Koller went to the telephone and spoke to the Fuehrerbunker to report his arrival at Fuerstenberg. The Fuehrer himself had retired and could not be disturbed. He spoke to Ritter von Greim. Greim told him not to attempt to fly to Berlin. The Fuehrer had not ordered it; it was quite unnecessary; and it was probably impossible. Even if it were possible to get in, it would be quite impossible to get out. Greim himself was doomed, lying in bed in the Bunker, with the Fuehrer talking at his bedside. . . .

Koller condoled. He condoled with Greim's plight, his wounds, his unprofitable appointment. He lamented the frustration of their efforts, and philosophized mournfully on the impending fate of Germany. "We shall not be able to work together for long, Herr Feldmarschall," he intoned lugubriously into the telephone; "we cannot make much out of the Luftwaffe now, and the end is approaching." Then he awaited a mournful echo from the Bunker. But the world was full of surprises for General Koller. Life in the Bunker seemed even madder than life in Fuerstenberg. Ritter von Greim, like everyone who had been drawn into the magic circle around Hitler, had been seduced away from his wits by that extraordinary personality. It had happened to them all—it had happened to Stumpfegger, who had forgotten Himmler and Gebhardt and all their interests and was now bowing before a new shrine; it had happened to Burgdorf, the regular officer who had deserted his caste and now, when overcome by wine, danced with Bormann and denounced treacherous field-marshals;[1] it had happened to Hewel,[2] Ribbentrop's liaison

[1] Burgdorf's dance with Bormann took place at a party at Rastenburg at which he committed many indiscretions. There is general agreement about his drinking habits.

[2] Walter Hewel had been an early Nazi. As a boy he had taken part in the Munich *Putsch* of 1923 and like Hitler had been imprisoned in the Landsberg fortress. On his release he had worked as a clerk in an English commercial firm in the Dutch East Indies. He was therefore regarded as an expert in foreign affairs and received the titular rank of 'ambassador'. As Ribbentrop's liaison officer with Hitler he seems to have fallen completely under Hitler's personal influence.

officer; it had happened to Himmler; even the sagacious Speer had not been able to resist that compelling enchantment; and now it had happened to Ritter von Greim. Instead of lugubrious admissions of defeat, Koller was astonished to hear hilarious promises of inevitable victory. "Just you wait," replied the voice of the stricken Field-Marshal. "Don't despair! Everything will be well! The presence of the Fuehrer and his confidence have completely inspired me. This place is as good as a fountain of youth for me!" Koller could not believe his ears. "The whole place is a lunatic-asylum!" he protested to himself. "I simply don't understand it. I often ask myself whether I am really too stupid to follow the spiritual soarings of these people and to recognize the way of salvation. Or perhaps they have a sixth sense and can see things to which we ordinary mortals are blind. One begins to doubt one's own sanity."

Shortly afterwards another telephone call gave Koller another breath from the Bunker. It was the voice of Hanna Reitsch. She wished Koller to give her last message to her family in Salzburg, explaining that she could not refuse Greim's appeal.[1] Then she gave a detailed description of her flight, omitting nothing and repeating everything. In vain Koller sought to stem the flood; nothing would stop her. After twenty minutes he hung up the receiver and left her rhapsodizing into the void. "That was the only line to the Bunker, and it was required for more urgent business."

Nevertheless not everyone in the Bunker was equally mad, or equally inspired by the fountain of youth. On this same day, April 27th, one man at least showed signs of sanity. Unfortunately for him, it is as inadvisable to be sane in a madhouse as mad in a sane world; and such was the experience of Fegelein.

Fegelein was Himmler's personal representative at the Fuehrer's headquarters. Like Himmler, and all the more destestable of the Nazis, he was a Bavarian. He had begun his career as a gentleman of the turf. There the elegancy of his

[1] In fact Greim had not appealed at all; Reitsch had insisted on accompanying him.

horsemanship had excited the admiration of Christian Weber,[1] 'the uncrowned king of Bavaria', who had himself been a groom in a fashionable stable before the favour of the Nazis had raised him to magnificence and the vast increase of his girth had incapacitated him for the saddle. Through the good graces of Weber, Fegelein's promotion had been rapid. He had joined the Waffen SS, and soon had the command of a cavalry division. Lucky in all his enterprises except the last, he attracted Hitler's notice by fortunate successes on the Eastern Front; and in 1944 he succeeded Wolff as Himmler's liaison officer with Hitler. In the same year he achieved what seemed to many his most brilliant success. Observing, with the keen eye of the opportunist, that the centre of power in the Nazi hierarchy had left the cabinet and the ministries for the court and the levée, he married Gretl, the sister of Eva Braun. Thus, at what seemed the most favourable moment, he detached himself from sole dependence on the fortunes of Himmler, now beginning to wane, and secured his position in the family circle of the Fuehrer. At the same time he did not omit to protect his rear by a judicious alliance with Bormann. From that time onwards, in the words of one who was well qualified to judge,[2] 'he thoroughly betrayed Himmler to the Fuehrer', whose side he rarely left.[3] It was he, says Schellenberg, who advised Hitler publicly to dishonour the SS division which had been massacred in a hopeless effort to conform to the Fuehrer's strategy—an insult which the soldiers never forgave to Himmler, who had been powerless to prevent it.[4] He was, says Speer, "a very unpleasant type," and exercised "a pernicious and radical influence" at court; and the loyal subordinates of

[1] Weber, one of the most corrupt and fraudulent of the Nazi bosses, was President of the municipal council of Munich. He amassed a colossal fortune by various forms of privileged speculation. The stables which he built for his ten racehorses (some of them looted from French racing stables) have been described as 'a horses' paradise'. He was murdered during the Bavarian rising of April–May 1945.

[2] Ohlendorf.

[3] According to Berger, 'Bormann, Fegelein, and Burgdorf formed a very close circle round Hitler, and it was hardly possible for an outsider to penetrate it, especially after the attempt on his life.' Speer has said the same.

[4] See above, p. 133, n.1.

Himmler—men not unfamiliar with the infinite varieties of human depravity—are unanimous in their delineations of the vices of Fegelein.

Nevertheless, if Fegelein was a cad, he was not a fool; or at least not such a fool as Ritter von Greim. His actions, his loyalties, his betrayals, had always been inspired by a calculated, almost intellectual self-interest, quite unencumbered by principles or scruples. If he had deserted Himmler for Hitler, that was not because he, like so many less critical spirits, had been bewitched by that hypnotic influence; it was because Himmler was losing his value and the personal court of Hitler promised more advantages to a resourceful climber. His allegiance, his alliances, his marriage—all these had been based upon expediency: they were the methods by which he hoped to share the privileges of the family circle. But on April 25th, when Fegelein returned to the Bunker from his last visit to the outside world,[1] it was clear to that lucid mind that the privileges of the family circle were becoming daily less enviable; for the declarations of Hitler and Eva Braun on that subject had been painfully explicit. Fegelein did not hesitate. He had not secured his adoption into the family circle merely in order to burn on the family pyre. Leaving the other inhabitants of the Bunker to cluster hysterically round the Fuehrer and beg participation in the sacrament of his death,[2] Fegelein seized a favourable opportunity, slipped unnoticed out of the Bunker, and disappeared.

From the timeless records of the Bunker, and the dark, lugubrious secrecy in which the whole episode was enclosed, it is impossible now to extract with certainty the dates and stages of this last, uncharacteristic episode in the life of Fegelein: his failure. His ordinary residence in the Chancellery was not in the Fuehrerbunker, but in one of the other two

[1] Fegelein had left Berlin by car, with SS Hstuf. Bornholdt of the *SS Begleitkommando* to visit Ogruf. Juettner, head of the *SS Fuehrungshauptamt*, at Fuerstenberg. On April 25th return by car was impossible, and Fegelein had flown back, leaving Bornholdt at Fuerstenberg. (Statement by Bornholdt.) Fegelein's last words to Juettner had been, 'I certainly don't intend to die in Berlin' (Juettner).

[2] At least this is the picture ascribed to Hanna Reitsch, although less rhetorical witnesses have not recorded the same details.

bunkers, and his disappearance was for some time unnoticed by Hitler's immediate *entourage*. Occasional telephone calls, in which he asked for the latest news, were at any rate evidence that he was still in Berlin; and they inquired no further. It was apparently on April 27th, late in the afternoon, that Hitler demanded his presence and learnt that Fegelein was no longer in the Chancellery. Inquiries were made. None knew whither he had gone. In that unnatural atmosphere suspicion was quickly aroused, and once aroused, became certainty. Suspicion was anyway part of Hitler's nature now. It had become chronic after the Generals' Plot, and every recent experience had confirmed it. At once he went for the head of his personal police guard, the trained detectives who shadowed him and every other high Nazi leader. This officer, SS Standartenfuehrer Hoegl, was ordered to go out into the city, taking with him a party of armed guards from the SS Escort.[1] He was to find Fegelein, and to bring him back into the Bunker. Hoegl went out into the Charlottenburg area of Berlin, where Fegelein lived, and there, in his own house, found him quietly resting on his bed, in civilian clothes. Free at last, as he thought, from the safe but stormy atmosphere of the Bunker, Fegelein was able, in this more civilized *milieu*, quietly and dispassionately to survey the world; to compare, in philosophical detachment, the relative advantages of life and death, and to choose, freely, the alternative which seemed more attractive to his opportunist mind. He explained to

[1] Hitler had two distinct guards: (1) *Reichssicherheitsdienst* (*RSD*) an organization under the command of Brigf. Rattenhuber (who remained in the Bunker), which consisted of separate units (*Dienststellen*) allocated to the personal protection of high Nazi leaders. *Dienststelle* 1 of this organization, under the command of SS Staf. Hoegl, was Hitler's personal guard, and was at this time partly at Obersalzberg, partly in the Bunker. The *RSD* guard was composed of trained detectives from the Criminal Police (*Kripo*), who also (since the whole German police was under Himmler) held SS ranks. The guards who witnessed the burning of Hitler's body came from this force. (2) The *SS Begleitkommando* or Escort, under the command of SS Ostuf. Franz Schedle. This was a purely military guard, consisting of smart and loyal, but unintelligent soldiers, who kept watch over official buildings and were regarded with some disdain by the more observant but less obtrusive *RSD*.

Hoegl that he had chosen survival, and suggested that, with his assistance, an airplane might be found to take him away from the doomed city to his wife and pleasant family life in Bavaria. This suggestion aroused no response from the obedient Hoegl. No such arrangement was thinkable, he replied, without the explicit authority of the Fuehrer. Fegelein was not dismayed. Picking up the telephone, he put through another call to the Bunker and spoke to his sister-in-law, Eva Braun. There had been a misunderstanding, he explained; would she smooth the matter over, use her influence with the Fuehrer, and obtain the necessary sanction? Alas, the cool exercise of the intelligence, which could so easily be indulged in the free, if somewhat sulphurous atmosphere of Charlottenburg, was quite impossible in the cramped, subterranean Bunker of the Chancellery, where threats and promises, preachings and protestations, high-pitched oratory and meaningless generalities (if we are to believe Hanna Reitsch) excluded all rational noises. Eva Braun replied curtly that such a proposal could not be considered; Fegelein must return to the Bunker; and while Fegelein was marched back to the Chancellery under armed guard, she wrung her hands at yet another betrayal. "Poor, poor Adolf!" she would declare, "deserted by everyone, betrayed by all! Better that ten thousand others die than that he be lost to Germany!" The Fuehrer was spared nothing, she said sadly; Goering had wickedly betrayed him; and now, at the end of his life, he had been deserted even by his old and trusted friend Fegelein. On his return, Fegelein was degraded from his rank of Gruppenfuehrer and kept, for the time being, under armed guard in the second bunker.[1]

That night, the night of April 27th–28th, the Russian bombardment of the Chancellery reached its highest pitch. To those who cowered in the Bunker and heard the shells falling above them, the accuracy seemed deadly; every shell, it seemed, fell exactly in the centre of the Chancellery buildings. At any moment they now expected the Russian ground troops to

[1] Details from Frl. Krueger (quoting Beetz) and von Below. The exclamation of Eva Braun is ascribed to Reitsch, who now says that the words were to that effect, though not exactly as given.

arrive and overrun the ruins. During the night (if we are to believe the report of Hanna Reitsch), Hitler called his court around him, and in this macabre conclave all rehearsed their plans for suicide and considered, in maudlin detail, the various methods in which their corpses might be destroyed. The first appearance of Russian soldiers, they agreed, would be the signal for the execution of this ritual self-sacrifice. Then everyone made a short speech, swearing perpetual allegiance to the Fuehrer and Germany. If such was really the climate of the Bunker, few sensible people will blame the prudent decision of Fegelein.

In fact, of course, it was mostly humbug: the artificial emotion and corresponding verbiage so easily generated, and once generated so easily accepted as both true and moving, by the immature Teutonic mind. The competitive servility of a court is always odious; combined with eloquent humbug, it is nauseating. In fact, as will appear, very few of those who thus professed a desire for communal death gave effect to their heroic resolutions. Ritter von Greim, it is true, when a month had passed and his untended wound made further movement impossible, swallowed his poison in captivity; and one or two others may possibly have done the same in Russian hands. But it is interesting to reflect how many whose resolve to die has been recorded have since been found in continued health and restored sanity, eagerly explaining to their British and American captors that they never really owed any allegiance to Nazi Germany.

Of Hitler at least it can be said that his emotions were genuine. He at least intended to die if Berlin fell. And yet—such was the extraordinary confidence which still alternated with his despair—even now he still believed that the city might be saved. Though he was prepared to die if it fell, nevertheless it seemed impossible that the capital of the Reich really could fall with the Fuehrer inside it. He regarded himself, it seems, as a kind of palladium, a totem whose presence rendered any citadel impregnable, so long as he stayed. "If I leave East Prussia," he had told Keitel at Rastenburg, "then East Prussia will fall; if I stay, it will be held." Keitel had persuaded him to leave East Prussia, and East Prussia had duly fallen; but he did not intend to leave Berlin, and Berlin therefore could not fall. So he deluded himself as he held out, in an ever-contracting pocket of the city, awaiting the arrival of Wenck's army, for which the Hitler Youth were desperately holding the bridgeheads on the Havel. Wenck's army was in fact already a defeated force; but Hitler had long been accustomed, from underground bunkers, to direct the operations of non-existent armies, to dictate their strategy and tactics, dispose their forces, calculate their gains, and then to denounce the treachery of their generals when the actual results failed to correspond with his private conclusions. So in these days he would expound the tactics whereby Wenck would relieve the city. Pacing up and down in the Bunker (according to the dramatic report of Hanna Reitsch[1]) he would wave a road map, fast decomposing with the sweat of his hands, and explain to any casual visitor the complicated military operations whereby they would all be saved. Sometimes he would shout orders, as if himself directing the defenders; sometimes he would spread the map on the table, and stooping over it, with trembling hands he would arrange and rearrange a set of buttons, as consolatory symbols of relieving armies. In the tropical climate of a court, emotions and beliefs quickly change their direction. No one except Hitler still believed in Wenck's army, but no one disagreed with his assurances; and in a moment of time the chorus which had been chanting *lamentoso*, the dirge of despair and suicide, would suddenly break out *allegro vivace*, with a triumphant welcome for the army of Wenck.[2]

The most obstinate illusions are ultimately broken by facts. On April 28th the Russians were already fighting near the centre of Berlin, and still there were no signs of Wenck.

[1] Hanna Reitsch is now much less dramatic on this point.

[2] Hans Fritzsche, head of the radio department of the Propaganda Ministry, described at Nuremberg (June 27th, 1946) how 'in the days when Berlin was surrounded by the Russian Army, the people of Berlin was told that a relief army, the Wenck army, was marching on Berlin . . . and leaflets were printed in Berlin containing approximately this text: "Soldiers of the Wenck army, we Berliners know that you have reached Potsdam. Hurry! Help us!"' These leaflets were scattered in Berlin, as if by mistake, to raise the morale of the citizens.

Hysterical telegrams began to flow outward from the Bunker. 'I expect the relief of Berlin', Hitler wired to Keitel. 'What is Heinrici's army doing? Where is Wenck? What is happening to the Ninth Army? When will Wenck and the Ninth Army join?'[1] All day the inhabitants of the Bunker waited for news, and since none came, repeated rumours instead. What could be the explanation of Wenck's failure? One explanation, the obvious, the true explanation, was that Wenck's army, as a fighting force, no longer existed; but obvious truth was unlikely to be heard among the conflicting noises of the Bunker. There only one explanation could be entertained. Whatever the problem, the answer was always the same: it was treachery. As the day proceeded, this explanation seemed more obvious. Communication with the outer world was diminishing; only the radio-telephone to the Combined General Staff still served as a channel of information, but could even Keitel now be trusted? At eight o'clock that night Bormann sent a telegram which vividly illustrates the temper now prevailing in the beleaguered Bunker. It was sent to Admiral von Puttkamer in Munich, to be relayed to Doenitz. 'Instead of urging the troops forward to our rescue with orders and appeals', it ran, 'the men in authority are silent. Treachery seems to have replaced loyalty! We remain here. The Chancellery is already in ruins.' An hour later authentic news at last reached the Bunker from the outside world. It was brought over from the Propaganda Ministry by the official of the Press Service whose duty it was to translate and deliver to the Fuehrerbunker such items of foreign news as seemed important. This official was Heinz Lorenz, and the news which be brought was the news of Himmler's negotiations with Count Bernadotte. There had been a leakage to the Press.

[1] Keitel has given the text of this telegram from memory, saying that he received it at Waren on April 28th. (It is possible that he has mistaken the date, as his dates are sometimes incorrect; but I have given him the benefit of the doubt.) Generaloberst Gotthard Heinrici had succeeded Himmler in command of the Army Group Vistula, now fighting west of Berlin.

CHAPTER SIX

ET TU BRUTE

SINCE he had left Luebeck after his last meeting with
Bernadotte, Himmler had thought no more of his, or
rather Schellenberg's complicated conspiracies; those he had
left to Schellenberg, who, for the next three days, waited
eagerly in Flensburg and Denmark, his delicate antennae
quivering in the direction of Stockholm, ever ready to catch
the first faint message of success. Thence, on April 27th,
Bernadotte had returned, bringing with him the news which
the head of any but a Nazi intelligence service might have
expected: that neither Himmler nor a limited surrender was
acceptable to the Western Powers. With a sinking heart
Schellenberg had heard the news of this, to him, quite unexpected failure. For so long now he had admired his own
subtlety, his diplomatic virtuosity and Swedish connections,
that it had never occurred to him that he would fail utterly.
He had staked his reputation, and Himmler's, on success.
How could he now face Himmler, whom he had so pertinaci-
ously and (as it now appeared) so indefensibly forced into this
false and vulnerable position? He was relieved when Bernadotte offered to accompany him into Himmler's presence and
give him countenance; but when he telephoned to Himmler's
office and explained to Dr Brandt, Himmler's secretary, that
the result had been negative, and that Count Bernadotte was
anxious to come and see Himmler, the answer was an absolute
refusal. Himmler had seen quite enough of Count Bernadotte,
and never wished to see him again.

Trembling with apprehension, Schellenberg made diplomatic excuses to Bernadotte, and then set out alone to face
his master. On the way, he reflected on the reception he was
likely to have. His thoughts were gloomy; but once again his
ever-resourceful diplomacy came to his aid. 'As I knew,' he
writes, 'that my position with Himmler was now very difficult,

and that in certain circumstances I must expect to be liquidated, I hit on the idea of sending for an astrologer from
Hamburg, personally known to Himmler, whom I took with
me, in order that an astrological session might absorb some
of the bitterness of disappointment; for I knew that Himmler
had a great opinion of this particular gentleman.'[1] By such
ingenious expedients did the high politicians of the Third
Reich lubricate their personal diplomacy. It is agreeable to
record that when Schellenberg faced Himmler, in the early
hours of April 29th, he was not liquidated, although his
situation had now become even worse, since the news of the
negotiations had by this time become public. Himmler was
not unnaturally irritated, and expressed bitter disappointment.
He saw that nothing but ill could come of the whole business;
he feared that his letter to the Swedish Foreign Minister
would now be published; he pointed to the consequences
which this affair would have in his relations with Hitler; and
he blamed Schellenberg as the moving spirit in the whole
matter. 'Nevertheless,' records the complacent Schellenberg,
'I managed, with the help of the aforementioned astrologer,
to put forward the proposals for a more limited solution so
convincingly that he withdrew for an hour to think it
over.' Ultimately Himmler agreed to pursue this more
limited solution, which entailed a cessation of hostilities
in Norway and Denmark, and instructed Schellenberg
accordingly. He did this the more confidently because he
still felt sure of the future. Hitler was taking a long time to
die, but the end must come soon; and then, as the new
Fuehrer, Himmler would have power to make all necessary
decisions.

For all this time it had never occurred to Himmler to doubt
that he was the heir-apparent to Hitler's throne. He was
Reichsfuehrer; he had his private army; his numerous offices,
his long record, his hitherto undisputed loyalty all emphasized
his claims; and one reason why he would never conspire to
seize power lay in his confidence that it would automatically
devolve upon him. He even had a programme prepared for
the occasion—though not of course by himself; such origin-

[1] The astrologer was of course Wulf. Cf. above, p. 129.

ality was not within his narrow faculties. He contemplated a new party, for which Schellenberg had obligingly supplied a name—the Party of National Union;[1] and he had a shadow government composed of high police leaders and others who, like Schellenberg, believed that a government headed by Himmler could both survive and enable them to survive under the favour of the Western Allies.[2] Among these optimists we must include the murderous Ohlendorf and the asinine Schwerin von Krosigk; neither the record of the one, nor the intellect of the other, was considered incompatible with political office under the rule of the supreme crank and prime criminal of the Nazi system.

Such illusions may seem to us desperate; but it was not only Himmler's subordinates who entertained them. Almost every Nazi recognized in Himmler the natural successor to Hitler, once Goering had fallen. On the very day when his relations with Bernadotte were published, Himmler described to one of his followers how he intended to exercise his new authority, adding that he had spoken to Doenitz, and that Doenitz, who equally regarded Himmler as Fuehrer-designate, had volunteered to work under his command.[3] On the same day, Schwerin von Krosigk discussed the same question with two of Doenitz's supporters. Since both Goering and Hess were out of the question, they agreed, there were three possibilities. Either Hitler would make no alteration in his so-called 'will',[4] in which case only Himmler would fulfil the conditions of inheritance; or Hitler would alter his will—and then, they agreed, he could name only Himmler as his successor; or the decision would be left to the emergency provision of the constitution—but when they considered what that would entail, they found that it only led to Himmler again. Even two days later, when Himmler's negotiations were known throughout the world, Speer and others were solemnly

[1] *Nationale Sammlungspartei.*
[2] This shadow government is mentioned by Ohlendorf and Speer as well as by Schellenberg.
[3] Ohlendorf.
[4] This does not of course refer to the testament of April 29th, which was not known in Ploen, but to Hitler's pre-war declaration.

discussing the same problem, and agreeing that there was no conceivable alternative to Himmler.[1]

Like so many in those last days, they forgot that Hitler was not yet dead. Besieged in the shattered capital, cooped up fifty feet below the ground, cut off from ordinary communication, a physical and mental wreck, without power to enforce, or reason to persuade, or machinery to execute, Hitler still remained, in the universal chaos he had caused, the sole master whose orders were implicitly obeyed. Goering, imprisoned under an SS guard at Mautendorf, now had leisure to reflect on the dangers of anticipating that fatal inheritance. Soon Himmler was to learn the same lesson. The power of the Fuehrer was a magic power, and no profane hand might reach out to touch it until the reigning priest was really dead.

We turn our attention therefore back to the underground Bunker whither Lorenz had brought from the Propaganda Ministry the British Reuter report of Himmler's negotiations with Count Bernadotte. In the Bunker, Lorenz found Bormann, Goebbels, and Hewel sitting together, and to them he gave one copy of the text. They told him that Hitler was in conference with Ritter von Greim. He therefore gave a second copy to Heinz Linge, Hitler's personal servant, to be handed to the Fuehrer.

The scene which followed the delivery of that note has been variously described, according to the opportunities of knowledge, and the resources of vocabulary, possessed by the various witnesses of it. All agreed that it was a dramatic scene. Hitler was white with indignation. This was the last, the unkindest cut of all: *der treue Heinrich*—faithful Heinrich—had betrayed him; the one Nazi leader whose loyalty had always been above suspicion had now stabbed him in the back. As the news spread round the Bunker, the obedient chorus again echoed the voice of its leader, and men and women competed to denounce the traitor. Then Hitler withdrew with Bormann and Goebbels behind locked doors and a conference began.

What occurred, or was decided, at that conference we shall probably never know in detail. The participants are all dead

[1] Schwerin von Krosigk.

or missing; and although Krebs and Burgdorf may afterwards have been called in, they are missing too. But from that moment the events in the Bunker acquired a new momentum; the period of waiting for Wenck was followed by a period of decision and action comparable with the crisis of April 22nd; the last phase of the comedy had begun.

There can be no doubt that to Hitler the treachery of Himmler, as he conceived it to be, was the signal for the end. Always he had hesitated before his decisions; he had wavered and waited, and by his wavering had perplexed his impatient followers; then he had made his decision, and it had been final. He had wavered for two days before deciding whether to stay in Berlin or not, and then he had decided to stay, and had stayed, and no pressure, no persuasion had shaken that decision. After that he had waited for a week before deciding how to make an end of it; now he faced that decision. During the night of April 28th–29th he disposed finally of Himmler's claim to the succession; he wrote his last will and testament; and he married Eva Braun.

First he sent for Fegelein. Since the incredible news of Himmler's defection had been brought to him, old problems had suddenly assumed a new complexion. Now he realized why the Steiner attack had failed on April 21st; Himmler had never meant that it should succeed and had ordered Steiner not to move. Now he knew why Fegelein had deserted from the Bunker; it was part of an elaborate SS plot. Fegelein was closely questioned, apparently by Gruppenfuehrer Mueller, head of the Gestapo.[1] It is said that he admitted to a knowledge that Himmler had had meetings with Count Bernadotte. That may easily be true, for Himmler's meetings with Bernadotte were no more secret than those of Kaltenbrunner or Ribbentrop. Whatever he may have known or admitted, he

---

[1] Mueller is mentioned by Frau Junge, Kempka and Axmann as having conducted the examination of Fegelein and others have referred to his appearance in the Bunker during the last days; but the whole Fegelein incident is somewhat obscure. As a high SS officer, Mueller might have been suspect after Himmler's treachery; but his position was by now almost independent of Himmler, and he was never trusted by Himmler's other subordinates.

can hardly have confessed (as overheated minds afterwards imagined) to a plot by Himmler to murder Hitler, for no such plot existed. Though some high members of the SS had envisaged such a plot,[1] Himmler, as we have seen, had never countenanced it; only the wishful thinking of Schellenberg had made him so imagine. And though Steiner himself desired negotiation with the West, the failure of his attack needs no political explanation and certainly was not intended by Himmler, who believed in its necessity.[2] Nevertheless it was not justice that Hitler required, but revenge. Himmler's defection, he declared,[3] was the worst act of treachery he had ever known; Fegelein's attempted escape was in itself sufficiently criminal; and he wanted blood. Dr Brandt had escaped his clutches at the last minute: Fegelein should not. After a brief formality, Fegelein was taken out of the Bunker by guards of the Escort, led into the Chancellery garden, and shot.[4]

Relieved by this incident of blood-letting, Hitler turned aside to consider the military situation. Russian tanks had now been reported in the Potsdamer Platz, and Greim was ordered to ensure that every available plane was sent forward to attack them. Greim gave his orders to General Christian by telephone; but more personal supervision would soon be possible. For on April 28th, after nearly three days of imprisonment in the Bunker and against all expectation, a plane had at last made its way into Berlin to take the new commander-in-chief of the Luftwaffe back to his operational headquarters.

[1] Apart from Schellenberg, such a coup was certainly contemplated by certain other police and SS leaders (including Steiner, Ohlendorf, Gottberg, and Hildebrant); but it seems never to have developed beyond the stage of loose talk.

[2] Steiner's political views are given by Ohlendorf, but it is clear from Schellenberg's complaints that Himmler believed in the necessity of the Steiner attack, and intended it to succeed. 'Himmler was still,' he says (on April 22nd), 'convinced of the necessity of this order of the Fuehrer [ie for the attack], while I agreed with his military adjutant Grothmann that it was an unnecessary spilling of blood. My protests were ignored, as I was supposed to understand nothing of military matters.

[3] To Axmann.

[4] See note on *The Execution of Fegelein*, p. 277.

It was an Arado 96 training plane, and the sergeant-pilot who had brought it in from Rechlin had circled down from a height of 13,000 feet to land it upon the East-West Axis.

Shortly after midnight, Hitler came into Greim's room to convey to him his last orders. His face was white, and sitting on the edge of the bed he explained to Greim the twofold nature of his mission. Firstly, he was to mount an attack by the Luftwaffe against those Russian positions from which the assault on the Chancellery would be made. With the help of the Luftwaffe, Wenck might yet force his way to Berlin. Secondly, he must order the arrest of the treacherous Himmler. As he mentioned that name, Hitler's voice became more unsteady, and his lips and hands trembled. "A traitor must never succeed me as Fuehrer," he shouted; "you must go out to ensure that he does not?"

Both Greim and Reitsch protested; they wished to stay; the attempt, they said, would be futile; they would never reach Rechlin. . . . But Hitler insisted that they must go. It was the only chance of success. To this Greim yielded; but Hanna Reitsch continued her expostulations, and left the Bunker, as she had entered it, in a profusion of tears, rhetoric, and abstract nouns. With her she carried hastily-written letters from the inhabitants of the Bunker—official letters from Hewel to the headquarters of the Foreign Office at Schloss Fuschl, near Salzburg, and from Bormann to the Party Chancery at Obersalzberg, and private letters from Goebbels and his wife to her son, and from Eva Braun to her sister Frau Fegelein. Goebbels' letter contained some fine phrases about his exemplary devotion to the Fuehrer's pure and holy cause. The letter from Eva Braun does not survive. It was, says Hanna Reitsch, 'so vulgar, so theatrical, and in such poor, adolescent taste' that its survival could only do harm; and she tore it up. In this eloquent, egotistical letter it is to be observed (if Hanna Reitsch has remembered the text aright) that no reference was made to the health of Frau Fegelein's husband, whose body, at the time of writing, was being buried in the Chancellery garden.

When Greim left the Bunker, he carried with him one consolation for his wounded spirit. For many months Hitler had stormed at the incompetence and cowardice of the high command of the Luftwaffe, had insulted its officers, demanded the impossible, and threatened savage revenge. Now that Goering had gone, his resentment seemed to have evaporated too. To Greim he praised the Luftwaffe with particular and redeeming emphasis; it had fought best of all the Armed Forces, he said, from the beginning to the end. Even the enemy had allowed that everybody, even the ground personnel, had fought with exceptional bravery. For its technical inferiority others, he said pointedly, were to blame. He even, in the course of this *amende honorable*, threw a dewdrop to poor old General Koller, who had so often wrung his hands unavailingly under the torrent of inspired abuse that had formerly been discharged upon that universal scapegoat, the Chief of Staff of the Luftwaffe.[1]

The later history of Greim and Reitsch can be shortly described. They flew out of Berlin, as they had entered it, amid scenes of destruction and experiences of danger which lose nothing of dramatic property in the narrative of Hanna Reitsch. Explosions tossed the plane to and fro like a feather, till they had climbed to a height of 20,000 feet, and, looking down, could see Berlin like a sea of flame beneath them. From Rechlin Greim gave his orders for all available aircraft to support the relief of Berlin. Thence they flew on to Ploen, to Doenitz' headquarters; and we are favoured with a graphic, but perhaps inaccurate, account of an interview between Hanna Reitsch and Himmler, in which the loyal denunciations of the stage heroine glanced ineffectually away from the hard, cold skin of the stage villain, until a dramatic air raid terminated the argument. After a few days at Ploen, Greim and Reitsch, the wounded hero and the devoted heroine, set out on their travels again, flying to Koeniggraetz, to Graz, to Zell-am-See, with patriotic messages for Schoerner and Kesselring. At Zell-am-See they met the plodding General Koller; and from his more pedestrian pen we have a last glimpse of this curious couple—Greim, now a total wreck, his skin

---

[1] Greim, quoted by Koller (May 8th, 1945). Part of the foregoing account, which is based largely on the statements of Greim (to Koller) and Reitsch, is also confirmed by von Below.

yellow, hobbling on two crutches; Reitsch tenacious and tear-
ful; and both singing their tedious duet, now a ferocious
denunciation of Goering, now a devout litany about the
Fuehrer and the Fatherland. "In these circumstances," complained Koller, "it is very difficult to discuss practical matters."

After the dismissal of Ritter von Greim,[1] Hitler turned to
the next item of business. He married Eva Braun. For this
symbolic ceremony, Goebbels had introduced into the Bunker
a certain Walter Wagner, a Gau Inspector who worked under
him in his capacity of Gauleiter of Berlin, and who, having an
honorary position as an official of the city administration, was
therefore considered a proper person to officiate at this civil
ceremony. He appeared in the Bunker, where he was completely unknown except to Goebbels, in the uniform of the
Nazi Party and the armband of the Volkssturm. The ceremony
took place in the small conference room or 'map room' in the
private part of the Bunker.[2] Besides Hitler, Eva Braun, and
Walter Wagner, Goebbels and Bormann were present as
witnesses. The formalities were brief. The two parties declared
that they were of pure Aryan descent and were free from
hereditary disease. In consequence of the military situation
and other extraordinary circumstances, they proposed a wartime wedding, by simple word of mouth, and without any
delay. In a few minutes the parties had given assent, the
register had been signed, and the ceremony was over. When
the bride came to sign her name she began to write 'Eva
Braun', but was checked before completing it. Striking out the
initial letter B, she corrected it to 'Eva Hitler, *née* Braun'.
The ceremony over, the bride and bridegroom walked out

[1] Both Greim and Reitsch disowned any knowledge of the marriage,
which I have therefore placed after their departure. Since they were
actually in the Fuehrerbunker, it is inconceivable that it could have
taken place without their knowledge; and it seems certain from several
sources that they left soon after midnight. Zander and Lorenz both
say that the marriage took place between 0100 and 0300 in the morning;
and the marriage certificate itself is clearly dated April 29th (*ie* after
midnight). In these circumstances I have rejected the statements of
von Below, Fraeulein Krueger, and Frau Christian that the ceremony
took place before midnight.

[2] Room 21 in the diagram (p. 150).

into the conference passage. There a few generals and secretaries were waiting. They shook hands with all in turn, and then withdrew into their private apartments for a wedding breakfast. Shortly afterwards, Bormann, Goebbels, Frau Goebbels, and Hitler's two secretaries, Frau Christian and Frau Junge, were invited into the private suite. There they sat for some hours, drinking champagne and talking. The conversation was of old times and old comrades, of Goebbels' marriage which Hitler had witnessed, in happier days; now the position of the parties was reversed, and the happiness was reversed too. Hitler spoke again of his plans of suicide. National Socialism was finished, he said, and would never revive; death would be a relief to him now that he had been deceived and betrayed by his best friends. A temporary gloom overcame the party; and one of the secretaries left the room. There was a good deal of coming and going, for it was a long session, and there was other business to be done. For part of the time Krebs and Burgdorf and von Below came in and joined the party, and Guensche, the SS adjutant, and Fraeulein Manzialy, the vegetarian cook; and for some time Hitler was absent with Frau Junge in an adjoining room, to which other members of the party were also occasionally summoned. He was dictating his will.[1]

Thus, after many years, Eva Braun's position was at last defined. The ambiguity of her status was at last terminated; and when a servant, in a moment of crisis next day, broke the ban on speech with 'E. B.', and addressed her as 'Gnaediges Fraeulein', she could at last answer, "You may safely call me Frau Hitler."[2]

The reasons which impelled Hitler to this belated ceremony are unknown; but they may be conjectured without great fear of error. It was clearly Eva Braun's wish to be married. She had long been embarrassed by her undefined position at court, and would have welcomed such a solution long ago had Hitler been prepared to countenance it. But Hitler was unwilling.

---

[1] This account of the wedding ceremony is taken from the statements of Fraeulein Krueger, Frau Christian, Frau Junge, Zander, Lorenz, von Below; and from the evidence of the certificate.

[2] Karnau.

Presumably he wished to avoid the imputation of humanity which the acknowledgment of wife or mistress would entail. At the end, he had not wished for her presence, and when she arrived in Berlin for the last time on April 15th, he had tried, ineffectually, to send her away. But since she had stayed, she was entitled to her reward. Her loyalty had increased her claims to consideration. Hitler had said that only she would remain faithful to him at the end, and she had not failed to justify his intuition. As all others fell away, her devotion became more conspicuous and more regarded. In conversation with his personal adjutants, Hitler contrasted her fidelity with the gross treachery of Goering and Himmler in whom he had trusted.[1] Signal devotion deserves signal recognition; and there is no doubt what recognition she most desired—the status which would separate her from all other women of the court and would entitle her to that honour which she now most affected, of sharing in the ritual death of the Fuehrer. It was an easy request; at this last hour there was little danger of misinterpretation; and it was granted.

Meanwhile, in the intervals of the social gathering which followed the wedding, Hitler was continuing the succession of business which preoccupied him throughout this active night. He had sent for his secretary, Frau Junge, and was dictating two documents: his personal and his political testaments, which should be his final appeal to posterity and the textual basis of the Nazi myth.

Since this was clearly their purpose, these documents are extraordinarily interesting; for in this last advertisement of the Nazi movement, designed as a dignified valediction to the world and a message to later generations, there is nothing but the old hollow claptrap, the negative appeal, the purposeless militarism, of the Revolution of Destruction; the protestations of innocence, and the recriminations of failure.

The political testament is in two parts; the first general, the second particular. 'It is untrue that I, or anybody else in Germany, wanted war in 1939. It was wanted and provoked exclusively by those international politicians who either came of Jewish stock, or worked for Jewish interests. After all my

[1] von Below.

offers of disarmament, posterity cannot place the responsibility for this war on me. . . .' The mind goes back from the testament to *Mein Kampf*, from the epitaph to the prospectus of the Nazi Party, from the disclaimer of responsibility for defeat to the promise of glorious victory. Then comes the cry of despair. 'After a six-years' war, which in spite of all setbacks will one day go down in history as the most glorious and heroic manifestation of a people's will to live, I cannot forsake the city which is the capital of this state. Since our forces are too small to withstand any longer the enemy's attack on this place, and since our own resistance will be gradually worn down by an army of blind automata, I wish to share the fate that millions of others have accepted and to remain here in the city. Further, I will not fall into the hands of an enemy who requires a new spectacle, exhibited by the Jews, to divert his hysterical masses. I have therefore decided to remain in Berlin, and there to choose death voluntarily at the moment when I believe that the residence of the Fuehrer and Chancellor can no longer be held. . . .' Then the valediction to those forces on which the Nazi Party had relied is coupled with a sidelong stab at the force which he charged with failure: 'In future may it be a point of honour with German Army officers, as it already is in our Navy, that the surrender of territory and towns is impossible, and that, above all else, commanders must set a shining example of faithful devotion to duty until death.' In the first World War, Hitler was a soldier; and when it failed, he blamed the politicians for betraying the soldiers. In those days he could not praise the German General Staff highly enough. 'The organization and leadership of the German Army was the mightiest thing that the world has ever yet seen.' In the second World War he was a politician; when it failed, he blamed the soldiers for betraying the politicians, and all for betraying him.

After the generalities, the particulars. The second part of the political testament, like the first, is stronger in recrimina-tion and negation than in positive statement. 'Before my death,' it begins, 'I expel from the Party the former Reich Marshal, Hermann Goering, and withdraw from him all the rights conferred upon him by the Decree of June 29th 1941, and by my Reichstag speech of September 1st 1939. In his place I appoint Grand Admiral Doenitz as Reich President and Supreme Commander of the Armed Forces.'

It was now clear what had been decided behind the locked doors of the Fuehrerbunker after the news of Himmler's treachery had been brought. The question of the succession was at last resolved. Since the politicians had betrayed him, and the Army had betrayed him, and the SS had betrayed him, a sailor should succeed. The Navy, if its operations had not always been spectacular, at least was always Nazi. 'In future may it be a point of honour with German Army officers, *as it already is in our Navy . . .*' In that phrase Hitler had found the solution to the problem which had so long seemed insoluble.

The next paragraph is in form like its predecessor. It concerns the other arch-traitor. 'Before my death I expel from the Party and from all his offices the former Reichsfuehrer SS and Reich Minister of the Interior, Heinrich Himmler. In his stead I appoint Gauleiter Karl Hanke as Reichsfuehrer SS and Chief of the German Police, and Gauleiter Paul Giesler as Reich Minister of the Interior.

'Goering and Himmler, by their secret negotiations with the enemy, without my knowledge or approval, and by their illegal attempts to seize power in the state, quite apart from their treachery to my person, have brought irreparable shame on the country and the whole people.'

Having disposed of the traitors and appointed his own and their successors, Hitler then dictated the government which they should accept. 'In order that the German people may have a government of honourable men who will continue the war by all methods', he usurped the privilege of his successor and appointed his own nominees to nineteen cabinet offices. Apart from Deonitz, who was to be Reich President, Supreme Commander of the Armed Forces, Minister of War, and Commander-in-Chief of the Navy, the most interesting appointments are those of Goebbels as Reich Chancellor, Bormann as Party Chancellor, and Seyss-Inquart, the Austrian quisling and oppressor of Holland, as Foreign Minister. Thus Ribbentrop, the second Bismarck, was at last dropped from the position he had so unskilfully occupied. Another who was silently omitted was Albert Speer. He was succeeded as Armaments Minister by his deputy, Saur. To the end a certain favour was accorded to the erring Benjamin of the court; his transgressions were passed over in silence, and he was displaced not in anger but in pain. Field-Marshal Schoerner, on whose unbroken Army Group the defence of Bohemia might yet depend, was appointed Commander-in-Chief of the Army. In the general change, one name at least remains constant—the Minister of Finance, Count Schwerin von Krosigk. In the great crises of his time he could boast of the achievement of the abbé Sieyès: *J'ai survécu*.

To this new government, imposed by testament, Hitler then dictated his orders. Though some of them, such as Bormann and Goebbels, had come to Berlin of their own will, wishing not to desert the capital but to fall there with their Fuehrer, nevertheless they must obey his orders and survive to carry on the Nazi administration, the Nazi war, the Nazi myth. Finally (so this strange document ends) they must 'above all else, uphold the racial laws in all their severity, and mercilessly resist the universal poisoner of all nations, international Jewry'.

Hitler's personal will is a shorter, less grandiose document; it is the testament not of the revolutionary genius, the angel of destruction, but of the Austrian petty-bourgeois, the picture-going host of Obersalzberg, the husband of Eva Braun. It explained his marriage, disposed of his property, and announced his impending death.

'Although during the years of struggle I believed that I could not undertake the responsibility of marriage, now, before the end of my life, I have decided to take as my wife the woman who, after many years of true friendship, came to this town, already almost besieged, of her own free will, in order to share my fate. She will go to her death with me at her own wish, as my wife. This will compensate us for what we both lost through my work in the service of my people.

'My possessions, in so far as they are worth anything, belong to the Party, or if this no longer exists, to the State.

If the State too is destroyed, there is no need for any further instructions on my part.

'The paintings in the collections bought by me during the course of the years were never assembled for private purposes, but solely for the establishment of a picture gallery in my home town of Linz on the Danube.

'It is my most heartfelt wish that this will should be duly executed.

'As executor, I appoint my most faithful Party comrade, Martin Bormann. He is given full legal authority to make all decisions. He is permitted to hand over to my relatives everything which is of worth as a personal memento, or is necessary to maintain a petty-bourgeois standard of living;[1] especially to my wife's mother and my faithful fellow workers of both sexes who are well known to him. The chief of these are my former secretaries, Frau Winter, etc, who helped me for many years by their work.

'My wife and I choose to die in order to escape the shame of overthrow or capitulation. It is our wish that our bodies be burnt immediately in the place where I have performed the greater part of my daily work during the course of my twelve years' service to my people.'[2]

At four o'clock in the morning the two documents were ready for signature. There were three copies, for delivery was uncertain, and such important documents must not be lost to posterity. After Hitler had signed them, the political will was witnessed by Goebbels, Bormann, Krebs, and Burgdorf. The

---

[1] The German phrase is 'zur Erhaltung eines kleinen buergerlichen Lebens'.

[2] At the time of their discovery and first publication, the authenticity of Hitler's testaments was doubted by the writer of a letter to the *Daily Telegraph*, and others, who referred to un-German characteristics in the typescript. These characteristics are not in the original documents, but were introduced into the photographic reproductions printed in the newspapers by sub-editors who wished to restore the blurred lettering. The argument therefore had no basis in fact. In fact, the authenticity of the documents has been established without the possibility of doubt by a mass of internal and circumstantial evidence, expert scrutiny of the signatures, and the testimony of those who knew of them, including one of the signatories of the Personal Testament (von Below), and the secretary who typed both documents (Frau Junge).

personal will was witnessed by Goebbels, Bormann, and Colonel Nicolaus von Below, Hitler's Luftwaffe adjutant, who was summoned for this purpose as one who had been a member of his personal *entourage* for the last eight years.

After the signature, Hitler retired to rest. But for Bormann and Goebbels there was still work to do. Both had been present at that secret conclave which had met after the announcement of Himmler's treachery, and at which, we must presume, the question of the succession and its attendant problems had been faced and resolved. Both, according to Hitler, had wished, or stated a wish, to remain and die in Berlin. Both had been ordered by Hitler to survive and carry on the Nazi administration. Each now had a decision to make: which of these two voices to obey.

Martin Bormann was an unromantic man. Neither statesman nor soldier, neither prophet nor priest, neither champion nor devotee, he loved one thing only, power; and the power that he loved consisted not in its outward semblance, its trappings and deference, nor in its material rewards, but in its reality, in the quiet assurance of its exercise. Under Hitler he had enjoyed that assurance; now that Hitler had resolved to die, what hope had he of continuance? He did not really wish to die, he had always given his voice for survival and escape; but if he were to survive, how could he retain the power he loved? He was himself a cipher, dependent entirely on his master. There were only two possibilities of his survival as the 'Brown Eminence' behind the Throne. Either he must himself succeed, or the successor must be one who would still make use of his indispensable services. Whether Bormann ever hoped personally to succeed, we cannot say; but it is improbable. His gifts were those of the secretary, not of the ruler: of Father Joseph, not of Cardinal Richelieu; and Hitler doubtless considered him, like Himmler, 'too inartistic' to be the Fuehrer of Germany. If then he was to be not successor, but adviser to the successor, it was essential to him that the appointed successor should be a man who would make use of his services. This Goering would certainly never do, and Goering had therefore been displaced. To make doubly sure, Bormann had recently taken, or now took, an additional precaution. He sent to his trusted servants in Obersalzberg a telegram of unmistakable significance. 'The situation in Berlin,' it read,[1] 'is more tense. If Berlin and we should fall, the traitors of April 23rd must be exterminated. Men, do your duty! Your life and honour depend upon it!' This telegram was duly delivered to the commandant of the fortress where Goering was imprisoned; but the commandant refused to recognize the authority of Bormann, and Goering was spared from that form of death.

It was equally certain that Himmler would never employ Bormann as his adviser; Himmler already had too many eager competitors for that office. But the danger of Himmler's succession had also been averted by the events and decisions of this eventful and decisive night. The chosen successor was now Doenitz. Doenitz was not a politician, but a sailor. He was also a Nazi. He had no political experience, but was devoted to Hitler and the ideals of Hitler. He would certainly need a good Nazi adviser, who understood the mysteries and was experienced in the habits of government and administration. What advice Bormann had given about the succession, if he was consulted, we do not know; but there can be little doubt that the nomination of Doenitz was welcome to him, and Hitler's testamentary command that he should not die but live fell, in such circumstances, on open and appreciative ears. Under Doenitz, Bormann decided that his duty lay in obedience; obeying, he might still wield the authority without which life would hold no sweetness for him.

Goebbels was a very different character. As the intellectual of the Party, the substance and justification of his life lay not in the power that he wielded, nor in the rewards that he drew from it, but in the myth of which he was the prophet, and which he alone could lucidly and cogently express. To him survival meant the survival not of his person, but of the myth; and with his clear understanding, he had realized that the

---

[1] The text of this telegram is given by Koller (May 1st) as having been received 'yesterday' (*ie* April 30th); but since the text has been vouched for by Zander, who left the Bunker on April 29th, it must have been sent earlier. Frau Christian knew of the telegram; she did not know whether Hitler had authorized it.

survival of the one meant the annihilation of the other. Hitler himself had realized this important psychological truth, and was himself adopting the course which he had forbidden to his prophet. But why should Hitler thus monopolize all the virtue of the Party? If, by his death, he was to go down to history as the leader, was there not room, by his side, for the true follower? If the God of Destruction was to immolate himself in his ruined heaven, should not the priest of destruction do the same, in his ruined shrine—less magnificently of course, less obtrusively, as befitted his junior status? Survival in such circumstances would be not only an anticlimax, but a logical inconsistency.

In all his last actions, speeches, and writings, Goebbels had borne witness to this philosophy. When Bormann had advised flight, he had protested that he would stay. In the last days, the Bunker had rung with his tedious oratory. Hobbling about his room, or clasping the back of a chair like a rostrum, he had denounced the treacherous survival of Goering, and glorified, in the name of future historians, the great and fertile example which would be set by a well-staged death.[1] In his letter to his stepson, which Hanna Reitsch had carried out of the Bunker, Goebbels had expressed the same philosophy. 'Germany will outlive this terrible war,' he had written, 'but only if it has examples by which to guide its reconstruction.' By 'reconstruction' he meant, of course, the reconstruction not merely of German industry or independence or greatness, but of Nazism; and his statement, thus interpreted, has a profound psychological truth. After any great defeat there are always men who will say that the prime need is to continue the administration. They can adduce good arguments in support of this view, which is convenient to the victors. But if it is not merely survival under a different system, but the revival of a defeated ideology that is required, this is a short-term view, and will fail, as Marshal Pétain discovered, and those

[1] Hanna Reitsch's account of Goebbels' behaviour in the Bunker, like all her accounts, is highly coloured by personal bias and an incorrigible love of rhetoric; but basically it is probably true. At any rate the sentiments correspond with those expressed by Goebbels in his letter to his stepson, Harold Quandt (of which the text survives), and in his *Appendix*, of which Hanna Reitsch knew nothing.

who supported him. The revival of a myth requires not continuity but a gesture; even if that gesture is suicide.

After witnessing Hitler's two statements, Goebbels therefore withdrew to his own apartment, and there composed his personal apologia in the form of an 'Appendix to the Fuehrer's Political Testament'.

'The Fuehrer has ordered me,' he wrote, 'should the defence of the Reich collapse, to leave Berlin, and to take part as a leading member in a government appointed by him.

'For the first time in my life I must categorically refuse to obey an order of the Fuehrer. My wife and children join me in this refusal. Otherwise—quite apart from the fact that feelings of humanity and loyalty forbid us to abandon the Fuehrer in his hour of greatest need—I should appear for the rest of my life as a dishonourable traitor and common scoundrel, and should lose my own self-respect together with the respect of my fellow citizens; a respect I should need in any further attempt to shape the future of the German nation and State.

'In the delirium of treachery which surrounds the Fuehrer in these most critical days of the war, there must be someone at least who will stay with him unconditionally until death, even if this conflicts with the formal and (in a material sense) entirely justifiable order which he has given in his political testament.

'In doing this, I believe that I am doing the best service I can to the future of the German people. In the hard times to come, examples will be more important than men. Men will always be found to lead the nation forward into freedom; but a reconstruction of our national life would be impossible unless developed on the basis of clear and obvious examples.

'For this reason, together with my wife, and on behalf of my children, who are too young to speak for themselves, but who would unreservedly agree with this decision if they were old enough, I express an unalterable resolution not to leave the Reich capital, even if it falls, but rather, at the side of the Fuehrer, to end a life which will have no further value to me if I cannot spend it in the service of the Fuehrer, and by his side.'

It was half past five in the morning when Dr Goebbels put his signature to this, the last of his famous broadsheets addressed to the German nation. At least we must admit that at the end he was not deserted by the psychological acumen of his mind, the Latin clarity of his expression.

Thus the night of April 28th–29th, like the afternoon of April 22nd, was a time of formidable decisions. The day which followed was occupied by their execution. The first business was the despatch of Hitler's testaments to his successors. At about eight o'clock in the morning General Burgdorf sent for Major Willi Johannmeier, Hitler's Army adjutant, and told him that an important mission had been entrusted to him. He was to carry a copy of the Fuehrer's political testament out of Berlin, through the Russian lines, and deliver it to Field-Marshal Schoerner, the newly appointed Commander-in-Chief of the Army. With him would go two other messengers, bearing similar documents, SS Standartenfuehrer Wilhelm Zander, Bormann's personal adviser, representing Bormann, and Heinz Lorenz, the official of the Propaganda Ministry who had brought to the Bunker the news of Himmler's treachery, as representative of Goebbels. These two men would receive separate instructions. As an officer of the Wehrmacht, a soldier with a distinguished fighting record and a reputation for bravery and resourcefulness, Johannmeier was charged to escort the party on their difficult journey through the enemy lines. Burgdorf then gave to Johannmeier a copy of Hitler's political testament. With it was a covering letter from Burgdorf to Schoerner, written in his own hand:

DEAR SCHOERNER,—Attached I send you by safe hand the Testament of our Fuehrer, who wrote it today under the shattering news of Himmler's treachery. It is his unalterable decision. The Testament is to be published as soon as the Fuehrer orders it, or as soon as his death is confirmed. All good wishes and *heil Hitler*.—Yours, WILHELM BURGDORF.

Major Johannmeier will deliver the Testament.

Schoerner at least would understand, if he received the

letter, that Hitler, like Julius Caesar, had died with *Et tu Brute* on his lips.

About the same time, Bormann summoned his adviser Wilhelm Zander, and gave him similar instructions. He was to take copies of the Fuehrer's will to Admiral Doenitz. When Zander heard this, his heart sank. A half educated, stupid, but honest man, in these last days, he had looked with a philosophical eye upon the history of the past twelve years; he had seen his own part in that history in a new and clearer perspective; and he had come to a decision. An idealist, as he assured himself, who had joined the Party long ago, and served it steadily, abandoning his comfortable business in Italy not to refresh himself with the perquisites, but to bow at the altar of the new God, he had learnt at last, and too late, whither idealism leads its uncritical devotees. Now, when the true consequences had become apparent to him, Zander had seen that there was no turning back. It was too late to change. He had dedicated his life, and could not recover it; and now by an inversion of his former idealism, he only wished, by a silent death, to end a wasted life and expiate the illusions which it was too late to shed. A week ago, when the convoy of planes and trucks had carried the fugitives from the Party Chancellery to Obersalzberg, he had refused to go. He was determined to share in Berlin the doom of Nazism. Now, on the eve of this great event, he was ordered out to begin again, without guidance or purpose, his half wasted life. All this he explained to Bormann, and explaining, begged to be excused. Bormann went to Hitler and described the hitch that had interfered with their plans. Returning, he told Zander that his objections had been overruled. It was the Fuehrer's order; he must go. Thereupon he handed him his papers—copies of Hitler's personal and political testaments, and the certificate of the marriage of Hitler and Eva Braun. To cover these documents Bormann scribbled a short note to Doenitz in which, as in all his last communications, he expressed his bitterness at the failure of the relieving army:

DEAR GRAND ADMIRAL,—Since all divisions have failed to arrive, and our position seems hopeless, the Fuehrer dictated last night the attached political Testament. *Heil Hitler.*—Yours, Bormann.

Meanwhile Johannmeier had found Lorenz and had told him that a special mission awaited him. Lorenz went into the general dining-passage in the outer part of Hitler's Bunker for breakfast; there he met Zander, who gave him a similar message and advised him to go to Goebbels or Bormann at once. Lorenz reported to Goebbels, and was told to go to Bormann and then return. From Bormann, Lorenz received copies of Hitler's personal and political testaments. On his return, Goebbels gave him the Appendix which he had himself composed. Lorenz was told to take these documents and escape to Doenitz's headquarters, or elsewhere in British or American territory. Ultimately they were to be taken to Munich, the cradle of the Nazi movement, there to be preserved as documents of the Heroic Age. With an eye to history, Goebbels had attached his own manifesto to this set of papers; it was not to generals or admirals that he appealed, but to posterity.

The rest of the morning was spent in hurried preparation for the journey, and at about noon the three men, Lorenz, Zander, and Johannmeier, accompanied by a corporal called Hummerich, left the Bunker. They were an ill-assorted, ill-equipped party, and their mission showed every sign of hasty improvisation. Neither food nor money nor papers were issued to them; each took what he could find as his *viaticum*. Lorenz had reported to Hitler and taken his leave, but Hitler had said nothing to him, only shaken hands in silence. Zander had no time to say goodbye to Bormann, and when he telephoned to do so, he was merely asked angrily why he had not left and ordered to start at once. Their dress was equally miscellaneous: Johannmeier and Zander were in military and SS uniform respectively; Lorenz in plain clothes. They left the Chancellery through the garages in the Hermann Goering Strasse and worked their way westward through the Tiergarten and Charlottenburg towards Pichelsdorf, at the north end of the Havel Lake. Johannmeier and Hummerich went ahead; Lorenz and Zander followed, directed by hand signals.

On their way they had to penetrate three Russian rings thrown round the centre of the city, the first at the Victory Column, the second at the Zoo station, the third before Pichelsdorf. Between four and five in the afternoon they reached Pichelsdorf, where a battalion of Hitler Youth was holding the bridge against the expected arrival of Wenck's army. There the battalion commander accommodated them in his bunker and they slept till night. At ten o'clock that night, after consultation with the battalion commander, they took two boats and pushed out into the lake, heading southwards for the Wannsee bridgehead, held by units of the German Ninth Army. In the early hours of April 30th they landed independently, Johannmeier on the Wannsee bridgehead, Lorenz and Zander on the Schwanenwerder Peninsula. There they remained, resting all day in underground bunkers; and in the evening they reunited, and sailed together to the Pfaueninsel, an island in the Havel. From the Wannsee bridgehead Johannmeier had been able to send a radio message to Doenitz, informing him of their position and asking that an airplane be sent to fetch them. On the Pfaueninsel Johannmeier and Zander obtained civilian clothing and disposed of their uniforms. There too they were overtaken by three other men, who had come, like them, from the beleaguered Reich Chancellery.

For in the morning of April 29th, when the three bearers of Hitler's testament left the Bunker, all telephone communication between Berlin and the outside world had ceased; the balloon upon which the radio-telephone to the Combined General Staff had depended had been shot down, and a conversation between Krebs and Jodl had died unfinished. The adjutants and ADC's of the generals at court no longer had any function to perform. This being so, three of them, Major Baron Freytag von Loringhoven, adjutant to General Krebs, Rittmeister Gerhardt Boldt, his ADC, and Lieut-Colonel Weiss, adjutant to General Burgdorf, decided to escape, if possible, from the Chancellery and go to join the still awaited army of General Wenck. They studied their maps; they applied to their generals; and their generals promised to seek permission from Hitler.

At midday on April 29th the usual situation conference was held in the Bunker. It was attended by Hitler, Bormann, Goebbels, Krebs, Burgdorf, Hewel, Voss, von Below, Freytag von Loringhoven, and Boldt. Krebs reported the latest news. The Russians had advanced in Grunewald, in Charlottenburg, at the Anhalter railway station; from the other fronts there was silence. Of Wenck there was no news. The supply of ammunition from the air during the night was inadequate; and not all the containers had been found in the debris of Berlin. After the conference, General Burgdorf asked whether Hitler would allow the three officers to make an attempt to reach Wenck's army. Hitler agreed, and the three officers were summoned and given their orders. They were to find General Wenck and to tell him to hurry; for the Chancellery would soon have fallen. Early in the afternoon, Freytag von Loringhoven, Boldt, and Weiss took their leave and left the Bunker. They followed the route of their predecessors, and with the help of a guide from the Hitler Youth reached the bridge at Pichelsdorf early on the morning of April 30th. Thence they sailed down the Havel in a folding-boat to the Wannsee Peninsula and the Pfaueninsel, where they overtook the three bearers of the testament. At the Reichssportfeld they had already been overtaken by yet another fugitive from the Bunker, by Colonel Nicolaus von Below, Hitler's Luftwaffe Adjutant, the last man to leave the Fuehrerbunker before the death of Hitler.

Colonel von Below had served in the Fuehrer's *entourage* for eight years and was by now a familiar, if junior, member of the court. Thanks to this personal connection, he had been invited to participate in the wedding reception on the morning of April 29th and to witness Hitler's personal testament. But although he had received from Hitler, at his own request, a phial of poison, he had no ambition to participate in the final act; and when, after the midday conference, he heard the Fuehrer approve the departure of Freytag von Loringhoven, Boldt, and Weiss, he reflected that he too was an adjutant who had no further functions to perform in the doomed and isolated Reich Chancellery. The example of the other adjutants encouraged him. Evidently it was not compulsory to stay in the Bunker. Krebs and Burgdorf had stated that they would stay and die, but they had let their adjutants go; might not Hitler do the same? And in spite of the public vows of suicide witnessed, or at least recorded, by Hanna Reitsch, three men had already left the Bunker that morning, three more were preparing to leave, and both Hewel and Voss had discreetly assured von Below that they saw no reason to contemplate such drastic action, but intended, if they could, to escape.

At the afternoon conference at four o'clock, von Below heard from Krebs that the situation was as before, only worse. Then he approached Burgdorf and asked whether he too might not be permitted to escape. Burgdorf replied that this was a matter for the Fuehrer to decide. Von Below went to Hitler, and put his request to him. Hitler agreed at once. He seems to have agreed to everything that day: April 29th, it seems, was like April 23rd, when he had forgiven Speer. Both were days of calm after a crisis of decision. But Hitler had another reason for allowing von Below to leave the Bunker. He wished to send yet another document out of the Bunker, to add, as it were, a postscript to his testament. He told von Below that he must seek to reach the headquarters of the Combined General Staff, now at Ploen in Schleswig-Holstein, and to deliver a document to Field-Marshal Keitel. He was to be ready to start after the evening conference.

This conference began at ten o'clock that night. It was attended by Hitler, Goebbels, Bormann, Krebs, Burgdorf, Hewel, Voss, von Below, and General Weidling, the commandant of the city. General Weidling described the military situation in Berlin, which had deteriorated according to expectation. The Russians had advanced in the Saarlandstrasse and the Wilhemstrasse, almost as far as the Air Ministry. West of Berlin they had penetrated from the north into the streets between the Bismarckstrasse and the Kantstrasse, and from the south into the northern border of the suburb of Grunewald and the Reichssportfeld; only a small German force was still holding a bridgehead on the Havel at Pichelsdorf—the Hitler Youth detachment which had forwarded the two parties of fugitives on their way. On the other fronts Weidling described other Russian successes; the advance was universal. The Russians would reach the Chancellery by May 1st, at the latest. Now or never, said Weidling, the troops in Berlin might seek to break through the Russian ring and escape from Berlin. Hitler replied that this was impossible. Retreat was barely possible for individual fugitives; for larger units of soldiers, battle-weary, ill-armed, and without ammunition, it was hopeless. With these words the subject was closed. As always, Hitler's word was final.

After the conference, von Below sent for his batman, Heinz Matthiesing,[1] whom he ordered to prepare himself for the journey. Then he took his official leave. Hitler shook hands with him, but, as with Lorenz, in silence. Von Below then said goodbye to all the others in the Bunker. General Krebs asked him to greet his wife for him, if possible, and gave her address; he also handed him a letter to General Jodl. In this[2] Krebs informed Jodl that the situation in Berlin was desperate; the encirclement of the city was complete, arms and ammunition were lacking, supplies dropped from the air were inadequate, it was no longer possible to land in Berlin, nothing had been heard of Wenck, and relief by his army was no longer expected. Resistance in Berlin could last only a few days. The Fuehrer expected other fronts to fight on to the last man.

Hitler's postscript was handed to von Below by Burgdorf; it was addressed to Keitel, and was Hitler's valediction to the German Armed Forces. In it (if Below has correctly reconstructed it) Hitler stated that the fight for Berlin was now drawing to its close, that he intended to commit suicide rather than surrender, that he had appointed Doenitz as his successor, and that two of his oldest supporters, Goering and Himmler, had betrayed him at the end. Then he turned to the achievements of the Armed Forces, which his strategy had led to destruction. The Navy he praised; by its high morale it had wiped out the disgrace of 1918, and it could not be blamed for its defeat. The Luftwaffe he excused; it had fought bravely; it was Goering who had failed to maintain its initial supremacy. But the Army—when Hitler considered the Army

---

[1] Matthiesing has been interrogated, and his story used to check and confirm that of von Below.

[2] According to von Below. (The original text was destroyed.)

he saw there two nations: the common soldiers, to whose ranks he had once belonged, who trusted in him and in whom he still trusted, and the generals who had misdirected this great weapon, who had resisted his strategy, undermined his policy, and conspired against his person. In his last message to the world, he could not omit, once again, to utter his hatred of that Army General Staff which he had once considered the mightiest thing the world has ever seen. 'The people and the Armed Forces,' he wrote (according to von Below's version of the letter[1]), 'have given their all in this long and hard struggle. The sacrifice has been enormous. But my trust has been misused by many people. Disloyalty and betrayal have undermined resistance throughout the war. It was therefore not granted to me to lead the people to victory. The Army General Staff cannot be compared with the General Staff in the first World War. Its achievements were far behind those of the fighting front.' The letter ended with a repetition of the now futile dream of the Pan-Germans, the ultimate, the only positive and consistent message of *Mein Kampf*: 'The efforts and sacrifices of the German people in this war have been so great that I cannot believe that they have been in vain. The aim must still be to win territory in the East for the German people.'

At midnight on the night of April 29th–30th, von Below and his batman left the Chancellery. They followed, with variations, what was by now the classical route, by the Hermann Goering Strasse, through the Brandenburger Tor, up the Charlottenburger Chaussee, to the Tiergarten railway station; then by the Kantstrasse, under Russian fire, and the Masuren Allee to the headquarters of the Hitler Youth, whence a guide led them by the Reichsstrasse to the Reichssportfeld. There they found Freytag von Loringhoven, Weiss, and Boldt; and following them to the bridgehead at Pichelsdorf, thence, in the next evening, they sailed, like their predecessors, down the Havel and landed on the western bank between Gatow and Kladow.

[1] The original text of this document was also destroyed, and it is given here as reconstructed by von Below. On internal evidence, Below's version seems genuine.

CHAPTER SEVEN

THE DEATH OF HITLER

WHEN VON BELOW left the Bunker, Hitler was already preparing for the end. During the day the last news from the outside world had been brought in. Mussolini was dead. Hitler's partner in crime, the herald of Fascism, who had first shown to Hitler the possibilities of dictatorship in modern Europe, and had preceded him in the stages of disillusion and defeat, had now illustrated in a signal manner the fate which fallen tyrants must expect. Captured by partisans during the general uprising of northern Italy, Mussolini and his mistress Clara Petacci had been executed, and their bodies suspended by the feet in the market place of Milan to be beaten and pelted by the vindictive crowd. If the full details were ever known to them, Hitler and Eva Braun could only have repeated the orders they had already given: their bodies were to be destroyed 'so that nothing remains'; 'I will not fall into the hands of an enemy who requires a new spectacle to divert his hysterical masses'. In fact it is improbable that these details were reported, or could have strengthened an already firm decision. The fate of defeated despots has generally been the same; and Hitler, who had himself exhibited the body of a field-marshal on a meathook, had no need of remote historical examples or of a new and dramatic instance, to know the probable fate of his own corpse, if it should be found.[1]

[1] It has often been stated, by those whose imagination is stronger than their memory, that Hitler's decision was affected by the fate of Mussolini. An account of the table-talk of the prisoners at Nuremberg, ascribed to the chief psychiatrist at the Trial and printed in the *Sunday Express*, August 25th, 1946, even quotes Goering as saying, 'You remember the Mussolini incident? We had pictures of Mussolini dead in the gutter with his mistress, and hanging in the air upside-down. They were awful! Hitler went into a frenzy, shouting: "This will never happen to me!"' A glance at the dates disposes of this romance.

In the afternoon, Hitler had had his favourite Alsatian dog, Blondi, destroyed. Professor Haase, his former surgeon, who was now tending the wounded in his clinic in Berlin, had come round to the Bunker and killed it with poison. The two other dogs belonging to the household had been shot by the sergeant who looked after them. After this, Hitler had given poison capsules to his two secretaries, for use in extremity. He was sorry, he said, to give them no better parting gift; and praising them for their courage, he had added, characteristically, that he wished his generals were as reliable as they.[1]

In the evening, while the inhabitants of the two outer bunkers were dining in the general dining-passage of the Fuehrerbunker, they were visited by one of the SS guard, who informed them that the Fuehrer wished to say goodbye to the ladies and that no one was to go to bed till orders had been received. At about half past two in the morning the orders came. They were summoned by telephone to the Bunker, and gathered again in the same general dining-passage, officers and women, about twenty persons in all. When they were assembled, Hitler came in from the private part of the Bunker, accompanied by Bormann. His look was abstracted, his eyes glazed over with that film of moisture which Hanna Reitsch had noticed. Some of those who saw him even suggested that he had been drugged; but no such explanation is needed of a condition upon which more familiar observers had often commented. He walked in silence down the passage and shook hands with all the women in turn. Some spoke to him, but he said nothing, or mumbled inaudibly. Ceremonies of silent handshaking had become quite customary in the course of that day.[2]

When he had left, the participants in this strange scene remained for a while to discuss its significance. They agreed that it could have one meaning only. The suicide of the Fuehrer was about to take place. Thereupon an unexpected

[1] Frau Junge.   [2] Von Varo.

Goering saw Hitler for the last time eight days before Mussolini's death. Goering may have seen pictures of Mussolini's body in captivity; Hitler never. Such is the value of unchecked human testimony, on which, however, much of written history is based.

thing happened. A great and heavy cloud seemed to roll away from the spirits of the Bunker-dwellers. The terrible sorcerer, the tyrant who had charged their days with intolerable melo-dramatic tension, would soon be gone, and for a brief twilight moment they could play. In the canteen of the Chancellery, where the soldiers and orderlies took their meals, there was a dance. The news was brought; but no one allowed that to interfere with the business of pleasure. A message from the Fuehrerbunker told them to be quieter; but the dance went on. A tailor[1] who had been employed in the Fuehrer's head-quarters, and who was now immured with the rest in the Chancellery, was surprised when Brigadefuehrer Rattenhuber, the head of the police guard and a general in the SS, slapped him cordially on the back and greeted him with democratic familiarity. In the strict heirarchy of the Bunker the tailor felt bewildered. It was as if he had been a high officer. "It was the first time I had ever heard a high officer say 'good evening'," he said; "so I noticed that the mood had com-pletely changed." Then, from one of his equals, he learned the reason of this sudden and irregular affability. Hitler had said goodbye, and was going to commit suicide. There are few forces so solvent of class distinctions as common danger, and common relief.

Though Hitler might already be preparing for death, there was still one man at least in the Bunker who was thinking of life: Martin Bormann. If Bormann could not persuade the German armies to come and rescue Hitler and himself, at least he would insist on revenge. Shortly after the farewell ceremony, at a quarter past three in the morning of April 30th, he sent another of those telegrams in which the neurosis of the Bunker is so vividly preserved. It was addressed to Doenitz at Ploen; but Bormann no longer trusted the ordinary communications, and sent it through the Gauleiter of Mecklen-burg. It ran:

DOENITZ!—Our impression grows daily stronger that the divisions in the Berlin theatre have been standing idle for several days. All the reports we receive are controlled, sup-

[1] W. O. Mueller.

228

pressed, or distorted by Keitel. In general we can only communicate through Keitel. The Fuehrer orders you to proceed at once, and mercilessly, against all traitors.— BORMANN.[1]

A postscript contained the words: 'The Fuehrer is alive, and is conducting the defence of Berlin.' These words, containing no hint of the approaching end—indeed seeming to deny its imminence—suggest that Bormann was reluctant even now to admit that his power would soon be over, or must be renewed from another, less calculable, source.

Later in the same morning, when the new day's work had begun, the generals came as usual to the Bunker with their military reports. Brigadefuehrer Mohnke, the commandant of the Chancellery, announced a slight improvement: the Schlesischer railway station had been recaptured from the Russians; but in other respects the military situation was unchanged. By noon the news was worse again. The underground railway tunnel in the Friedrichstrasse was reported in Russian hands; the tunnel in the Vossstrasse, close to the Chancellery, was partly occupied; the whole area of the Tiergarten had been taken; and Russian forces had reached the Potsdamer Platz and the Weidendammer Bridge over the river Spree. Hitler received these reports without emotion. At about two o'clock he took lunch. Eva Braun was not there; evidently she did not feel hungry, or ate alone in her room; and Hitler shared his meal, as usually in her absence, with his two secretaries and the cook. The conversation indicated nothing unusual. Hitler remained quiet, and did not speak of his intentions. Nevertheless, preparations were already being made for the approaching ceremony.

In the morning, the guards had been ordered to collect all their rations for the day, since they would not be allowed to pass through the corridor of the Bunker again; and about lunchtime Hitler's SS adjutant, Sturmbannfuehrer Guensche, sent an order to the transport officer and chauffuer, Sturmbannfuehrer Erich Kempka, to send 200 litres of petrol to the

[1] In the German text the name of Keitel is represented by his codename 'Teilhaus'.

Chancellery garden. Kempka protested that it would be difficult to find so large a quantity at once, but he was told that it must be found. Ultimately he found about 180 litres and sent it round to the garden. Four men carried it in jerricans[1] and placed it at the emergency exit of the Bunker. There they met one of the police guards, who demanded an explanation. They told him that it was for the ventilating plant. The guard told them not to be silly, for the plant was oil-driven. At this moment Hitler's personal servant, Heinz Linge, appeared. He reassured the guard, terminated the argument, and dismissed the men. Soon afterwards all the guards except those on duty were ordered to leave the Chancellery, and to stay away. It was not intended that any casual observer should witness the final scene.

Meanwhile Hitler had finished lunch, and his guests had been dismissed. For a time he remained behind; then he emerged from his suite, accompanied by Eva Braun, and another farewell ceremony took place. Bormann and Goebbels were there, with Burgdorf, Krebs, Hewel, Naumann, Voss, Rattenhuber, Hoegl, Guensche, Linge, and the four women, Frau Christian, Frau Junge, Fraeulein Krueger, and Fraeulein Manzialy. Frau Goebbels was not present; unnerved by the approaching death of her children, she remained all day in her own room. Hitler and Eva Braun shook hands with them all, and then returned to their suite. The others were dismissed, all but the high-priests and those few others whose services would be necessary. These waited in the passage. A single shot was heard. After an interval they entered the suite. Hitler was lying on the sofa, which was soaked with blood. He had shot himself through the mouth. Eva Braun was also on the sofa, also dead. A revolver was by her side, but she had not used it; she had swallowed poison. The time was half past three.[2]

[1] A jerrican is a German petrol can containing $4\frac{1}{2}$ gallons.
[2] The method of death chosen by Hitler and Eva Braun has been reported identically by Fraeulein Krueger and Frau Junge (who had it from Guensche) and Frau Christian (from Linge), and by others who heard it from the same sources. It is also described by Axmann, who personally inspected the bodies. Kempka, who carried out the body of Eva Braun, unblanketed, observed no signs of blood.

Shortly afterwards, Artur Axmann, head of the Hitler Youth, arrived at the Bunker. He was too late for the farewell ceremony, but he was admitted to the private suite to see the dead bodies. He examined them, and stayed in the room for some minutes, talking with Goebbels. Then Goebbels left, and Axmann remained for a short while alone with the dead bodies. Outside, in the Bunker, another ceremony was being prepared: the Viking funeral.

After sending the petrol to the garden, Kempka had walked across to the Bunker by the subterranean passage which connected his office in the Hermann Goering Strasse with the Chancellery buildings. He was greeted by Guensche with the words, 'The Chief is dead'.[1] At that moment the door of Hitler's suite was opened, and Kempka too became a participant in the funeral scene.

While Axmann was meditating among the corpses, two SS men, one of them Hitler's servant Linge, entered the room. They wrapped Hitler's body in a blanket, concealing the bloodstained and shattered head, and carried it out into the passage, where the other observers easily recognized it by the familiar black trousers. Then two other SS officers carried the body up the four flights of stairs to the emergency exit, and so out into the garden. After this, Bormann entered the room and took up the body of Eva Braun. Her death had been tidier, and no blanket was needed to conceal the evidence of it. Bormann carried the body into the passage, and then handed it to Kempka, who took it to the foot of the stairs. There it was taken from him by Guensche; and Guensche in turn gave it to a third SS officer, who carried it too upstairs to the garden. As an additional precaution, the other door of the Bunker, which led into the Chancellery, and some of the doors leading from the Chancellery to the garden, had been hastily locked against possible intruders.

Unfortunately, the most careful precautions are sometimes unavailing; and it was as a direct result of this precaution that two unauthorized persons in fact witnessed the scene from which it was intended to exclude them. One of the

[1] 'Der Chef ist tot.' Hitler's personal servants referred to him as 'der Chef'.

police guards, one Erich Mansfeld, happened to be on duty in the concrete observation tower at the corner of the Bunker, and noticing through the opaque, sulphurous air a sudden, suspicious scurrying of men and shutting of doors, he felt it his duty to investigate. He climbed down from his tower into the garden and walked round to the emergency exit to see what was afoot. In the porch he collided with the emerging funeral procession. First there were two SS officers carrying a body wrapped in a blanket, with black-trousered legs protruding from it. Then there was another SS officer carrying the unmistakable corpse of Eva Braun. Behind them were the mourners—Bormann, Burgdorf, Goebbels, Guensche, Linge, and Kempka. Guensche shouted at Mansfeld to get out of the way quickly; and Mansfeld, having seen the forbidden but interesting spectacle, returned to his tower.[1]

After this interruption, the ritual was continued. The two corpses were placed side by side, a few feet from the porch, and petrol from the can was poured over them. A Russian bombardment added to the strangeness and danger of the ceremony, and the mourners withdrew for some protection under the shelter of the porch. There Guensche dipped a rag in petrol, set it alight, and flung it out upon the corpses. They were at once enveloped in a sheet of flame. The mourners stood to attention, gave the Hitler salute, and withdrew again into the Bunker, where they dispersed. Guensche afterwards described the spectacle to those who had missed it. The burning of Hitler's body, he said, was the most terrible experience in his life.[2]

Meanwhile yet another witness had observed the spectacle. He was another of the police guards, and he too came accidentally upon the scene in consequence of the precautions which should have excluded him. His name was Hermann Karnau. Karnau, like others of the guard who were not on duty, had been ordered away from the bunker by an officer of the SS

[1] This account is given independently by Kempka and Mansfeld, who agree. Kempka mentions the incident when a guard (ie Mansfeld) collided with the procession in the porch and was dismissed by Guensche. Some of the details were accidentally noticed by Schwaegermann.

[2] Fraeulein Krueger, Frau Junge.

Escort, and had gone to the Chancellery canteen; but after a while, in spite of his orders, he had decided to return to the Bunker. On arrival at the door of the Bunker, he had found it locked. He had therefore made his way out into the garden, in order to enter the Bunker by the emergency exit. As he turned the corner by the tower where Mansfeld was on duty, he was surprised to see two bodies lying side by side, close to the door of the Bunker. Almost at the same instant they burst, spontaneously it seemed, into flame. Karnau could not explain this sudden combustion. He saw no one, and yet it could not be the result of enemy fire, for he was only three feet away. "Possibly someone threw a match from the doorway," he suggested; and his suggestion is essentially correct.

Karnau watched the burning corpses for a moment. They were easily recognizable, though Hitler's head was smashed. The sight, he says, was 'repulsive in the extreme'. Then he went down into the Bunker by the emergency exit. In the Bunker, he met Sturmbannfuehrer Franz Schedle, the officer commanding the SS Escort. Schedle had recently been injured in the foot by a bomb. He was distracted with grief. "The Fuehrer is dead," he said; "he is burning outside"; and Karnau helped him to limp away.

Mansfeld, on duty in the tower, also watched the burning of the bodies. As he had climbed the tower, after Guensche had ordered him away, he had seen through a loophole a great column of black smoke rising from the garden. As the smoke diminished, he saw the same two bodies which he had seen being brought up the stairs. They were burning. After the mourners had withdrawn, he continued to watch. At intervals he saw SS men come out of the Bunker and pour more petrol on the bodies to keep them alight. Some time afterwards he was relieved by Karnau, and when Karnau had helped him to climb out of the tower, the two went together to look at the bodies again. By now the lower parts of both bodies had been burned away and the shinbones of Hitler's legs were visible. An hour later, Mansfeld visited the bodies again. They were still burning, but the flame was low.

In the course of the afternoon a third member of the police guard sought to watch the spectacle of the burning bodies.

His name was Hans Hofbeck. He went up the stairs from the Bunker and stood in the porch; but he did not stay there. The stench of burning flesh was intolerable and drove him away.

Late that night Brigadefuehrer Rattenhuber, the head of the police guard, entered the Dog-bunker where the guards were spending their leisure, and spoke to a sergeant of the SS Escort. He told him to report to his commanding officer, Schedle, and to pick three trustworthy men to bury the corpses. Soon afterwards Rattenhuber returned to the Dog-bunker and addressed the men there. He made them promise to keep the events of the day a holy secret. Anyone talking about them would be shot. Shortly before midnight Mansfeld returned to duty in the tower. Russian shells were still falling, and the sky was illuminated by flares. He noticed that a bomb crater in front of the emergency exit had been newly worked upon, and that the bodies had disappeared. He did not doubt that the crater had been converted into a grave for them; for no shell could have piled the earth around it in so neat a rectangle. About the same time, Karnau was on parade with the other guards in the Vossstrasse, and one of his comrades said to him: 'It is sad that none of the officers seems to worry about the Fuehrer's body. I am proud that I alone know where he is.'[1]

That is all that is known about the disposal of the remnants of Hitler's and Eva Braun's bodies. Linge afterwards told one of the secretaries that they had been burned as Hitler had ordered, 'till nothing remained'; but it is doubtful whether such total combustion could have taken place; 180 litres of petrol, burning slowly on a sandy bed, would char the flesh and dissipate the moisture of the bodies, leaving only an unrecognizable and fragile remainder; but the bones would withstand the heat. These bones have never been found. Perhaps they were broken up and mixed with the other bodies, the bodies of soldiers killed in the defence of the Chancellery,

[1] In their narratives of the burning of the bodies, Karnau and Mansfeld agree on facts, but differ on dates and times. Both mistake the date. Mansfeld's times are correct where they can be checked, while Karnau's are hopelessly erratic. If Mansfeld is reliable throughout, the bodies were set alight at about 4 pm (this is almost certainly correct), and were still burning at 6.30; Rattenhuber's orders for burial were given 'late at night'; and the bodies had been buried by 11 pm.

and the body of Fegelein, which were also buried in the garden. The Russians have occasionally dug in that garden, and many such bodies have been unearthed there. Perhaps, as Guensche is said to have stated, the ashes were collected in a box and conveyed out of the Chancellery. Or perhaps no elaborate explanation is necessary. Perhaps such investigations as have been made have been somewhat perfunctory. Investigators who left Hitler's engagement diary unobserved in his chair for five months may easily have overlooked other relics which were more deliberately concealed. Whatever the explanation, Hitler achieved his last ambition. Like Alaric, buried secretly under the riverbed of Busento, the modern destroyer of mankind is now immune from discovery.

While these last rites and pieties were being observed by guards and sentries, the regents of the Bunker were busy with more practical matters. Having set the bodies alight and paid their last summary respects, they had returned to safety underground, there to contemplate the future. Once again, as after Hitler's first leavetaking, a great cloud seemed to have been lifted from their spirits. The nightmare of ideological repression was over, and if the prospect before them remained dark and dubious, at least they were now free to consider it in a businesslike manner. From this moment nobody seems to have bothered about the past or the two corpses still sizzling in the garden. That episode was over, and in the short space of time remaining they had their own problems to face. As the tragically-minded guard observed, it was sad to see everyone so indifferent to the Fuehrer's body.

The first evidence of the changed atmosphere in the Bunker was noticed by the secretaries, who had been dismissed during the ceremony, but who now returned to their stations. On arrival they learned the details from Guensche and Linge; but it was not from such secondhand information only that they knew that Hitler was dead. Everyone, they observed, was smoking in the Bunker. During Hitler's lifetime that had been absolutely forbidden; but now the headmaster had gone and the boys could break the rules. Under the soothing influence of nicotine, whose absence must have increased the nervous tension of the past week, they were able to consider the

administrative problems which the Fuehrer had left them to
face.

First, there was the succession. With Hitler's death, the
centre of power had moved automatically from the Bunker to
the distant headquarters of the new Fuehrer in Schleswig-
Holstein. It was mortifying to Bormann, who for so long had
given orders and exercised authority in the name of Hitler,
to admit that now he had no position at all, unless Doenitz
should confirm his appointment as Party Minister in the new
government. On the other hand it was improbable that any
copy of Hitler's will had yet reached Doenitz, who was therefore unaware not only of Hitler's death, but also of his own
right of succession. It was clearly Bormann's duty to inform
the new Fuehrer of these facts by telegram; and it is interesting
to notice the ambiguous manner in which this was done.

After Hitler's death, Bormann sent the following telegram
to Doenitz:

> GRAND ADMIRAL DOENITZ,—In place of the former Reich-
> Marshal Goering the Fuehrer appoints you, Herr Grand
> Admiral, as his successor. Written authority is on its way.
> You will immediately take all such measures as the situation
> requires.—BORMANN.

The important and relevant fact that Hitler was already dead
was not mentioned. It seems as if Bormann wished to prolong
yet a little longer the authority which he loved, but could no
longer legally exercise.

The arrival of this document caused something like con-
sternation at Ploen. The appointment was entirely unexpected.
Only two days before, Doenitz had gone to Himmler and
offered his support to him as Hitler's most obvious successor,
and Himmler was even now preparing his government. Now
the position was suddenly reversed. "Not Himmler but
Doenitz!" exclaimed the astonished Schwerin von Krosigk,
who as usual had backed the wrong horse, though his genius
for survival guaranteed his own appointment in either events.
Doenitz himself was not only surprised but mortified. Almost
alone among the Nazi leaders, he had entertained no ambitions
of the succession, and now the succession had been thrust

upon him. Ever since his appointment to the command of the northern area, Doenitz had been in a nervous state; on receipt of this telegram, says one of his *entourage*,[1] his condition became obviously worse. Nevertheless, since it was the Fuehrer's order, no one thought of disobeying it. There was no coup, no question. Himmler's cumbrous bodyguard, which seemed to dominate the whole headquarters, stood idle, while Himmler, reluctantly abandoning his hopes of supreme power, offered to serve under Doenitz; and Doenitz, reluctantly assuming his new responsibility, replied thus by telegram to the Fuehrer whom he supposed still alive:

MY FUEHRER!—My loyalty to you will be unconditional. I shall do everything possible to relieve you in Berlin. If Fate nevertheless compels me to rule the Reich as your appointed successor, I shall continue this war to an end worthy of the unique, heroic struggle of the German people. —GRAND ADMIRAL DOENITZ.

What was Bormann's purpose in thus concealing the fact of Hitler's death, while covering himself by authorizing Doenitz to assume responsibility? To speculate deeply on human motives is an unprofitable undertaking; but in this instance one thing at least is certain. Bormann was determined, one way or another, to reach Ploen. He was already considering alternative means of making that journey. It therefore seems probable that he intended, if possible, himself to be the first bearer of the news. Thus, having reduced to a minimum the period of his temporary eclipse, he might hope, by his personal presence at the decisive moment, to reinforce his claim to continued authority.

Bormann's first plan for such a journey consisted of a mass escape through the Russian lines; and at first the survivors of the court were told to be prepared for such an attempt in the darkness of the coming night. But such a mass escape would certainly be dangerous and might fail—Hitler had already declared it impossible on the previous day, when the situation was less desperate than now—and in the course of the afternoon

[1] Julius Weitmann, Press Referent at Doenitz's headquarters.

another, less hazardous possibility suggested itself. Since Goebbels and Bormann were, by virtue of Hitler's will members of the new government, might not the Russian military authorities recognize their status, and, if they offered surrender, send Bormann to Ploen to have it ratified by Doenitz? Bormann would thus be sent to Ploen by the Russians as a privileged envoy, would join the new government, and would take up his position as one of the rulers of the new Reich. Such a hope seems ridiculous to us; but in the fools' paradise of Nazism nothing seemed ridiculous. It was certainly no more ridiculous than the political plans of Himmler, or of Schellenberg, or of Ribbentrop, or of Schwerin von Krosigk, all of whom assumed the possible survival of a Nazi, or at least a semi-Nazi Government; and it did not seem ridiculous to Bormann.

This project of a treaty with the Russians was worked out in the course of a long conference in the evening of April 30th. Bormann and Goebbels were there, with Krebs, Burgdorf, and Axmann; possibly also Mohnke. Contact was made with the Russian headquarters by wireless, and a messenger was then sent to inquire whether Marshal Zhukov would receive a representative of the German Government. The reply was favourable; and at midnight Krebs himself set out from the Bunker carrying a letter from Goebbels and Bormann. He was a suitable emissary. From his long experience as military attaché in Moscow, he knew the Russians, and spoke their language; he was reputed a strong advocate of Russo-German friendship; and Bormann and Goebbels might reasonably expect a civil reception at Russian headquarters for a man who had once been publicly embraced by Stalin.[1] In their letter they informed Zhukov of Hitler's death, and quoted, as their authority for writing, the positions to which they had been appointed by Hitler's will. They authorized the bearer, General

[1] This was in March 1941, when Matsuoka, the Japanese foreign minister, was leaving Moscow for Berlin. The incident has been described to me by General Heim, who had it from Krebs. It is also described in Semler's diary (*Goebbels*, p. 26). According to Semler, Stalin 'embraced him [Krebs] in Russian fashion and said: "If we stand together like brothers, then nothing can happen to us in the future. You see to it that we remain good friends".'

Krebs, to negotiate an armistice or truce, pending the decision of the new President Admiral Doenitz.[1]

For the rest of the night, and throughout the following morning, Goebbels and Bormann awaited the issue of Krebs's mission to Zhukov. At eleven o'clock in the morning they had received no satisfaction[2]; and now at last Bormann decided, or agreed to inform Doenitz that his reign had begun. Even so, he still avoided an explicit admission of Hitler's death. His laconic telegram was more concerned with his own position. It ran:

GRAND ADMIRAL DOENITZ,—The Testament is in force. I will join you as soon as possible. Till then I recommend that publication be held up.—BORMANN.

With this brief and not entirely satisfactory communication, Doenitz had, for the time, to be content.

At noon, or soon afterwards, Krebs returned to the Bunker from Marshal Zhukov's headquarters. The reply which he brought was not satisfactory. It demanded unconditional surrender, and the delivery of all persons present in the Bunker. There was clearly no question of privileged status, no possibility of an accredited journey to Schleswig-Holstein. Another meeting was held in the Bunker, and it was decided to send a message to the Russian headquarters that the negotiations were closed. There was now no alternative. The mass escape must be attempted.

At quarter past three, a third and last telegram was sent to Doenitz to supplement the meagre messages of Bormann. It was signed by Goebbels. Having now no personal ambitions, Goebbels, unlike Bormann, had no need of the ambiguities and reticences of policy; he could afford to be explicit. His telegram was as follows:

[1] Frau Christian, Fraeulein Krueger.
[2] [*Author's note*, 1956: According to Lt-Col Troyanovsky, the correspondent of the Russian Army newspaper *Red Star*, Zhukov, speaking through Gen. Chuïkov, insisted on unconditional surrender. Krebs then returned to the Bunker and was sent back by Goebbels and Bormann with an offer of surrender provided that their 'government' was recognized by the Russians. This proviso was rejected, and he returned finally to the Bunker.]

GRAND ADMIRAL DOENITZ—

Most secret—urgent—officer only.

The Fuehrer died yesterday at 15.30 hours. Testament of April 29th appoints you as Reich President, Reich Minister Dr Goebbels as Reich Chancellor, Reichsleiter Bormann as Party Minister, Reich Minister Seyss-Inquart as Foreign Minister. By order of the Fuehrer, the Testament has been sent out of Berlin to you, to Field-Marshal Schoerner, and for preservation and publication. Reichsleiter Bormann intends to go to you today and to inform you of the situation. Time and form of announcement to the Press and to the troops is left to you. Confirm receipt.—GOEBBELS.[1]

On receiving this telegram, Doenitz assumed the burdens, but also the rights which it conferred. These included the right to accept or to reject advice from the ministers of his predecessor and the right to choose his own government. He decided not to accept the ministers imposed upon him by telegram (for he had not received, and never did receive, the full list contained in the testament), and not to wait for Bormann's arrival before making an announcement. At half past nine in the evening, Hamburg Radio warned the German people that 'a grave and important announcement' would be made; then, heroically accompanied by strains from Wagner's operas and the slow movements of Bruckner's Seventh Symphony, came the news of Hitler's death, fighting to the end against Bolshevism. At 10.20 Doenitz himself announced both Hitler's death and his own succession. The Fuehrer, he said, had fallen 'this afternoon'; he had died fighting 'at the head of his troops'. Both statements were untrue, for Hitler had fallen yesterday, not today, and since Doenitz had never been

[1] [*Author's note*, 1956: This telegram as received by Doenitz was undoubtedly signed by Goebbels only, but possibly this is an error. Doenitz's cypher-clerk, Edmund Kraft, afterwards deposed on oath that he had accidentally omitted to transcribe the signature of Bormann, and Doenitz's adjutant, Walter Ludde-Neurath, in his book *Regierung Doenitz* (Göttingen, 1950), while quoting only the signature of Goebbels, writes that he cannot be certain that the telegram was not signed by Bormann also.]

informed of the manner of his death, any account of it was necessarily speculation. The former inaccuracy was probably a mere error; the latter was probably designed. Had Doenitz known, and said, that Hitler had committed suicide, how would the troops have received such a statement? Might they not have felt that they had been betrayed, that the Fuehrer had deserted his post, and that their oaths of loyalty to him had been dissolved by his desertion? Such had been the attitude of Koller and of Jodl on April 22nd, when Hitler had announced his intention of suicide, and such, on this same day, was the attitude of General Weidling. Weidling had arrived as usual in the Bunker and had been told that 'the Fuehrer had committed hara-kiri'; he had returned to his command-post in disgust and released his soldiers from their oaths. As the new Fuehrer, who regarded the soldiers' oaths to his predecessor as still binding them to him,[1] Doenitz could not afford such consequences. If he was to negotiate a successful peace with the West, the support of the Armed Forces must strengthen him in negotiation; and therefore, though he had no knowledge, he had no doubt thought it most prudent to suppose that the Fuehrer had died a soldier's death.

Meanwhile, in the Bunker, Bormann and his colleagues were planning the details of the mass escape which was to bring them to deliverance and himself to power. Not all of them, for there were some who had by now given up all hope of life, or all interest in it, and who preferred, as Zander would have preferred, to meet their end now in the ruined Chancellery. Among these was Goebbels. His decision had long been taken; he had published it in his Appendix to the Fuehrer's testament; his wife had received a last decoration from the Fuehrer; and now the time of fulfilment had arrived. After sending his last telegram, Goebbels returned to his own apartments in the Bunker, with his wife and family. A few friends visited them to take their leave, among them Axmann and Kempka. Then they prepared themselves for the end.

[1] This was the argument adopted by Doenitz in his broadcast to the German people on the evening of May 1st. Owing to the interruption of communications it was physically impossible for him to exact a new oath of loyalty from the Army.

This time there was no Wagnerian drama; Goebbels did not attempt to compete with his master. As a tribal chief, Hitler might enjoy a spectacular, symbolic funeral; but Goebbels, as a secondary figure, would follow him, at a decent interval, unobtrusively to the shades. He had worked out his formula; the answer was nought; and self-annihilation was the logical consequence of his ideological nihilism. First, the six children were poisoned with capsules long prepared for the purpose. Then, in the evening, Goebbels called his adjutant, Guenther Schwaegermann. "Schwaegermann," he said, "this is the worst treachery of all. The generals have betrayed the Fuehrer. Everything is lost. I shall die, together with my wife and family. You will burn my body. Can you do that?" Schwaegermann promised to do so, and Goebbels took leave of him, only pressing upon him a silver-framed photograph of the Fuehrer from his writing-desk. Frau Goebbels also said goodbye. Then Schwaegermann sent Goebbels' driver and SS orderly to fetch petrol for the burning; for the grotesque scene of yesterday was to be re-enacted on a smaller stage. Shortly afterwards (it was now about half past eight in the evening) Goebbels and his wife walked through the Bunker. At the foot of the stairs they passed Schwaegermann and the driver, Rach, who were standing there with the petrol; but they passed them without a word and walked up the stairs into the garden. Almost immediately, two shots were heard; and when Rach and Schwaegermann reached the garden, they found the two bodies lying dead on the ground. The SS orderly, who had shot them, was standing by. Obediently, they poured four cans of petrol over the bodies, set it alight, and withdrew. It was a perfunctory cremation, and the charred bodies were found next day by the Russians; no attempt had been made to destroy or to bury them. On the way back through the Bunker, Rach and Schwaegermann met Brigadefuehrer Mohnke, who ordered them to set the Bunker on fire. They emptied one remaining can of petrol in the conference room, and set it alight. Then they left the Fuehrerbunker; for it was nine o'clock, and the mass escape from the New Chancellery was about to begin.[1]

[1] This account is based largely on the statement of Schwaegermann, supplemented by statements of Axmann and Kempka.

In the Bunker of the New Chancellery a disorderly group of Party officials, soldiers and women were gathered together. They were under the general command of Bormann; yet, as one of the participants said, "There was never any real command; they all ran around like chickens with their heads off."[1] When they were all assembled, the order of their exodus was described to them. They were to move in a succession of compact groups, through vaults and tunnels, into the underground station in the Wilhemsplatz. Thence they would walk along the tracks of the underground railway as far as the Friedrichstrasse station, where they would regain the surface. In the Friedrichstrasse they would attach themselves to the remains of Mohnke's battlegroup, which had been defending the Chancellery area, and with its aid they would attempt to force a way over the river Spree, and through the Russian lines, in a north-westerly direction. Once in the north-western suburbs of Berlin, individuals would make their way, as best they could, to German headquarters or to personal safety.

Such was the plan; the execution was different. It was eleven o'clock before the party was ready to move. They left, as planned, in groups. The first group included Mohnke, Guensche, Hewel, Admiral Voss, Hitler's pilot Baur, the three secretaries, and the cook. The rest followed at intervals, in four or five other groups. Bormann was in one of the central groups; in his pocket he carried the last copy of Hitler's private testament;[2] he intended to take it to Schleswig-Holstein as the certificate of his claims. When the last group left the Chancellery there were still three men left behind. They were General Krebs, General Burgdorf, and the commander of the SS Bodyguard, Hauptsturmfuehrer Schedle. These preferred to stay and to shoot themselves when the Russians entered the Chancellery; and it is most probable that they are either prisoners or dead. Schedle was wounded in the foot, and could hardly have escaped had he wished. When the others

[1] W. O. Mueller.

[2] Statement by Bormann to Axmann. The documents must have been the single copy of the private testament which is unaccounted for.

left the Chancellery, flames were rising from the deserted Fuehrerbunker—the funeral flames of Dr Goebbels.[1]

Arrived at the Friedrichstrasse station, the first group of fugitives emerged into the street and found a formidable and bewildering prospect before them. Everywhere the ruins of Berlin seemed to be in flames, and shells were falling all around. Nevertheless, this group kept together. Creeping forward by devious tunnels, they reached the river Spree and crossed it by an iron footbridge running parallel to the Weidendammer Bridge; then, pushing gradually ahead, they reached the Charité hospital and paused there, while their leaders, Mohnke and Guensche, looked for the groups which should have followed them. It was in vain. No other group had been able to advance beyond the river Spree.

The groups behind them had also regained the open air at the mouth of the Friedrichstrasse station; but there all cohesion had been lost in the confusion they had found, and the members made their way as individuals along the blazing Friedrichstrasse to the Weidendammer Bridge. At the north end of the bridge was an anti-tank barrier; and beyond this no one could pass for heavy Russian fire. Drawing back therefore to the old Admiral's Palace near the south end of the bridge, they waited till the arrival of a few German tanks offered hope of forcing the barrier. Gathering round the tanks, they moved forward again—a miscellaneous group including Bormann, Stumpfegger, Axmann, Kempka, Beetz (Hitler's second pilot), Naumann, Schwaegermann, and Rach. Some of these passed the barrier with the leading tanks and reached the Ziegelstrasse, about three hundred yards ahead; but there a *Panzerfaust*, falling upon the tank, caused a violent explosion. Beetz and Axmann were wounded; Kempka was

[1] It must have been between the exodus of the main party and the capture of the Chancellery by the Russians on May 2nd that an incident took place wihich was described at Nuremberg (on June 26th, 1946) by Hans Fritzsche. As the only high official left in Berlin, Fritzsche had collected the remaining government employees in the ruins of his office, and had prepared (in defiance of Hitler's order to fight on) to offer capitulation with Marshal Zhukov. 'When I was sending the emissary to cross the battleline. Hitler's last adjutant, General Burgdorf, appeared and wanted to shoot me in fulfilment of Hitler's orders.'

knocked out and temporarily blinded; Bormann and Stumpfegger were thrown to the ground, perhaps unconscious, but escaped injury. The advance was frustrated, and the parties retreated once more to the bridge.

Defeated in their attempt to advance as a group, each individual now sought only to save himself. Kempka succeeded in crossing the river by a footbridge, and after hiding for a whole day among Yugoslav women in a railway arch, while the Russians celebrated the fall of Berlin in their midst, he was captured by the enemy; but escaping, swam the Elbe and achieved instead an American captivity. Of Beetz nothing has been heard, he probably perished or fell silently into Russian hands. As for the rest, Bormann, Naumann, Schwaegermann, Axmann, Stumpfegger, Rach, and one other kept at first together, following the tracks of the railway line to the Lehrter station. There they divided, and while Bormann and Stumpfegger walked eastwards along the Invalidenstrasse towards the Stettiner station, the others went westwards towards Alt Moabit. These walked separately, and were soon divided. Schwaegermann and Rach escaped, the former into American captivity; Naumann also escaped. But Axmann, coming upon a Russian patrol, turned back and followed in the direction in which Bormann and Stumpfegger had gone. Before long he overtook them. Behind the bridge, where the Invalidenstrasse crosses the railway line, he found both of them lying outstretched on their backs, with the moonlight on their faces. Stopping for a moment, he saw that both were dead; but Russian fire prevented closer examination. There were no obvious wounds, no signs of a shattering explosion. He assumed they had been shot in the back. Axmann continued on his way alone, and ultimately escaped to join the relics of his Hitler Youth, which survived for six months in a secret fold in the Bavarian Alps, until he too was captured and told his tale.[1]

[1] These incidents have been described by Axmann, Kempka, and Schwaegermann. The account of the death of Bormann rests on the evidence of Axmann only; but since Axmann's account (apart from accidental errors of time) has proved accurate in other particulars, it is probably correct here also, unless he is deliberately lying to protect Bormann. After consideration of all other evidence on the subject, I have decided to accept this statement as being at least consistent with

Meanwhile the first group, which had passed the river Spree, had fared ultimately no better. Leaving the Charité Hospital they had made their way northwards along the Friedrichstrasse and the Chausséestrasse to the Maikaefer Barracks. There the fire of a Russian tank drove them underground, and when they emerged, some hours later, Admiral Voss was no longer with them; he had been captured by the Russians.[1] The remainder of the party moved purposelessly eastwards, gathering and shedding stragglers as they went, to the Schoenhaeuser Allee. There they all took refuge in a cellar. Mohnke, Guensche, Baur, and Hewel were there, and the four women; and Rattenhuber, who had been carried wounded to join them. It was their last refuge. In the afternoon of May 2nd, the Russians arrived at the cellar and demanded immediate surrender. Resistance was impossible, and the party gave themselves up. The four women were allowed to go free, and three of them ultimately reached the British and American zones.[2] When they left the cellar, Rattenhuber, Hewel, Guensche, and Mohnke had all stated their determination to commit suicide, which they may well have done, although the Russian communiqué reported the capture of Rattenhuber; for Russian captivity can have offered little hope to such men.[3] Baur was captured alive, but seriously wounded.[4] Of the other characters who had known the secrets of the Bunker, and who have not been mentioned in this account of the exodus, Hoegl was killed at the

[1] [*Author's note*, 1956: Voss, together with Field-Marshal Schoerner, was released by the Russians at Christmas 1954 and returned to Germany in January 1955.]

[2] Frau Christian, Frau Junge, and Fraeulein Krueger. Fraeulein Manzialy became separated from the party soon after leaving the cellar.

[3] [*Author's note*, 1956: In fact Rattenhuber and Guensche were both captured alive and returned to Germany in 1955 and 1956 respectively.]

[4] The Russian communiqué of May 6th mentioned the capture of Baur and Rattenhuber. Information from Frau Baur, obtained in October 1945, showed that Baur was then in a Russian military hospital, recovering from the amputation of a leg.

all available information although the evidence of a single witness can never be final [*Author's note*, 1978: Axmann's account is now confirmed. See above, pp. 28–9, 51–2.]

Weidendammer Bridge; Linge was captured by the Russians.[1]

Thus ended, in total failure, the attempted escape from Berlin. With it ended the hopes of Bormann to participate in the new government and to give it a link of continuity with the old; and the last chance of delivering to Doenitz the testament of Hitler.

For meanwhile the three other bearers of that treasured document were making but slow progress in their westward journey. We left them on the Pfaueninsel, an island in the Havel lake, on the night of April 30th. There they waited all the next day, vainly hoping that Doenitz would send a plane to fetch them; but no plane arrived. During the following night the Russians bombarded the island, and the four men, Johannmeier, Lorenz, and Zander, with their companion Hummerich, seized a canoe and paddled out into the lake to avoid the fire. Finding a small yacht at anchor, they took refuge in it; but the yacht had no sails, and they dared not move in any other way lest the Russians should see them from the shores; for a munition ship lay blazing on the Havel, shedding a bright light over the water. As they waited on the stationary yacht, a three-engined Junkers 52 seaplane alit upon the water—the plane, no doubt, sent by Doenitz to fetch them. From their position they could only see the shadow of the plane upon the water and hear the roar of the engines. They determined to reach the pilot. Zander set out towards it in a boat; Lorenz and Hummerich followed in another boat; and Johannmeier remained on the yacht, signalling to the plane with his pocket-lamp. Their efforts were unavailing. Zander and Lorenz drew up alongside the plane and sought to speak with the pilot; against the roar of the engines they shouted that Major Johannmeier was with them, and the pilot told them to bring him out. At that moment Zander upset his boat, and the efforts of his companions were diverted to his rescue; the Russians began to shell the plane; and while the

[1] He was seen and recognized in a group of Russian prisoners by Fraeulein Krueger and Frau Christian. The Russians have not been able to comply with requests for the identification of Rattenhuber, Baur, and Linge; but by now there is little that they could add to the story, although Rattenhuber (if alive) would know about the burial of Hitler's and Eva Braun's bodies.

emissaries returned to fetch Johannmeier, the pilot took fright and flew away. He returned to Doenitz and reported that he had failed to find the party. By such a narrow margin did Johannmeier and his companions fail in their mission.

The party spent another day on the Havel, sometimes on the Pfaueninsel, sometimes on the yacht; then before dawn on May 3rd, they set out again, and landing at the Wannsee swimming-bath made their way to Potsdam and Brandenburg, crossed the Elbe at Parey, between Magdeburg and Genthin, and passed ultimately, as foreign workers, into the area of the Western Allies. By this time the war was over; Doenitz had surrendered; and they easily convinced themselves that their mission had now no purpose or possibility of fulfilment. Zander made the long journey to Bavaria, and there, having hidden his documents in a trunk deposited in the village of Tegernsee, he cast off, or sought to cast off, all the traces and associations which bound him to his disastrous past. He changed his name, his identity, his status; his few friends let it be known that he was dead; and he began an altogether new life under the name of Wilhelm Paustin. Johannmeier went to his family's home in Iserlohn, in Westphalia, and buried his documents in a bottle in the back garden. Had the fate of the papers depended upon these two men, they would never have been found by the Allies; for one was too proud, too courageous to yield the truth, the other had too successfully withdrawn from human cognizance. It was the garrulous journalist, Lorenz, whose vanity and indiscretion led accidentally to the discovery of these important documents.

Nor was von Below more successful in delivering his documents. In the early morning of May 1st, he, with his batman Matthiesing, had landed on the west bank of the Havel. Thence they pursued their way westwards, hiding in remote forests by day and moving by night. In a few days he too gave up hope of fulfilling his mission, and in a lonely wood he burned the documents which he was to have delivered to Keitel and Jodl. A few days later, in a hut near Friesack, von Below and Matthiesing met a sergeant-major from their old office in Berlin. His name was Pardau, and he had escaped from the cellar in the Schoenhaeuser Allee when Mohnke and the rest had been captured. Pardau told the story of the death and burning of Hitler and Eva Braun; then they parted. Von Below made his way to Bonn University, there to begin a new life as a law student; Matthiesing to his home near Osnabruck; both ultimately into British captivity.

Freytag von Loringhoven, Boldt, and Weiss also continued their journey; though having no papers to deliver, their escape interested only themselves. After parting from Johannmeier and his party on the Pfaueninsel, they had rejoined the Wannsee garrison only in time to see the whole garrison captured or destroyed in an attempt to break out; for their ammunition was exhausted. Only Freytag von Lorignhoven and Boldt escaped; and that night, while hiding in a slittrench in a wood, Boldt tried to commit suicide by taking an overdose of morphine. Freytag von Loringhoven forced him to vomit the whole dose, and thus saved his life. Thereafter they moved westward, dodging the Russian patrols, and swimming rivers, till they parted, in western territory, into western captivity.

Thus, with the scattering of the disciples after Hitler's death, ended the last days in Berlin. The Fuehrer was dead; his testament was lost; his companions were killed or captured, or wandering as anonymous fugitives in the forests of central Germany. The old centre of power had dissolved without a trace; and a new centre had arisen in Schleswig-Holstein that had no other continuity with the old than the text of the two telegrams which informed Doenitz of his appointment, and the sinister, everpresent shadow of the disappointed Himmler.

For if Doenitz had accepted with chagrin the unwelcome appointment, it was with even greater chagrin that Himmler learned of his failure to gather the inheritance. All his plans had now failed; his brief moment of recovered certainty was past; the purpose had once again gone out of his life. He had sold his soul to the Devil—he had lapsed from the faith and forgotten the unconditional terms of his loyalty—and now he had not been paid the price. Though he went to Doenitz and offered to serve under him, it was without relish, and without assurance of acceptance. Between him and Doenitz there was no common idiom, except political insufficiency. As Himmler's secretary explained, "in the Grand Admiral's purely military circles, Himmler's political approach to the Western Powers was not understood". That night Himmler contemplated resignation—he did not know that Hitler had already dismissed him, and did not dream that Doenitz might dismiss him; he even contemplated suicide.

Himmler did not commit suicide—at least not yet. To the unrealist everything is possible, and that night an absent spirit returned from the north to reawaken his sleeping fantasies. It was Schellenberg. To Schellenberg the situation presented no difficulty at all; everything would turn out well if only it were left to him. Wherever he went, he saw only evidence of the importance attributed to himself and to his political opinions. Had not Doenitz 'on the strength of my original suggestion' dismissed Ribbentrop and appointed the good Schwerin von Krosigk as his successor? Did not Schwerin von Krosigk ask Schellenberg for his collaboration? Did not everyone seem to listen attentively to his large and subtle views on the Northern Question and the Czech Problem? Did not Keitel and Jodl plainly regard him as 'the most experienced in foreign affairs'? Schellenberg offered himself as an envoy to Sweden, or to General Eisenhower. Everything now seemed possible to him; why then should Himmler despair? Himmler agreed not to despair. Indeed, if Schellenberg is to be believed, he joined in the universal admiration of Schellenberg's genius. Within a few days (we learn from this partial source) they had 'a short but significant talk together, the gist of which was, "If only I had listened to you sooner", and "Perhaps you are the first German to be permitted to do something for his poor country again"'. As Samuel Butler says, "the advantage of doing one's praising for one's self is that one can lay it on so thick, and exactly in the right places."

Nor were Schellenberg and Himmler alone in their strange and irresponsible optimism. The air of Schleswig-Holstein was after all still the gaseous air of Nazi Germany, which had generated so many fantastic notions in the heads of those who had become acclimatized to it. Just as Bormann expected to wield authority under Doenitz, so Ribbentrop, though dismissed, did not despair of future political influence. The day after his dismissal, he drafted a document for submission to Doenitz in which he suggested that an independent German government in Schleswig-Holstein might obtain Allied recognition and serve as the nucleus of a new 'national and national-socialist' Germany.[1]

Narrow-minded and fanatical though he was, Doenitz at least had some of the ordinary common sense of the practical man. If he was politically ignorant, at least he was not politically silly. When he surveyed the legacy which had been thrust upon him, at first he trembled to contemplate it. He ordered elaborate proofs to be made of the legality of Hitler's, and therefore of his own authority; he ordered an examination, upon oath, of all the clerks responsible for the reception and decoding of the last telegrams from the Bunker, to be sure of their authenticity; and while these measures of justification were in progress, he prepared to modify the commitments which he had accepted. Like all conservatives, he intended to rely, in this critical posture of defeat, on a ministry of non-political specialists. Hitler's will, or rather the short abstract of it which he had received by telegram, imposed upon him a government including Bormann, Goebbels, and Seyss-Inquart. Doenitz knew nothing of the fate of Goebbels and Bormann; but not even Hitler's will could force upon him such Nazi notorieties. The telegram informing him of his appointment had authorized him to take at once 'all such measures as the situation requires'; on the assurance of that authority he had already appointed Schwerin von Krosigk as his Foreign Minister: and now, on the same assurance, he decided to ignore the later, more inconvenient order. At the same time he resolved gradually to disburden himself of the compromising Nazis who still surrounded him, and in particular of Himmler.

On May 2nd, Doenitz moved his headquarters from Ploen to Flensburg, on the Danish frontier. With him, as an unofficial member of the new government, went Albert Speer. Now that Hitler was dead, Speer was able to carry out the plan he had

[1] This draft was among documents captured at Flensburg.

jeden einzelnen verpflichtet, immer dem gemeinsamen
Interesse zu dienen und seine eigenen Vorteile dem-
gegenüber zurückzustellen. Von allen Deutschen,
allen Nationalsozialisten, Männern und Frauen
und allen Soldaten der Wehrmacht verlange ich, daß
sie der neuen Regierung und ihren Präsidenten treu
und gehorsam sein werden bis in den Tod.

Vor allem verpflichte ich die Führung der
Nation und die Gefolgschaft zur peinlichen Ein-
haltung der Rassegesetze und zum unbarmherzigen
Widerstand gegen den Weltvergifter aller Völker,
das internationale Judentum.

Gegeben zu Berlin, den 29. April 1945, 4.00 Uhr.

so long projected but which, in the Fuehrer's lifetime, he had not ventured to execute. On May 3rd, the speech which he had recorded at Hamburg was at last broadcast to the German people, who now, after years of abstract slogans and political mythology, heard the sane voice of the technocrat telling them not to despair, not to let political disillusion breed practical apathy, but to keep famine at bay and the life of the nation undestroyed. They must repair the railways, 'in so far as the enemy allows or orders it'; industry and trade must continue; agricultural work must go on, and the producers of food must have first claim to fuel and power for production and distribution. If the 'biological substance' of the German people was to be saved, this at least was a more practical means of saving it than the complacent political virtuosity of Schellenberg.

At the same time Doenitz sent Admiral von Friedeburg to Field-Marshal Montgomery with the first offer of surrender.

Himmler also moved his headquarters to Flensburg.[1] In spite of all the omens which, to a more sensitive observer, might have portended his decline, he had now recovered from his momentary depression and was more confident than ever. His huge bodyguard was undiminished; a retinue of staff cars followed him around; high SS officers jostled cumbrously about him; one of them, Pruetzmann, once head of the infelicitous Werewolves, was now liaison officer with Doenitz. In incautious conversation with his indiscreet subordinates, Himmler mentioned his ambition: he would be Prime Minister of a defeated Germany, under Doenitz—and perhaps not always under Doenitz either, for Doenitz, he hinted, was old, while he himself had many years of life and power ahead of him. Meanwhile he was painfully eager to impress upon Doenitz his own indispensable gifts, and begged his friends to represent to the new Fuehrer, by this or that argument, the advantages of his admission to power. He even anticipated the answer, turning up uninvited at Doenitz's staff confer-

---

[1] The above account of Himmler's last days at Flensburg is based mainly on statements by Ohlendorf, Juettner, von Woyrsch, and von Herff.

ences. He could not believe that he was unwanted, and embarrassed even the SS leaders by his insensitivity to the most obvious hints.

On May 5th Himmler held, at Flensburg, his last staff conference. Like obsolete dinosaurs, moving inappropriately in the wrong geological age, they gathered at his headquarters —high SS and police leaders, Obergruppenfuehrer and Gruppenfuehrer, heads of now defunct organizations, sustained only by portentous titles, the memory of vanished authority, and absurd illusions. Himmler entered, attended by his secretary and his adjutant, and delivered a speech on the political situation. He mentioned that he had been reproved for having negotiated with the Western Powers without the late Fuehrer's authority—for Ritter von Greim and Hanna Reitsch had arrived in Schleswig-Holstein and discharged upon him their angry rhetoric; but he was indifferent to that now. He still saw political possibilities, he said—"although I can tell you," says one who heard him, "the possibilities of which he spoke made me clutch my head". He intended to establish a 'reformed' Nazi administration in Schleswig-Holstein, which would conduct peace negotiations with the Western Powers as an independent government in its own territory. Then he went into the details of administration which so delighted that strange, bipartite mind. The SS head offices were to be dissolved, and their leaders to join Himmler's staff as advisers. The chief of the ordinary police, Obergruppenfuehrer Wuennenberg, was ordered to continue his duties: policemen detailed for duty in the area of the new 'government' were to be selected carefully for their smart and soldierly appearance. Other tasks and titles were allotted to others of his followers. As for himself, he had no intention of committing suicide, he assured them, or of being killed. On the contrary, he was full of plans and vitality. All he wanted now was an interview with Field-Marshal Montgomery. He had plans, he seemed to imply, of bargaining for life and authority with the Western Powers; and he seemed confident that his plans would succeed. When the meeting was over, even the SS leaders shook their heads sadly at the illusions of the Reichsfuehrer.

Next day the illusions were clearly exposed. Doenitz wrote a letter to send to Himmler. It ran:

To the Reich Minister of the Interior, Reichsfuehrer SS Himmler.

DEAR HERR REICH MINISTER,—In view of the present situation, I have decided to dispense with your further assistance as Reich Minister of the Interior and Member of the Reich Government, as Commander-in-Chief of the Replacement Army, and as Chief of the Police. I now regard all your offices as abolished. I thank you for the service which you have given to the Reich.[1]

Parallel letters were addressed to Goebbels, whose death was not yet known in Flensburg; to Rosenburg, who still held the ironical title of Minister for the Occupied Territories in the East; and to the Nazi Minister of Justice, Thierack. Bormann, since he had no ministerial post, did not need to be dismissed; he could be ignored. Doenitz had decided to break with the past; he had dismissed the Nazis. Within a week of the death of Hitler, who from his underground bunker, by the mere force and terror of his name, had artificially prolonged its existence, the *detritus* of the Party could be thus easily swept away. Two days later, the instrument of unconditional surrender was signed at Rheims, and the Thousand-Year Reich was over.

Still Himmler remained. No longer Reichsfuehrer, or High Priest, or Inquisitor, but a purposeless, vacillating, ignorant man who had lost the principle of his life, and yet could not admit his unreality, he hung on in Flensburg, an embarrassment to his successors, an enigma to his now meaningless staff. Still he kept up his pretentious establishment: a staff of 150 men, a radio detachment, an escort of four cars to protect

---

[1] [*Author's note,* 1956: It is now clear that this letter was never actually delivered to Himmler. The original text (which was captured in Doenitz's files) has a MS note *Auf Befehl des Grossadmirals gestrichen* ('Cancelled by order of the Grand Admiral'). In 1947 the word *gestrichen* was misread as *zu schicken* ('To be sent by order of the Grand Admiral'). It is therefore clear that Doenitz (as stated by Ohlendorf) conveyed the news of his dismissal to Himmler in a personal interview.]

him; but to what end he did not know. Sometimes he consulted his friends for advice. Should he commit suicide? Should he give himself up? Should he go to ground? Perhaps one of the Nazi field-marshals would protect him—Busch, for instance, or Schoerner. He went to Busch; but after a few days Busch sent him back; and Schoerner was now out of reach.[1] Himmler could not understand that the respect which had once been offered to his power would not extend to his weakness. One day he disappeared again, quite silently; but again he returned. He wrote to Field-Marshal Montgomery, and inquired daily whether a reply had come; but no reply came. Now there was not even Schellenberg to comfort him with false hopes; for Schellenberg was away in Sweden. Himmler asked daily for news of him; "but Schellenberg," says one of his staff, "did not dream of returning. He had made far too many promises to Himmler which he could never fulfil." Himmler had to rely for comfort on the detestable Gebhardt; and Gebhardt, like everyone else in these last days, thought only of himself. It should be added that Schellenberg did not, of course, ascribe the failure of his ingenious political schemes to any defects in his own conception or handling of them; his complacent nature was proof against such a conclusion. When he looked back, from Sweden, upon his universal failure, his judgment spared his own pride. "It was the indecision of the Reichsfuehrer," he said, "that had ruined everything."

The Reichsfuehrer remained undecided. For another fortnight he led a purposeless life in the outskirts of the Flensburg administration; then one day he left, with his adjutant and his secretary. He was dressed as a common soldier, and for disguise had a patch over his eye. Undecided to the end, he did not even know whither he was going. In fact he walked into a British control post; and there, revealed, stripped, and searched, when the doctor's fingers reached his mouth, and his last chance of determining the manner of his death would soon have gone, he at last made a decision. He bit the poison

[1] [*Author's note*, 1956: Schoerner abandoned his army and fled to the American Army in Bavaria on May 9th. He was handed over to the Russians who released him at Christmas 1954.]

capsule which was concealed behind his teeth, and was dead in a few seconds.

It was an appropriate death, as appropriate as the barbaric funeral of Hitler and the silent, secondary death of Goebbels; appropriate to his character—for it was squalid and delayed—and appropriate to the functions which he could no longer exercise. The terrible high-priest of Hitler, who had once served the altar, expounded the mysteries, and presided over the human sacrifices with such undeviating devotion, having once yielded to doubt, had become a mere wandering shadow, a ghostly sacristan, fitfully haunting the shrine he could no longer tend. Now the god himself had perished; the temple had been utterly destroyed; the faithful had been scattered, or converted; and the suicide of the exiled priest is the natural end of a chapter in history: the history, it seems, of a savage tribe and a primitive superstition.

EPILOGUE

THE ORIGINAL purpose of the inquiry which caused this book to be written was to establish the facts of Hitler's end, and thereby to prevent the growth of a myth; and certainly Hitler's own exploitation of mythology in politics has been sufficiently disastrous for the world to apprehend a repetition. The facts are now clear, and if myths, like the truth, depend on evidence, we are safe. But myths are not like truths; they are the triumph of credulity over evidence. The form of a myth is indeed externally conditioned by facts; there is a minimum of evidence with which it must comply, if it is to live; but once lip-service has been paid to that undeniable minimum, the human mind is free to indulge its infinite capacity for self-deception. When we consider upon what ludicrous evidence the most preposterous beliefs have been easily, and by millions, entertained, we may well hesitate before pronouncing anything incredible.

Therefore, though the facts in this book are confidently asserted, for their original purpose I only timidly prophesy success. Many men saw Nero die; but within a year several false Neros arose and were believed. In our own history, the Princes were clearly murdered in the Tower, but there were many who afterwards found it convenient to discover their survival. From such discouraging examples we turn with relief to the story of the Greek philosopher Empedocles, who, in the interests of his reputation, plunged secretly down the crater of Mount Etna, confident that his bereaved fellow citizens, remembering his own judicious prophecies, would suppose him translated to Heaven. But the citizens of Girgenti came to no such conclusion. Finding a shoe of the prophet casually ejected by the volcano, they satisfied their curiosity without recourse to miracles. This analogy, if true, is certainly more promising; but it is only fair to add that the Greeks of Sicily, who so creditably disbelieved the impossible, were favoured by a sceptical education and a high standard of

259

living. The Germans have long been without the former; and they are unlikely, for some time, to enjoy the latter.

Nevertheless, I believe that the facts given in this book do belong to the category of the undeniable minimum, of which even the most extravagant myths must take account. Nazism may revive; the ancient froth of Nibelung nonsense, whose exhalations had poisoned German political thought even before Hitler, may well find another vent; a new party may appeal to a myth of Hitler; but if so, it will be to a myth of Hitler dead, not of Hitler living. This is perhaps small comfort; but it is as much as mere truth is capable of supplying. To prevent political myths from arising is the function not of historical inquiry but of practical politics.

Turning aside, therefore, from the inappropriate task of seeking to control the future, we may here consider what further lessons are to be derived from this extraordinary chapter of history. Some of these lessons will already have been apparent in the course of the narrative, but in this epilogue it will perhaps be of value to resume and summarize them; for no one, I think, can have read this account of life in a monkey-house without asking at least two questions to which he may expect an answer: firstly, how did such monkeys succeed in seizing and retaining power; and secondly, how did they so nearly win the war? The first of these questions involves us in a consideration of the nature of dictatorial power.

Thomas Carlyle supposed that power should be entrusted unconditionally to great men, heroes who were laws to themselves, not responsible to the institutions or prejudices of inferior men. When a nation is so fortunate as to breed a great man (he thought), it should not seek to limit the expression of his greatness; it should be happy to forward his design. This doctrine rang musically in German ears, in a time of gloom and defeat, when Germans despaired of political institutions and their own capacity to use them. It was acceptable to Hitler, whom we have seen listening with egotistical relish to readings from Carlyle's *History of Frederick the Great* in the Bunker in Berlin. Hitler, like Carlyle, believed in 'historical greatness', which to him was more important than the happiness or survival of a people; and he conceived of himself as a great man—in which he was surely not mistaken; for it is absurd to suggest that one who made such a stir in the world was of ordinary stature. The Germans accepted him as the Messiah for whom they were waiting, and in the hours of his apparent success they sacrificed their political institutions to him; for they believed not in them, but in the man.

Now this doctrine of Carlyle, which the history of Nazism so aptly illustrates, depends upon two premises of doubtful validity: firstly, that 'greatness', or any other merely abstract conception, is desirable; secondly, that the human character is constant—for a great man can clearly be trusted with absolute power only if his qualities remain 'great'. The opposite doctrine to this is the doctrine summarized by Lord Acton in his famous aphorism, 'Power tends to corrupt, and absolute power corrupts absolutely': the doctrine that power is not merely the effective expression of a fixed character, but can affect and alter the character which exercises it. The history of Nazism suggests that this doctrine is true.

In the early days of Nazism, Hitler showed a political genius which we are in danger now of forgetting, but which it is very important that we should remember. His ultimate purpose was indeed clear to those who did not willingly deceive themselves: he aimed at the destruction of European civilization by a barbarian empire in central Europe—the terrible hegemony of a new, more permanent Genghiz Khan: 'a new Dark Age', as Mr Churchill called it, 'made more sinister, and perhaps more protracted, by the lights of perverted science'. But when we have admitted the bestiality of his ambition, we must admit that he set himself to realize it with political genius. He detected and exploited all the cruel impulses, the irrational beliefs, the atavistic prejudices, the memories and fears of a frustrated people; he discovered a new technique of exploitation; and he used it with skill and daring in the direction of his ultimate aims. His purpose was clear, his policy consistent, his methods various, adaptable, and effective. If the Germans wanted the same results as he, and if Carlyle's theory were correct, they might reasonably suppose (as too many of them did suppose) that the Fuehrer had found the secret of politics, and that institutions which limited or constrained the infallible power of the new Leviathan, the mortal god, were but the idols of a discarded faith, only fit for sacrifice.

In the years 1938–41 Hitler enjoyed his most spectacular successes; and with each success the German people burnt a new sacrifice before him, until, in 1941, he took his own infallibility for granted. With his armies a few miles from Moscow, and himself hailed as the greatest military genius of all time, he no longer felt the need of political skill, of that patience and flexibility which is, after all, merely a recognition of the possibility of weakness or error. In the autumn of 1941, when he demobilized 40 divisions and ordered industry to revert to the production of consumer-goods; in December 1941, when he wantonly declared war on America, that another victim might add splendour to his inevitable triumph; it was clear that he was no longer prepared to make such recognition. Political skill was judged unnecessary and had been discarded; and the institutions which might have corrected him, if he were wrong, had been discarded too.

It is with the recollection of this past history that we should now look at the last days described in this book. In them we see the last, the logical consequences of Carlyle's dream. After July 20th, 1944, the opposition of the Army, the last and only opposition in Germany, had been crushed. The power of the Nazis was now so absolute, its institutional channels so utterly destroyed, its divorce from political skill so complete, that we find ourselves examining a new spectacle: a situation in which politics, instead of being a skilful calculation of forces, have become the direct expression of irresponsible power.

The consequences of such irresponsibility are obvious. It is not only that the personal extravagances of a single corrupted man have unchallenged political effect: that Hitler's formula of *World Power or Ruin* could become a real policy, and his destroying spirit, when the outer world remained firm, could spend itself upon Germany. There are consequences independent of personality. Though dictatorship is sometimes defended as efficient, and under certain conditions may be efficient, real dictatorship is by definition unconditional, and inherently inefficient. Irresponsible power, without elaborate institutions, cannot be centrally exercised, even by a mortal god; it must tend to fall apart into manageable empires in the hands of his equally irresponsible subordinates. Furthermore, such a god, since he is mortal, must die; and there is therefore the problem of the succession. The candidates for the succession will inevitably be those who have contrived, at the moment of his death, to reserve the largest or most effective portion of power. Even those who cannot hope to succeed, must equip themselves to survive under the successor. Behind the façade of unanimity, all dictatorships are to a large extent centrifugal: the rule of a court conceals a political anarchy in which jealous feudatories, with their private armies and reservations of public resources, are secretly bargaining, and may openly fight, for the reversion or preservation of power. In fact, neither courts nor feudalism are nurseries of political intelligence; and therefore the ambitious sometimes ludicrously fail of their ambitions. The satraps of Cromwell, after a brief struggle, sold out to a more traditional authority; and Hitler's *Bonzen* plotted absurdly for a throne to which there could be no possible succession. The characteristics of modern dictatorship—its careful self-sufficiency, its deliberate intellectual isolation—reduce still further the likelihood of political intelligence within it: they lead directly to the political and intellectual fools' paradise in which such figures as Goering and Goebbels and Himmler, with their drugs and perfumes, their nihilism and mysticism, their flatterers and astrologers, could determine policy, and such ninnies as Ribbentrop, Schellenberg, and Schwerin von Krosigk could be regarded as experts in foreign affairs. We are reminded of the court-parasites of the Roman Empire, of whom Juvenal wrote: the bad jokes of Fortune—village pierrots yesterday, arbiters of life and death today, tomorrow keepers of the public latrines.

Nor is it only political intelligence which is killed by the lack of criticism inherent in absolute power; for technical progress, however unpolitical in its aim, is equally dependent upon the free opposition of minds and methods which the uniform patronage of a dictatorship must deny. Now that all German secrets have been disclosed, the decline of German science under the Nazis has become apparent. This book

263

illustrates one instance of it; for how could medicine advance when the direction of studies, the allocation of resources, the judgment of results, and the promotion of merit depended upon corrupt charlatans like Morell and Conti and the crack-brained fanatics of the SS? Even in military science the same decline is apparent. Hitler began the war with a group of generals trained to uniform efficiency in the greatest military tradition in the world; he ended it with a handful of obedient nonentities, and himself. The military historians of the future may have something to say about Beck and Halder, Manstein and Rundstedt; it is unlikely that they will waste much time on Keitel and Krebs or even on Kesselring and Schoerner. What will they say of Hitler himself?

It is customary to laugh at Hitler's strategical genius, which was certainly disastrous for Germany; but here again it is necessary to observe not merely the final issue, but the stages which led to it. Behind the military snobism of the professional generals, and through the smokescreen of official servility, it is possible to discern that Hitler's military talents were not really contemptible. The extent of his knowledge, and his amazing grasp of detail, have been universally, if sometimes reluctantly, admitted; his willpower, which ultimately doomed Germany, sometimes achieved results which the professional generals, on purely logistical grounds, thought impossible;[1] and his operational plans have at least the honour of controversy.[2] But Hitler's mind and method were erratic. The

[1] Speer believed that only Hitler's intervention in the first Russian winter saved the German armies from greater disaster, and that this incident confirmed Hitler in his belief that all his generals were inept. Certainly Hitler's willpower was extraordinary, and his confidence in it unlimited. His error lay in supposing that faith can move mountains by itself, instead of merely giving the decisive impetus to the spade.

[2] Hitler's critics insist that his strategical successes, such as the battle of France in 1940, were only made possible by the judicious mis-interpretations of the Army Command, and that his tactical successes, such as the battle of Kiev in 1941 and the Ardennes offensive in 1944, were strategic blunders. I am not competent to give any judgment in these matters. For some opinions of Halder and Keitel on Hitler's strategy, see above p. 61 note. Since Halder hated Hitler personally and politically, and despised him militarily (Halder is a military snob, believing that no amateur can ever understand the mysteries of war), his reluctant admissions must be respected.

intuition which, in politics, chose both Speer and Ribbentrop, in military matters chose both Guderian and Keitel. The correction of criticism, the opposition of both minds and facts, is essential to such a random genius; and it is the disappearance of criticism, not the inherent errors of his thought which made Hitler's strategy in the end as calamitous as his politics. Those who attended his staff conferences in the first two years of the war have described his earlier, more patient methods: how he would sit in silence, only now and then asking questions or eliciting opinions, feeling his way warily, and learning what he could from the experts whom he wished to despise but secretly feared. But gradually success bred confidence; the propaganda of Goebbels, the sycophancy of Keitel, nourished the self-delusions of unchallenged power; no mind, no fact was allowed to contest the dogmas of strategic genius;[1] and at the end, how different had the conference table become! Hitler was still there, still the central figure, still the ultimate authority; but a Chinese wall separated him from the outer world of reality. He listened not to other voices, but to echoes of his own; for none of the surviving courtiers dared speak, or even know the truth. He still interested himself in every detail, still moved armies by battalions and regiments; but it was on an imaginary battlefield. He was mounting the impossible Steiner attack, or marshalling the phantom army of Wenck.

Thus, in reading of the last days of Hitler's empire, we must remember that they were the last days, and were different from the first; otherwise we may forget the political lesson that they illustrate. Nevertheless, we should remember that the last days were implicit in the first. Most historical dictators have passed through similar stages of development. Starting with revolutionary power, based on a revolutionary idea which happens to symbolize the mood of a people, they convert it into military power based on success; when the revolutionary promise is betrayed, and the success runs dry, they resort to

[1] Hitler's repudiation of inconvenient facts would be incredible, were it not so well attested. According to Halder, Hitler often complained of the 'damned objective views' of the Army General Staff.

naked power, based on political expedients and secret police; but since these are inadequate in the long run, the system collapses, or is overthrown. In theory, of course, revolutionary power can become respectable and traditional, and develop along orderly lines, as happened in the Roman Empire; but most of the great modern dictators—Cromwell, Napoleon, Hitler, Mussolini—went the other way; and the reason is, I believe, the ultimate inefficiency of dictatorial power, which causes the success to run dry.[1]

These observations will perhaps answer the first question, how power came into the hands of such a set of monkeys; but the answer itself forces upon us another question. If these are the logical consequences of the separation of power from the institutions which should contain it, what forces, in a practical, not a logical world, allowed these merely logical consequences to emerge? Why was there no effective revolt or opposition, once the logical inevitability of their emergence had become plain? It is true the institutions of resistance had been sacrificed, and in the modern world the advantages are on the side of the government; it is true Goebbels sustained the Germans with the promise of miracles and millennia, of secret weapons and diplomatic somersaults; it is true dictatorship kills political intelligence in the governed as well as in the governors; but men are not blind automata; there is still an irreducible residue of common sense; men are after all the agents as well as the victims of governments; and the submission of eighty million men to a clique which was plainly and wilfully driving them to disaster calls for some attempt at explanation.

It is sometimes said that the Allied insistence on 'unconditional surrender' frightened the Germans into continued obedience; but if this implies that they would otherwise have

---

[1] The case of Cromwell is somewhat controversial. His personal character was of course entirely different from Hitler's, and he was never absolute; further, he sought to convert his power from revolutionary to traditional, but found such a change both logically and practically impossible. Nevertheless, the basis and nature of his power make it fundamentally similar to Hitler's (more similar than that of Napoleon or Mussolini); and in spite of all differences of circumstance, the same tendency is apparent.

revolted, I do not think it is true. Of those Germans who preferred the rule of the Nazis to unconditional surrender, how many would have been inspired to rebellion by an Allied assurance of moderation? Conditions can only be made with power-holders, or alternative power-holders, otherwise they are not conditions but promises; and what German was influenced by promises after twelve years of Dr Goebbels? Of alternative power-holders, the Army leaders might perhaps have been ready to bargain; but conditions which included the destruction of the German Army would have seemed no conditions to them; and anyway, even the Army failed in its politics. As for the 'democratic opposition', invented by virtuous journalists—it is a creature as fabulous as the centaur and the hippogriff. No doubt many Germans quietly grumbled about the Nazis and have since claimed to have been their enemies; but in time of war, bargains can be struck only with real political forces, not with whimpering shadows. Who of these 'democrats' ever concerted a programme or approached the Allies with concrete proposals? A few high-minded aristocrats, a few disappointed officials and dismayed parsons—were these really more promising than the Schellenbergs and the Schwerin von Krosigks? If we wish to explain the docility of the German people, we must look for some other explanation, and find it, perhaps, in that most discouraging German characteristic: the despair of politics.

In thus isolating German characteristics, we must not, of course, fall into the error of racialism. German characteristics do not spring from German blood or climate, but from the habits of thought and traditions of government to which Germans happen to have become accustomed. Now German history is characterized by a record of political failure so continuous as to have become a tradition—a tradition which in turn perpetuates the record by the appearance of inevitability. Who has succeeded among German politicians? a German may ask himself; and he will answer, Frederick the Great, and Bismarck—the men of blood and iron. On the other hand, what liberal or popular movements have ever succeeded in Germany? The romantic liberals of 1815–30, vapouring immaturely in provincial universities? the lawyers and businessmen of 1848, theorizing solemnly in Frankfurt? the Weimar Republic, silently destroyed from within by Bruening, and then ordered away by the Nazis, without even the show of a revolution? With these and such memories the Germans are easily persuaded that however reason will do for others, only force will succeed with them. The Kaiser indeed failed, but at least he had a run of success, unlike the Weimar Republic; and perhaps he failed for purely technical reasons—his personal policy, not his cardinal principles were at fault. That at least was Hitler's view, when he spoke of 'the fools of 1914–18', and promised to be more successful. Now he has failed even more catastrophically. But at one time he nearly succeeded; and if later 'liberal' governments are obvious failures, it may well be that the Germans will look back not to the disastrous failure of Hitler, but to the temporary prosperity and the nearly attained success.

This consistent tradition of political failure in Germany has other consequences besides a despair of reason and a reliance on force; and one of them is the elevation of politics into a mystery. If so few Germans have ever succeeded in politics, a German may say, it is clear that politics are beyond the reach of ordinary men, who will be more profitably and more happily employed in those tasks of commerce and agriculture, of manufacture and industry and military organization, in which their skill is acknowledged. Thus the political arena is left vacant, and any charlatan who professes to understand the mystery of politics is allowed to enter and to try his hand. Politics in Germany have long taken place in such a vacuum; the real ability of the people has been concentrated on industry or the army; and the direction of industry and the army, for peace or war, has been left to the adventurers who have occupied the neglected political stage. To salve their consciences, the Germans have invented comforting philosophies: the philosophy of Marxism, that all politics are but an immaterial reflection of social relations, and the philosophy of the technocrats, that politics are quite irrelevant. How fatally untrue those philosophies are has been shown by German history in this war, in which the crazy politics of a fully-developed and therefore calamitous dictatorship have not only controlled German industry and the German army, but have misdirected and ultimately ruined them. The answer to the question, why did the Nazis so nearly win the war? is then, that they did not win the war, or nearly. What nearly won the war was German industry and the German army which, in its early days, the days of its political skill, the dictatorship did indeed foster and serve; what lost it was the unchecked development of the dictatorship, in which the German people acquiesced, even to the end, through a fatal political tradition.

How fatal that tradition was, is clear from one personal history which is described in this book. In these pages, which describe and illustrate so many varieties of human corruption and human lunacy, one figure stands out in extraordinary isolation. Whatever the errors of judgment, and neutrality of conscience, which enabled him to acquire and retain the personal friendship of the most bloodthirsty tyrant in modern history, it is quite clear that in Hitler's court Albert Speer was morally and intellectually alone. He had the capacity to understand the forces of politics, and the courage to resist the master whom all others have declared irresistible. As an administrator, he was undoubtedly a genius. He regarded the rest of the court with dignified contempt. His ambitions were peaceful and constructive: he wished to rebuild Berlin and Nuremberg, and had planned 'at the cost of no more than two months' war-expenditure' (as he sadly protested in the dock at Nuremberg) to make them the greatest cities in the world. Nevertheless, in a political sense, Speer is the real criminal of Nazi Germany; for he, more than any other, represented that fatal philosophy which has made havoc of Germany and nearly shipwrecked the world. For ten years he sat at the very centre of political power; his keen intelligence diagnosed the nature and observed the mutations of Nazi government and policy; he saw and despised the personalities around him; he heard their outrageous orders and understood their fantastic ambitions; but he did nothing. Supposing politics to be irrelevant, he turned aside, and built roads and bridges and factories, while the logical consequences of government by madmen emerged. Ultimately, when their emergence involved the ruin of all his work, Speer accepted the consequences and acted. Then it was too late; Germany had been destroyed.

NOTE ON SOURCES

THE following is a list of the chief personal sources (excluding captured documents) on which the foregoing account is based:

A. *Personalities in Hitler's Court*

1. SPEER, ALBERT.—Reich Minister of Armament and War Production. In a series of statements and interrogations, Speer has given the completest and most objective account on this subject. He is also a valuable authority on his own policy of opposition to Hitler's plans of 'Scorched Earth', a subject on which his statements have been checked and confirmed by subsidiary sources, especially Karl Kaufmann, Gauleiter of Hamburg, and Koller (No 20 below), and on incidents in Hitler's Bunker on the occasions of his last visits on April 20th and 23rd–24th 1945. Further details have been given by Speer in the course of his defence at Nuremberg, where he was sentenced by the International Military Tribunal to twenty years imprisonment.

2. SCHWERIN VON KROSIGK, GRAF LUTZ.—Reich Minister of Finance. Krosigk's diary, written with an eye to history, records incidents which the writer thought significant during the period April 15th–May 5th, 1945. Condemned to 10 years imprisonment 1949.

There are numerous subsidiary sources on this subject, which have been used for matters of detail.

B. *Hitler's Relations with Army Leaders*

3. HALDER, FRANZ Generaloberst.—Formerly (till 1942) Chief of Army General Staff. Halder has given very full, factual, and objective accounts of the whole history of relations between Hitler and the generals, the development of the OKW, etc. These accounts have been supplemented by data from many other generals, including Field-Marshal Wilhelm Keitel (No 31 below), who believed in Hitler's strategical genius, and a much larger number who did not.

C. *Hitler's Physical Health and Personality*

The following doctors have been interrogated on Hitler's health and physical condition, and on other personal matters:

4. BRANDT, DR KARL.—Surgeon to Hitler's staff (Begleitarzt) until October 1944. Condemned and executed 1947.

5. VON EICKEN, PROFESSOR.—Ear, nose, and throat specialist. Attended Hitler in 1935, and again, after July 20th, 1944.

6. GIESING, DR ERWIN.—Ear, nose, and throat specialist. Attended Hitler after July 20th 1944.

7. VON HASSELBACH, DR HANS KARL.—Surgeon, deputy to Brandt (No 4 above) until October 1944.

8. MORELL, PROFESSOR THEODOR.—Personal physician (Leibarzt) to Hitler whom he last saw on April 22nd 1945. Died 1948.

D. *Himmler and his* Entourage

9. SCHELLENBERG, WALTER.—SS Brigadefuehrer, Head of RSHA, Amt VI (Foreign Intelligence). Though nominally subordinate to Kaltenbrunner, Schellenberg had direct personal relations with Himmler, which make him a valuable source. While in Sweden between the end of hostilities and his surrender to SHAEF, Schellenberg compiled a careful diary of the events of the last month of the war, which is very important. He has also been exhaustively interrogated. Condemned to 6 years imprisonment 1949. Died 1952.

10. GEBHARDT, PROFESSOR KARL.—SS Obergruppenfuehrer. Himmler's personal doctor. Condemned and executed 1947.

11. BRANDT, DR RUDOLF.—SS Standartenfuehrer. Himmler's secretary. Condemned and executed 1947.

12. GROTHMANN, WERNER.—Himmler's military adjutant.

13. BERGER, GOTTLOB.—SS Obergruppenfuehrer. Chief of SS Hauptamt and Kriegsgefangenenwesen. Condemned to 25 years imprisonment 1949.

14. OHLENDORF, OTTO.—SS Obergruppenfuehrer. Head of RSHA, Amt III (Sicherheitsdienst), and Ministerialdirektor in Reichswirtschaftsministerium. Condemned and executed 1948.

15. VON WOYRSCH, UDO.—SS Obergruppenfuehrer and General der Polizei.

16. VON HERFF, MAXIMILIAN.—SS Obergruppenfuehrer and General der Waffen SS. Head of Personalhauptamt.

17. JUETTNER, MAX.—SS Obergruppenfuehrer. Head of SS Fuehrungshauptamt.

18. KALTENBRUNNER, ERNST.—SS Obergruppenfuehrer. Head of RSHA. Kaltenbrunner was in south Germany at the end, and is therefore of little direct value for this subject; but he has been thoroughly interrogated, and his reports shed incidental light on

many matters. Condemned by International Military Tribunal and executed 1946.

Of the above, Nos 10, 14, 15, and 16 were with Himmler in Schleswig-Holstein during the last days; Nos 11 and 12 were with him when he was captured. Count Folke Bernadotte's book, *The Fall of the Curtain*, contains some useful information about the personal part played by the author in the last days. See also Felix Kersten, *Memoirs* (1956) and Norbert Masur, *En Jude talar med Himmler* (Stockholm, 1945).

E. *The Dismissal of Goering*

19. GOERING, HERMANN.—Reichsmarshall. Condemned by International Military Tribunal and committed suicide 1946.

20. KOLLER, KARL.—General der Luftwaffe. Chief of Staff of Luftwaffe. Koller's diary, covering the period April 16th to May 9th, 1945, is a detailed record of great value, not only for these events (in which he was the principal intermediary), but also for many other incidents during the period. Koller was with the OKW at Fuerstenberg, and in regular telephone communication with the Bunker. He also, on May 8th, received, and recorded, a first-hand account of events in the Bunker (April 26th–29th) from Ritter von Greim. He has since published a version of his diary under the title *Der letzte Monat* (Mannheim, 1949).

21. LAMMERS, HANS HEINRICH.—Head of Reichskanzlei. Lammers was present at Goering's conference on April 23rd, 1945, and has made a statement and produced documents relevant to this episode. Condemned to 20 years imprisonment 1949.

In addition to these, Speer (No 1 above) was an eyewitness of certain events in this connection, and Kaltenbrunner (No 18 above) has reported a conversation with SS Obersturmbann-fuehrer Frank, who both took part in Goering's conference and was responsible for his arrest.

F. *Events in the Bunker* (April 22nd to May 1st, 1945)

22. AXMANN, ARTUR.—Reichsjugendfuehrer. Axmann visited the Bunker on several occasions. He was there on April 30th 1945, and examined the dead bodies of Hitler and Eva Braun. He took part in the escape of May 1st, and claims to have seen the corpses of Bormann and Stumpfegger.

23. VON BELOW, NICOLAUS.—Oberst der Luftwaffe. Wehr-macht-attaché (Luftwaffe) at Fuehrer's headquarters. Was in

the Bunker till midnight April 29th–30th. Witnessed Hitler's personal will..

24. BOLDT, GERHARD FRIEDRICH WILHELM.—Rittmeister. ADC to General Krebs (Chief of Army General Staff). Left the Bunker on April 29th. He has since published his account as *Die letzten Tage der Reichskanzlei* (Hamburg, 1947).

25. CHRISTIAN, ECKARD.—General der Luftwaffe. Chef Luftwaffenfuehrungsstab. Was in the Bunker on April 22nd and 23rd, then with OKW at Fuerstenburg. Had contact with the Bunker, and with Ritter von Greim both during and after Greim's stay in the Bunker.

26. CHRISTIAN, FRAU GERDA (*née* DARANOWSKI).—Wife of No 25. Secretary to Hitler. Left the Bunker on May 1st.

27. FREYTAG VON LORINGHOVEN, BARON Major.—Adjutant to General Krebs. Left the Bunker on April 29th.

28. JOHANNMEIER, WILLI Major.—Wehrmachtattaché at Fuehrer's headquarters, assisting General Burgdorf. Left the Bunker on April 29th bearing a copy of Hitler's political testament addressed to Field-Marshal Schorener.

29. JUNGE, FRAU GERTRUD.—Secretary to Hitler. Left the Bunker on May 1st.

30. KARNAU, HERMANN.—Revieroberwachtmeister. Guard in Reichssicherheitsdienst, Dienststelle I, on duty in the Bunker. Left the Bunker on May 1st. Saw the burning of Hitler's and Eva Braun's bodies.

31. KEITEL, WILHELM Generalfeldmarschall.—Chef OKW. In the Bunker daily till April 23rd; then with OKW at Krampnitz and Fuerstenberg. Condemned by International Military Tribunal and executed 1946.

32. KEMPKA, ERICH.—SS Sturmbannfuehrer. Hitler's personal chauffeur and transport officer. Took part in burning of Hitler's and Eva Braun's bodies. Left the Bunker on May 1st. He has since published his account as *Ich habe Adolf Hitler verbrannt* (Munich, 1950).

33. KRUEGER, Fraeulein ELSE.—Bormann's secretary. Left the Bunker on May 1st.

34. LORENZ, HEINZ.—Official of Deutsche Nachrichtenbuero, working in Propaganda Ministry; reported frequently to Bunker, and left it on April 29th, bearing copies of Hitler's personal and political testaments, and Goebbels' Appendix, destined for Munich.

35. MANSFELD (alias SKRZIPCZYK), ERICH.—SS Hauptscharfuehrer. Guard in RSD Dienststelle I, on duty in the Bunker.

Witnessed burning of Hitler's and Eva Braun's bodies. Left the Bunker on May 1st.

36. MUELLER, WILLI OTTO.—Tailor, resident in Reich Chancellery. Observed some incidents of interest.

37. MATTHIESING, HEINZ.—Batman to von Below (No 23 above), whom he accompanied out of Berlin on April 29th.

38. POPPEN, HILCO.—Guard in RSD Dienststelle 1, on duty in Bunker. Left on May 1st.

39. REITSCH, HANNA.—'Flugkapitaen.' Test pilot and companion of Ritter von Greim. In Bunker April 26th till 29th.

40. SCHWAEGERMANN, GUENTHER AUGUST WILHELM.—SS Hauptsturmfuehrer. Adjutant to Goebbels. Was in the Bunker April 22nd till May 1st. Burnt bodies of Goebbels and his wife and children.

41. VON VARO BARONESS.—Was casually in second (SS) Bunker until May 1st. Was present at Hitler's first leavetaking at 02.30 hours on April 29th.

42. ZANDER, WILHELM.—SS Standartenfuehrer. Assistant to Martin Bormann. Left the Bunker on April 29th, carrying copies of Hitler's personal and political testaments, and marriage certificate of Hitler and Eva Braun, addressed to Admiral Doenitz.

APPENDIX I (1945)

THE EXECUTION OF FEGELEIN

(See p. 204)

THE real causes and circumstances of the execution of Fegelein provide one of the few subjects included in this book upon which final certainty seems unattainable. Both Greim (quoted by Koller) and Reitsch knew of Fegelein's execution, which must therefore have taken place before they left the Bunker (*ie* before about midnight on April 28th–29th); but both describe it as the punishment for his attempted escape, and say that it took place immediately after his recapture, which is certainly inaccurate. Reitsch says that Fegelein's absence was first noticed on April 27th, and the evidence from other sources, though never explicit, points to the same date. But it is certain that Fegelein was alive when the news of Himmler's treachery was brought to the Bunker, on the evening of April 28th, and that he was questioned on the subject. Explicit evidence of this has been given by Lorenz and von Below and others, and most sources agree that a day elapsed between the recapture of Fegelein and his execution. It seems necessary and reasonable therefore to agree with Lorenz (who elsewhere proves to be one of the most accurate of witnesses) that Fegelein was degraded in rank for desertion on April 27th, and executed on a second charge connected with Himmler's treachery on the night of April 28th–29th. His execution must then have taken place between the announcement of Himmler's treachery at about 9 pm and the departure of Greim and Reitsch soon after midnight.

We are therefore faced with the question, What was this charge, and was it true? No witness has given a clear answer to this question; and it seems clear that the whole matter was deliberately involved in secrecy in the Bunker—probably because Fegelein's former intimacy with Hitler, Bormann, and Burgdorf and his relationship to Eva Braun, made the discussion of his supposed apostasy distasteful. According to von Below, however, Burgdorf told him that 'Himmler had instigated a plot to hand over Hitler's dead body to the Western Powers', and that Fegelein was implicated in this. Others have also given evidence of a general belief that Himmler had plotted against Hitler's person, and that Fegelein's evidence, on the night of April 28th, proved both this plot and Fegelein's complicity.

Whether Burgdorf actually made this remark to von Below is uncertain; for von Below is very vague on the matter, and he may well have been influenced by the subsequent (and untrue) statements of Schellenberg, which were published while von Below was at liberty. But in any case the statement, as quoted, is incredible. It is quite certain that Himmler never considered any such plot; nor would it have been possible to convey Hitler's body to the Western Powers after April 25th. Nevertheless, it is clear that several SS leaders, including Steiner, were talking loosely about the possibility of such a plot, and that Fegelein must have known about such talk; he must also have known about Himmler's meetings with Bernadotte, which were ostensibly for quite legitimate purposes; and it is quite probable that under cross-examination on the night of April 28th he revealed his knowledge of both these facts. Since he had been in confinement since April 27th, and knew nothing of Himmler's treachery, he would not have been aware of the new significance which could now be attributed to such admissions.

It seems most probable to me that this in fact happened; that in the highly-charged atmosphere of the Bunker, and the universal suspicions of treachery, Fegelein's admissions were easily interpreted as knowledge, hitherto treasonably concealed, of an SS plot, subsidiary to Himmler's political schemes and connected with the presumably treacherous failure of the Steiner attack on April 21st; and that Fegelein's absences from the Bunker, culminating in his attempted escape on April 27th, were interpreted as the comings and goings of the indispensable agent between his employer and his victim. In fact, of course, Fegelein was only interested in escaping from the Bunker; but in such an atmosphere

Trifles light as air
Are to the jealous confirmations strong
As proofs of Holy Writ.

APPENDIX II (1978)

THE RUSSIAN EVIDENCE ON THE DEATH OF HITLER

(See Preface)

SINCE the last edition of this book was sent to Press certain new material on the death of Hitler has been published from Russian sources. In 1965, in the Russian periodical *Znamya*, Yelena Rzhevskaya published a somewhat fragmentary and rhetorical article entitled 'Berlinskie Stranitsy' ('Berlin Notes'), which she afterwards enlarged into a book. The author had been attached as an interpreter to the special unit of the Red Army which had been instructed to find Hitler 'alive or dead', and therefore had some first-hand experience; and for this article she had been allowed to see some of the documents of the Russian inquiry in Berlin which I describe on pp. 32–8. She did not however use any German or Western evidence. Three years later, another Russian writer, Lev Bezymenski, co-editor of the Russian periodical *Novoe Vremya*, published in West Germany a book entitled *Der Tod Adolf Hitlers* (English translation, *The Death of Adolf Hitler*, 1968). Mr Bezymenski's book was evidently written for export to the West only, for no Russian text has been seen and the book seems not to have been published in communist countries, although the author has been curiously reluctant to discuss his findings with Western scholars and has invariably failed to keep his appointments with them. Apart from the text of certain documents which Mme Rzhevskaya had seen but not quoted, Mr Bezymenski adds nothing to her account, on which it relies more heavily than is acknowledged. Like Mme Rzhevskaya, he completely ignores Western and German evidence. Like her, he insists that Hitler did not shoot himself but took poison; and he seems concerned to emphasize this distinction in order to argue that Hitler died not like a hero (which few had supposed) but 'like a dog'.

The moral distinction between death by revolver-shot and death by poison may seem to Western readers rather fine. Since all Nazi leaders were supplied with cyanide-capsules, and some (like Ritter von Greim, Himmler and Goering) used them, that form of death does not seem to have been regarded by them as cowardly. However, there is a distinction of fact, and a historian who aims at accuracy must examine the evidence. Mr Bezymenski's contribution to the evidence consists exclusively in the autopsy reports of the Soviet pathologists who examined the bodies discovered in the Chancellery, including those of Hitler and Eva Braun. These reports are printed by him 'in full'. As printed, they declare that the experts found in Hitler's mouth fragments of a crushed glass ampoule, and that this, together with the smell of bitter almonds, 'permitted them to conclude' that death was by cyanide poisoning. If we assume that the pathologists made a true report, and that their report is correctly and fully quoted and translated (for the Russian text has not been published), then we must agree with their conclusion, which has been, as I have stated, the official Russian version since 1949.

On the other hand certain reservations must be made. First of all, there is the difficulty presented by the German evidence. All the German witnesses interrogated by me, including those who had previously been interrogated by the Russians, agreed that Hitler had shot himself, and it is difficult to see why they should have lied in such a matter. None of them supposed that cyanide was a cowardly means of death; none of them felt concerned to defend Hitler, whose death anyway had severed their allegiance; all were factual and objective in their evidence. Therefore their evidence must be considered, and given its weight, along with the Russian evidence.

Secondly, the Russian evidence itself is not entirely satisfactory. On the face of it, it is clear and factual; but some doubts must be excused in view of its long concealment, its curiously oblique revelation, and the partisan purpose which that revelation is clearly designed to serve. Faked autopsies are unfortunately only too familiar in Russian history and this autopsy is in some respect incompatible with Hitler's authentic medical records. Besides, is it really revealed 'in full'? One passage, in so exhaustive and meticulous a document, is oddly brief and elliptical. I refer to a single sentence in the autopsy report on Hitler which Mr Bezymenski prints as a distinct paragraph and which reads, 'Part of the cranium is missing'. No explanation of this fact is offered, no more exact description, no conjectured cause. In an otherwise detailed professional document this isolated, casual statement must excite surprise, and we may legitimately wonder whether, at this point, part of the document is not missing too. However that may be, Mr Bezymenski in his commentary, ignores this part of the text. But he is evidently aware of the difficulty, for he advances—only to dismiss—a highly speculative hypothesis, for which there is neither evidence nor probability, but which (like so much else) is borrowed from Mme Rzhevskaya, *viz*: that Heinz Linge may conceivably have finished Hitler off with a bullet after he had taken poison. Since Linge was a Russian prisoner for eleven years, it seems odd that this little matter was not cleared up. Its only significance lies in the deduction which we are obliged to make, *viz*: that, although the printed autopsy report does not mention it, there was some inescapable evidence that Hitler had been shot.

The simplest conclusion, taking account of all the evidence, would still seem to be that, as I wrote in my Introduction in 1956, 'though Hitler may conceivably . . . have taken poison as well, he certainly killed himself with a revolver-shot'.

INDEX

Goering, Hermann, character, 63; successor-designate to Hitler, 63, 65, 135, 144; competes with Bormann, 65; declines into a voluptuary, 65–66, 130n.; responsible for failure of Luftwaffe, 80, 179 and n., 224; behaviour on July 20th, 1944, 82; leaves Berlin, 153; Hitler suggests that he take power, 161; Goering's conference and telegram, 168–70; receipt of his telegram by Hitler, 176; dismissed and arrested, 177–8; real reason for his fall, 179; superseded by Greim, 187; general indifference to his fate, 188–9; expelled from the Party, 210; execution ordered by Bormann, 215; mythical narrative by, 226n.; suicide, 273, 279

Gottberg (SS Ogruf.), 204n.

Grand Inquisitors, 69–70

Grawitz, Professor (head of German Red Cross), 163n.

Graziani (Marshal), 81

v. Greim, Ritter (Field-Marshal), 15, 177, 182–91, 196, 204–7, 254, 273, 279

Grothmann, Werner (Himmler's adjutant), 164n., 272

Guderian, Heinz (General), 123, 151, 265

Guensche (Hitler's SS adjutant), 20, 26, 43, 181, 208, 229, 230, 231, 232, 235, 243–4, 246

Haase, Professor, 106, 227

Haberzettel, Inge, 142 and n.

Hacha, Emil (President of Czechoslovakia), 121

Hagen, Kurt (stenographer), 158, 167

Halder, Franz (General), 59 and n., 60n., 61 and n., 84, 89, 117, 264, 271

Hanfstaengl, Frl., 129

Hanke, Karl (Gauleiter), 211

Hansen, Georg (Colonel), 83

v. Hasselbach, Hans Karl, Dr, 104, 106, 113, 174, 272

Hegel, Friedrich, 99

Heinrici, Gotthard (General), 198n.

Henderson, Sir Nevile, 88, 102

v. Herff, Maximilian (SS Ogruf.), 272

Herrgesell (stenographer), 158, 167

Hess, Rudolf, 64–65, 135

Heusemann, Käte, 32–33

Hewel, Walter, 182, 190 and n., 202, 205, 222, 223, 230, 243, 246

Heydrich, Reinhard, 75n.

Hildebrandt, Frl. (Goebbels' secretary), 142n.

Himmler, Heinrich, and the SS, 58; character and position, 68–75; takes over the *Abwehr*, 77; effect of the Generals' Plot on his career, 83–85; relations with Bormann, 86–87; rejects plan for resistance movement, 92; finds a new surgeon for Hitler, 114; begins to doubt, 128; pushed on by Schellenberg, 129–34; possible successor to Hitler, 135, 144; meets Schwerin von Krosigk, 145–6; further pressed by Schellenberg, 146–7; visits Bernadotte, 156–7; learns of Hitler's decision to stay in Berlin, 163; sends Gebhardt to Hitler, 165; last meeting with Bernadotte, 170–3; failure of negotiations with Bernadotte, 199–200; still expects to succeed Hitler, 200; his shadow government, 201; Hitler orders his arrest, 205; expelled from the Party, 211; learns of succession of Doenitz, 236; and Schellenberg, 250; his ambitions, 253; his last conference, 254; dismissed by Doenitz, 255; last days and suicide, 255–7, 279; sources, 272–273

Hitler, Adolf, fictitious versions of his end, 10–15; sources and witnesses for Hitler's fate, 15–18; his personal power, 54, 63, 88–90; his struggle with OKH, 58–63, 271; his court, 63, 81–83, 101n., 271; his theory of 'will-power', 60, 97n., 101; the problem of his successor, 63–65, 135, 144, 200–2; Hitler and the flight of Hess, 63–65; his interest in

CPSIA information can be obtained
at www.ICGtesting.com
Printed in the USA
LVOW04s1014110916

504133LV00018B/468/P